Why Did Japan Stumble?

Why Did Japan Stumble?

Causes and Cures

Edited by

Craig Freedman

Director, Centre for Japanese Economic Studies,
Macquarie University, Australia

In Association with the Centre for Japanese Economic Studies,
Macquarie University, Australia

Edward Elgar
Cheltenham, UK • Northampton MA, USA

Published by
Edward Elgar Publishing Limited
Glensanda House
Montpellier Parade
Cheltenham
Glos GL50 1UA
UK

Edward Elgar Publishing, Inc.
136 West Street
Suite 202
Northampton
Massachusetts 01060
USA

A catalogue record for this book
is available from the British Library

Library of Congress Cataloguing in Publication Data
Why did Japan stumble? : causes and cures / edited by Craig Freedman.
   'In association with the Centre for Japanese Economic Studies,
  Macquarie University.'
   Includes index.
   1. Japan—Economic policy—1989– 2. Japan—Economic
conditions—1989– 3. Banks and banking—Japan. I. Freedman,
Craig, 1950– . II. Macquarie University. Centre For
Japanese Economic Studies.
  HC462.95.W49 1999
  388.951—dc21

          99–25804
            CIP

ISBN 1 85898 834 9

Printed and bound by Creative Print and Design (Wales)

Contents

Figures

Tables

Contributors

Jenny Corbett
Nissan Institute of Japanese Studies, Oxford University

Peter Drysdale
Australia-Japan Research Centre, Australian National University

Craig Freedman
Centre for Japanese Economic Studies, Macquarie University

Michael Hutchison
Department of Economics, University of California, Santa Cruz

Takatoshi Ito
Institute of Economic Research, Hitotsubashi University

Ryutaro Komiya
Economics Department, Aoyama Gakuin University, Tokyo

Rita Madrassy
Department of Economics, University of California, Santa Cruz

Eileen Mauskopf
Board of Governors, Federal Reserve Bank, Washington, DC

Kathleen McDill
Department of Economics, University of California, Santa Cruz

Michio Morishima
Suntory and Toyota Institute, London School of Economics and Political Science

Mitsuaki Okabe
Faculty of Policy Management, Keio University

Hugh Patrick
Graduate School of Business, Columbia University

Kyoko Sheridan
Graduate School of Management, Adelaide University

Masaru Yoshitomi
Long Term Credit Bank of Japan Research Institute

A word before starting

. . . the triumph of hope over experience
Samuel Johnson

It is perhaps presumptuous of me to assume that there is any demand for a second conference volume. Certainly there seems to be no real need, given the volume of analysis that has enveloped us. All of it so sincerely seeks to reveal the true causes of Japan's current economic crisis that there seems no possible reason for me to add my own very modest commentary. But I think that the importance of this particular volume, and my only legitimate excuse for playing midwife to its birth, lies not in any small insights that I may be able to offer, but in the thoughts of the varied and remarkably interesting participants who agreed to contribute to the Centre for Japanese Economic Studies' fourth biennial attempt to prove that it exists.

This was my very first effort at organizing a conference. As beginners often are, I was partially assisted by my own naivety as to what was or was not possible and partially aided, with no such objective in mind, by Japan's Ministry of Finance. As I soon realized, when organizing a conference you have to start early. In this particular case it meant that the initial preparations for this August 1998 event began in the early months of 1997. I was taking a calculated risk in focusing on Japan's economic problems given the lead time and the unclear future Japan at that time faced. No one, including me, foresaw the extent of Japan's collapse. *Why Did Japan Stumble? Causes and Cures* suggests something less than a country on the brink of economic tomfoolery.

The reason for the title of this volume, and the theme of the conference, will become increasingly obvious as one reads through the papers and comments. It was clearly suggested by Michio Morishima's fascinating book *Why Did Japan 'Succeed'?*, written at the very start of the 1980s. I stumbled across this work back in those now distant days when I was working on my dissertation. It introduced me to many of the issues surrounding the Japanese economic system. What struck me about this book was Morishima's willingness to address big issues, no matter how daunting they might be. In contrast to the usual pedestrian approach taken by most economists, Morishima provocatively drew on history, philosophy, religion, politics and sociology to augment standard economic arguments. Accordingly, I invited Professor Morishima to do a follow up on his thoughts some 15 years down the road. I wondered how, if at all, he had changed his thinking, given recent economic history. I was pleasantly surprised to receive a fax accepting my invitation. It was then that I realized the only clearly personal benefit that comes from organizing a conference. You can in fact invite anyone you wish. Of course, people often refuse but some will say yes. This means you can sit through a conference and listen to people you want to hear. Given all the other energy-sapping details that go into producing a reasonable conference outcome, this is the one unalloyed pleasure open to a conference organizer. I can honestly say that in this respect the actual event met my expectations.

One quick point concerning the format of the book needs to be made. After all but the contribution by Masaru Yoshitomi, there are remarks by a discussant, followed in some cases by a reply from the beleaguered author. The discussant in each case is responding to the original draft of the paper as presented by the author. The paper which has finally found its way into this volume has been revised, sometimes in response to the discussant's critical remarks. This is important only to explain why at times a discussant may appear to be particularly thick.

As always there are many people to thank but I need to limit myself to just a few. Phillipa Brennan can't seem to stop herself providing the assistance I need when editing one of these volumes. It was largely thanks to her that it was done in such an expeditious fashion. Elaine Kent I need to thank most of all. Without her assistance in organizing the conference there would have been no volume to edit. Her endless optimism kept the project from sinking on many a Monday morning. Ngaire Chant proved that packaging remains an all-important element, while Debbie Jeffery as always was willing to pitch in at key moments. Edward Elgar seems determined to confound me by refusing to conform to all my preconceived ideas about publishers and editors. He continues to be encouraging, supportive and open to reasonable compromise. Without due care he might give publishing a good name. As for my daughters, they are now four years old and every bit as mystified about why I persist in banging away at my computer as when they were two. If only I had an answer.

CRAIG FREEDMAN

1. The catatonic economy

Craig Freedman

Success has ruined many a man.
Benjamin Franklin

By the 1980s many Japanese had come to believe in the inevitability of Japan as Number One. From an economically devastated country in 1946, by 1981 Japan had grown to become the world's second largest economy in an inexorable drive that saw the Japanese go from strength to strength. Western nations grew to fear them economically in a way never quite achieved by the Imperial Army. Japanese villains regained predominance in popular western books and films, a fashion not seen since the Second World War. This fear showed up in such aberrations as smashing Japanese consumer electronic goods on the steps of the Capitol in Washington, DC. People took seriously a joke by Japanese businessman Ryoei Saito, who said that he would take with him to his grave the two paintings (*Portrait of Dr Gachet* by Van Gogh and *Au Moulin de la Galette* by Renoir) purchased in 1990 for a record $US160.6 million. Behind the shudders was the belief that this economic juggernaut would dictate the world's economic future.

A decade later, decision-makers and professional pundits fear that a catatonic Japan will drag all the Asian economies (and perhaps the whole world) into a prolonged recession through their inscrutable inaction. A Japan that could do no wrong has become the clueless economy of the 1990s. How did this stunning reversal occur? How did the Japanese become convinced of their own infallibility and how did this contribute to their subsequent downfall? Only by responding thoughtfully to these questions can we begin to evaluate the future possibilities for Japan and only then does it become possible to shape them.

At one level the answer is straightforward.[1] A speculative boom led to the inevitable credit crunch, followed by the equally inevitable drop of asset prices as the 1990s began (to be exact, what the Japanese call with perverse pride their 'bubble economy' came to a juddering end as

1

1992 began). The subsequent asset deflation exposed a fundamental weakness in Japan's banking system that slowed the long-awaited recovery despite some serious fiscal injections by the Federal government. Like many aspects of the Japanese economy, decades of predictable growth had papered over the inadequacy of the financial nerve centre.

In a number of ways the Japanese economy had been run like an extended family, or perhaps more accurately, like a family business. In Japan, taking a family perspective means minimizing the risk individual members bear. The family looks after its own, regardless of any intrinsic ability, in exchange for hard work and obedience to the family head. Cash flow tends to ameliorate even disfiguring shortcomings of this family-like economic structure. In fact, success induces a certain generosity to even patently inefficient and ineffective sectors of the economy. However, by 1996, the collusive powers of the 'iron triangle' (businessmen, government bureaucrats and politicians) had lost its ability to shelter the Japanese economy from exogenous shocks. The unforgiving economics of the business cycle seemingly gained dominance over the course of Japanese economic affairs. It is at this point that Japan was struck by three interconnected blows that could be seen as a combination of bad luck and bad judgement:

- The budget deficit, which predictably had grown with the increase in countercyclical public spending, sent the Ministry of Finance mandarins into a nervous flurry of activity. Through their political mouthpieces, they announced an impending (1997) tax increase. Despite the need, however pressing, to put some brakes on the budgetary process, the timing was, to put it politely, curious. There seems to have been a serious miscalculation of the stage of recovery that the economy had entered. Consumption spending had kept the economy ticking over in the 1990s, although not without a life-support system of government expenditure. The tax increase and its prior announcement stopped consumer spending dead in its tracks in 1997 as planned spending was shifted backward into 1996 to avoid paying the scheduled extra tax. With deadly synchronicity, public spending also was slated to be significantly cut.[2]
- The Asian Miracle turned out to be the standard mixture of perfectly explicable economic growth combined with smoke and mirrors. Investors stopped ignoring that little man hiding behind the curtain and went retreating pell-mell back up the yellow brick road. This blow came as a particularly bitter and partially ironic

jolt to the fragile Japanese economy, which was trying to adjust to the eccentric strategy of raising taxes before an economic recovery was assured. The other Asian economies had become the implicit saviour of the ailing Japanese economy. Asia provided Japan with a destination that accepted a rapidly growing volume of exports. Tied with this was a significant amount of Japanese investment and loans. A rising yen increased the attractiveness of greater offshore production. The seemingly unlimited growth of this region made it a target for Japanese funds, which after the excitement of the 'bubble economy' was finding difficulty in locating domestic investments. Banks with their shaky asset base looked toward Asia as a way of recouping some of their losses. The irony is that it was this flow of funds pouring into the region (including the Japanese variety) that helped create the climate not only for the rapid boom but also for its subsequent collapse.

- The combination of domestic and regional recession meant that Japanese banks wouldn't be able to escape their own particular day of reckoning. Too many virtually insolvent banks made both fiscal and monetary policy ineffectual. A country with a paralysed banking sector is, to quote T.S. Elliot (1962: 13) out of context, 'spread out . . . like a patient etherised upon a table'. Until very late in the day, the Ministry of Finance, though aware of the problem,[3] put off taking any effective measures, perhaps in the hope that a resurgent economy would act as a patent cure-all for what ailed these increasingly fragile banks.
- Unfortunately, though these three aspects of the Japanese economy paved the way for an increasing deterioration in its performance, it does not explain why Japanese decision-makers in business and government seemed incapable of taking any decisive steps. In fact, by dwelling on these three immediate events we may succeed only in losing track of the more fundamental problems facing Japan. These problems may instead lie with the very institutional organization and associated incentive structures that differentiate the Japanese economy from that of other nations. We might term this Japan's business or economic culture. If this is the case, then Japan faces a need to make far-reaching and even radical reforms. Such reforms must of course have significant social and political consequences. It could be reasonably argued that the reformation Japan requires dwarfs the efforts made during the two other critical points in the development of modern Japan: the Meiji Restoration and the Post-war Recovery.

CULTURAL BIASES

> Economic structures and economic relations are also strongly conditioned
> by the national ethos. It is often the case that even though material conditions
> may be the same what may be possible in Japan may not be possible in the
> West and vice versa. (Morishima 1982: viii)

Economists share a reaction to the use of the word 'culture' not dis-
similar to that which reputedly characterized the late, but unlamented,
Hermann Goering.[4] There are two obvious reasons for this distinctly
negative reaction. Culture is usually an ill-defined, qualitative rather
than quantitative term. It is a variable that presents perhaps insurmountable obstacles to any attempt at meaningful measurement. As a result,
culture tends to be used to explain almost any anomaly. It can easily
be argued that variables which explain everything end up explaining
nothing at all. Culture is also an idiosyncratic or a specific rather than
a general explanation. For many economists, the objective of research
is to unlock those general relationships and causes which define all
economic functions, not just a favoured few. A case by case examination,
this veritable poring over of details, which a cultural approach implicitly
supports, is anathema to the research programme of the majority of
economists. It is narrative rather than science. For these academics and
professionals, similarities and the overwhelming importance of market
forces far outweigh the differences found when comparing specific
economies.

However, the frequent misuse of an analytical approach does not
automatically invalidate it. If by cultural differences we mean that
people in different countries respond differently to economic incentives,
we say nothing particularly startling or original. The implications are
then that different national economies can have special institutional
structures in order to provide the most effective set of incentives to
achieve a given objective or objectives.[5] This rather innocent observation underlines a fundamental problem. Economies operate most
effectively when the institutional structures in place (the cultural framework underlying an economy) promote the functioning of that economy.
Unfortunately, in a rather Baudelerian[6] way, markets and market
demands change far more rapidly than the structures which encourage
the appropriate economic responses to change. With changes in markets
occurring at ever more rapid rates, mismatches between a country's
business culture and economic necessity can become more severe and
more frequent. This potential problem becomes increasingly severe the
greater the success of a specific economic approach. It is difficult to

admit that former successful strategies are no longer worth pursuing. To tinker with, let alone to radically transform, a tried and proven formula appears to be a very high-risk option that surrenders certain returns for an unknown future.[7] The tendency is to stick with what is known best and to deny the need for change in order to justify basic inaction.

Japan has found change particularly difficult. The Japanese have lived in a country where mistakes are more costly, and thus risk is to be avoided at all costs. This is not some inexplicable manifestation of ill-defined cultural patterns but is rather grounded in the basic lack of available resources. The contrast with the US makes the difference clear,[8] especially the difference in risk preference. In the US, the traditional and fundamental belief, expanded and utilized throughout its history, is that it is a country with unlimited opportunity. Failure seems never to have precluded future success. We can contrast this fundamentally optimistic trait with the Japanese economy in the early nineteenth century, characterized by too many people trying to make do with too few resources, as opposed to the sparsely populated US where failure could be overcome by packing up and moving on. The corresponding static versus highly fluid societies meant different incentives were required to achieve economic objectives.

The implication is that in the aftermath of the Meiji Restoration the attempt to catch up with western industrialized nations did not necessarily require the simple adaptation of western institutional structures. In a highly capital constrained and resource-scarce economy emphasis would have to be placed on motivating and training the labour force. How to do this was not obvious, as Sheridan points out later in this volume (Chapter 4). Utilizing existing family or group ethics did produce a successful outcome. This did not represent the only possible alternative to assist industrialization. As Noguchi (1998) quite accurately emphasizes, Japan of the 1920s was moving rapidly toward a more western outlook both economically and socially before the strategic shift that occurred in the 1930s, preparatory to an all-out war economy, reversed this trend. But again, this dramatic shift in direction did successfully tap into an existing, older tradition. In other words, rather than some sort of simple imposition from above, this inward-looking move made use of an effective set of incentives.

It is impossible to play hypothetical guessing games and wonder if alternative business cultures could have been equally effective. Certainly the re-imposition of this economic approach which emphasized trust, loyalty and mutual obligation did not occur spontaneously. In the post-war era, the leading industrialists and their allies in the political and governmental spheres actively supported it. But despite being a successful solution generating some three decades of economic growth, it contained an inherent weakness. The very requirements needed to sustain growth, as Japan tried to expand in an ever more competitive international market environment, meant that the rigidity of its corporate structures would increase the difficulty of meeting the required rate of change.

For example, the Japanese have faced difficulties transplanting their culturally dependent corporate organizations. The need to reflect an international outlook puts strains on their pre-existing framework. To compete under these changed economic auspices, the Japanese moved steadily but rather slowly toward a more individualistic way of doing business. The need constantly to restructure, to move from mass manufacturing to a more targeted or niche approach, the transition to a more service-orientated economy, all placed an increased strain on nurtured Japanese relationships of trust and mutual obligation between firms and all their dependent constituencies. At the same time, the overwhelming success that these cultural norms had previously displayed in providing an efficient and flexible production system had caused a growing discontent among the Japanese with those traditional beliefs. Even in the prosperous 1980s a creeping disillusionment with a producer- rather than consumer-orientated economy started to spread. Discontent has of course grown, now that the economic system has stopped delivering assured growth. This failure has created an implicit feeling of betrayal. The Japanese people were assured that in return for their loyalty and hard work, business, political and government leaders would deliver a low-risk, middle-class society. Except for the illusion briefly created during the 1980s, such a result seems no longer self-evident. Moreover, a business and political governance system that depended on mutual trust and obligation seems to have lacked any effective oversight of those directing the economy. Ironically enough, a lack of accountability at one time was deemed to be a strength that specifically characterized the Japanese economy. It allowed business, financial and government managers to take a long-term developmental view of the economy and avoid the short-termism that was supposedly plaguing such countries as the US in the 1970s and 1980s.[9] As we can see with hindsight, such trust was largely misplaced. Long-term investment could at times become inseparable from personal advantage. Corruption and standard forms of rent-seeking behaviour seem to have flourished as the economy grew. This is perfectly reasonable, since as cash flow increases, the tolerance of corruption of any economic system expands. Growth tends to paper over poor judgement and corrupt practices.

It can be argued that much of Japan's success stemmed from a peculiarly hardworking, dependable workforce. Flexibility in the system came from having everyone pull together in times of hardship. For nearly 40 years, Japan was able to maintain a siege-like mentality. Sacrifices were ostensibly shared out equally. A deep-rooted cultural belief in harmonious actions and decisions promoted and sustained industrial strategy. The problem is that Japan's strength, this bond of loyalty and obligation, limits the ways in which corporations can adjust to change. A commitment to permanent employment need not prove a hindrance; but under the pressure of a stagnant economy, the degree to which such commitments slow down the necessary adjustment process may prove more serious.

> The kaisha have to depend on reduction first of temporary workers, then in subcontracted work, then pulling that work back into the plants of the company, then offering special retirement allowances to encourage workers to withdraw from the work force, and finally allowing attrition to do its work. Only in acute cases, only after exhausting other approaches, and only with full agreement of the union and work force, can actual layoffs or dismissals take place. (Abegglen and Stalk 1982: 201–2)

The logical conclusion to draw is that an economy cannot remain healthy if meeting market exigencies is constrained by an entrenched, institutional structure that is highly resistant to necessary change. The incompatibility will eventually bring on some degree of economic breakdown. Whether national belief systems or mythologies can survive these inevitable economic dislocations and transformations in a recognizable form is an unanswered question. Strict adherence to either the ideological individualism of the US or the communal ethic of Japan would seem to hinder rather than promote growth. Even the most dependable workhorse will eventually come up lame, given adverse conditions. The difficulty lies in knowing when and to what extent to desert the old proven ways. But whether desired or not, the optimal choice is not always attainable. Incentive structures, systems of cultural beliefs, cannot be traded in like last year's sedan. The impulse to change and the specific direction in which it leads is often outside any particular group's control. The transitional process itself is symbiotically related to more explicit economic or social change.

Given these considerations, the existing economic malaise and ingrained financial crisis is for Japan a symptom of a much deeper problem. The carefully constructed post-war economic system may be at its 'use-by date' in Japan. The inherent problems in that system were simply submerged by the misleading 'bubble economy' of the 1980s. It

was more of a question of when, not whether, problems would occur.
To look at just one aspect, it is ironic that the country which perfected
the *kanban* or 'just-in-time' inventory system also strictly followed the
'convoy system' in regards to business and especially financial failure.
The inventory system worked by exposing to the light of day weak
points in the production line so that these problem spots could be
instantly diagnosed and cured. The convoy system dragged down
healthy companies in order to insure that no firm, at least none of
significant size, would sink. When very strictly applied to the banking
sector, this in fact implied that the relative risks attached to financial
decisions could be, and were, badly distorted. The mentality that values
the survival of the group, as well as the Japanese need to reduce levels
of risk, at the very least contributed to the banking problems of the
1990s. The type of backroom deals that became part of this 'convoy'
system meant that access to relevant information was increasingly
limited to insiders. Without accountability, the resulting obscurity of the
decision-making process allowed corruption eventually to flourish. The
attempt to reduce risk ended up only in redistributing it at a systemic
economic level instead of limiting risk by localizing it.

 Given this analysis, Japan may be facing a challenge much greater
than those faced during the Meiji Restoration or immediately after the
Second World War. It is true that Japan is a wealthy country with
considerable savings, technological knowledge and accumulated capital
compared with its poverty and international vulnerability during those
previous periods. But at that time, as Morishima points out in his
contribution to this volume (Chapter 2), the necessary path to follow
was clearly marked out. Nor did the catch-up process involve radically
fundamental change. What makes Japan's future harder to sense is that
it must now prove capable of changing in a more dramatic fashion.
Whether Japan will prove able to do so is largely a matter of guesswork.

THE LONG AND SHORT OF THE JAPANESE ECONOMY

There is a spiritual void at the core of the Japanese nation, a moral degener-
ation that characterises everything that happens in this society . . . Japan
offers a glaring example of a highly developed level of cultural
achievement . . . supported by a pitifully mediocre . . . moral philosophy . . .
Postwar Japanese have been so alienated that they have been unable to
realise their responsibility and sense of duty as individuals and unable
to conceive a moral code. (Ishihara 1976: 75)

As noted, this volume is an attempt to understand the underlying causes behind Japan's current economic difficulties, to provide some sense of the problems it now faces, and how the Japanese might overcome them. The papers neatly divide themselves into two equal groups. In one case, Morishima, Komiya and Sheridan consider fundamental and long-range issues. Morishima reconsiders the ideological basis for the Japanese economy, an issue he first raised in his 1982 work, *Why Has Japan 'Succeeded'?* Komiya wrestles with demographic and political problems, some of which are raised, at least implicitly, by Morishima. Lastly, Sheridan dissects the development of the business culture now predominant in Japan.

Of more immediate concern, Yoshitomi, Hutchison *et al.* and Corbett worry about the recession with which Japan is currently trying to cope. All three essentially look at the financial sector as the prime cause of the continuing stagnation in Japan. While Yoshitomi provides a valuable overview which links the financial to the rest of the Japanese economy, Hutchison tries to pinpoint why the financial problems occurred in the first place, and Corbett evaluates attempts by Japanese regulators and politicians to deal with this growing difficulty.

THE LONG RUN

The Morishima paper is bound to prove controversial with many readers, especially those who claim some academic allegiance. It would be unfortunate if such readers' strong reaction to the work precluded them from considering dispassionately the issues raised. It is true that Morishima does not present any decisive arguments. There are valid criticisms to be made, as Patrick does in his response; but the fact that key parts of his thinking seem to depend on anecdotal information and tend toward the impressionistic is not reason enough to dismiss the paper out of hand. If we are honest, we will be forced to admit that we are often more persuaded by the anecdotal (especially our own experience) than by any volume of statistical evidence. But whatever we may individually find convincing, we should be willing to admit that Morishima does make us think deeply about some fundamental issues. It is imprudent to dismiss the paper as merely the pessimism of a grumpy old man. Its purpose is in fact to act as a catalyst for critical thinking, to stir things up. Economists, in particular, find this style uncongenial, at odds with a self-image of the profession as consisting of sober and methodical scientists. Current writers such as McCloskey and Mirowski do seem to upset some of the more excitable amongst their brethren by staking out strong, non-mainstream positions. But as a rhetorical approach, an attempt to overstate a case by removing all the possible myriad qualifications can, at least momentarily, shock a discipline out of its dogmatic sleep.[10] Taken in this spirit, Morishima's paper will serve as something of a litmus test for readers. Optimists are more likely to disagree violently. Professional pessimists, on the other hand, will find themselves nodding in agreement.

Morishima attempts to demonstrate how ideology can become at odds with economic necessity and hinder the progress of a given country. In the case of Japan, this leads him to conclude that the days of economic glory have passed the country by and are unlikely to return.[11] This result is due to changes in the external economic environment facing Japan coupled with ever-widening internal fissures in the existing institutional structure and prevailing ideology. Morishima, following the argument first laid out in his 1982 volume, sees the basic wartime economic structure as largely being preserved and further expanded during Japan's post-war recovery. This is what he terms 'state capitalism' or capitalism imposed from above. Confucianism, in this account, served as the moral base that oiled the wheels of the established system. Capitalism was imposed by a collaboration, consisting of business and government interests with politicians serving as the public face of the system. Those working the levers of the system had been schooled in the Confucianist beliefs that provided the necessary incentives and constraints to make the economy work. Given the post-war economic climate, the patronage of the US and the Korean and Vietnam Wars, this Japanese version of top-down economic activity was able successfully to exploit existing opportunities.

There were, however, problems which, temporarily submerged by economic success, would be sure to come to the surface if growth faltered. The key turns out to be the education system, which was imposed not by the Japanese themselves but by the Occupation forces in the immediate post-war era. As Morishima explains, the US wanted to replicate the style of education prominent in the US itself, one that cultivated individual initiative, values and actions. Confucianism ceased to be taught. Unfortunately, its replacement was only a poor imitation of a western-style education.[12] It was particularly inappropriate as Japanese society itself continued to reflect Confucianist values even if in a less conscious fashion. As generation followed generation, the ability to impose the restraint embodied by a Confucian ethic became increasingly weak. In a system based on trust but with insufficient accountability or inherent checks, corruption could only increase. This was assisted by a government that was at best only capable of village politics, namely political strategy that rewarded one's own supporters. This became a variety of politicking that forged links between rural constituents, the Liberal Democratic Party, construction companies and banks. By its own continued success, tendencies inherent in this type of capitalism from above were destroying its own basis for survival.

The complexity of the problem increases as Morishima claims that the comparative strengths of such a system, executing agreed-upon plans, are not the strengths needed in the current or foreseeable future economic environments. What is needed according to this analysis is the introduction of capitalism from below or market-driven capitalism in order to ensure the quick, flexible and innovative responses required in the new competitive environment. Unfortunately, according to Morishima, the failure to develop an educational system that either emphasized the Confucian belief system or truly developed westernized individualism means that the Japanese generation now beginning to dominate the economy, and the society in which they live, are ill suited to implement capitalism from below, or even to struggle along with some version of state capitalism.

This in itself would be enough to sink the future of Japan. The problem, however, will be aggravated in the coming decades by a generational clash. Politics remains the domain of an older generation (pre-war or transitional with a foot in both camps). Business, because of the prevailing retirement policy, is still for the most part led by an older generation, though perhaps not quite so old as the political leadership. However, the all-important government bureaucracy is now in the hands of the post-war generation who are the product of a poorly systematized educational policy. In this case, the old working partnership that symbolized Japan Inc. (business, government, politics) is breaking apart, given the lack of sympathy between generations. Just at a time when agreement and decisiveness are most needed, Japan is stuck with a poorly developed political system and an increasingly disgraced bureaucracy.[13]

Japan, as a result, has not been able to deal effectively with its most pressing problems. As an example Morishima presents the faltering financial system, an issue that is more thoroughly explored in the second half of the volume. The growing success of major Japanese corporations led to a realization that it was more efficient to raise funds via the equity or commercial paper markets. This deprived the main bank of a given horizontal *keiretsu* (grouping of firms and businesses allied to one another and mutually owning each other's shares) of its main function as well as its strategic leverage. The problem was that the main bank system worked in principle as a check on the prerogatives of management. In its weakened state, corporate governance came increasingly adrift. Even worse, most corporations maintained their drive for market share (cash flow ensuring viability) without the implicit oversight of their bankers keeping check on outstanding loans.[14] At the same time, banks, lacking the traditional outlet of corporate loans, looked more towards real estate and other sectors that aided and abetted the asset inflation characterizing the last half of the 1980s. Aggravating these problems, the protection of the banking sector by the government led to a deficient regard for risk. The assumed convoy system meant that no bank would be in danger of failing. Politicians, wanting to maintain the stream of loans to the construction industry which supported vote-getting public works in their rural constituencies,[15] looked the other way.

The issue then is not whether the Japanese will have to change their economic system. There is a consensus about this issue not only among the contributors to this volume but among many sectors of the Japanese economy itself, especially among corporate leaders. The issues raised by Morishima are rather whether, given their institutional and cultural structures, the Japanese will be able to transform themselves successfully and what the objective of such a transformation should be. Though it might be argued that the Japanese have demonstrated a remarkable degree of flexibility in the past, the type of change that Morishima describes, from a top-down to a bottom-up economy, measurably sur-passes previous accomplishments. The Meiji Restoration and the post-war re-industrialization largely adapted existing top-down institutions and a prevailing set of cultural beliefs to a well-defined objective. What Morishima and others seem to be arguing is for a distinct break with Japan's feudal past. Is this possible? It is here that we see clear disagree-ment. Morishima would say that the past decisions made by the Japanese mean that this basic capability is lacking.[16] Japan simply is not able to move quickly enough. Only when the core educational system changes will the potential at least be present. For educational reform, however, to have any significant effect we must wait for many decades until those just now entering school move to positions of some authority.

Can Morishima conclusively demonstrate this? Essentially, such proof must be elusive if not impossible. Hugh Patrick thus has legitimate grounds to mount an alternative vision of Japan's future. The point, however, when reading Morishima's gloomy premonitions is to realize the deep-rooted importance of the issues raised. Just being forced to consider the origins and implications of these fundamental problems is by itself a valuable contribution that is only negated if Morishima's work is dismissed out of hand.

Ryutaro Komiya eschews fundamental moral causes to examine more closely three of the overwhelming problems facing Japan: demographic, political and budgetary. The demographic issue is perhaps the most insidious since population control has long been one of the world's undisputed social and economic objectives.[17] Having one of the most rapidly ageing populations creates almost insurmountable difficulties in terms of the necessary transfer from future working population to those who are elderly and retired. Given the deep reluctance shown by the Japanese towards immigration, with only a handful allowed in each year, Komiya recognizes that child-bearing and child-rearing must be encouraged by lowering the opportunity cost of starting a family. This is a long-run solution, though evidence that this choice is sufficiently price sensitive doesn't abound.

What Komiya might emphasize equally is encouraging Japanese workers to continue in productive jobs.[18] Given the standard seniority system, early retirement relieves employers of paying generous salaries to long-serving employees. Moving away from this system would more easily open up the opportunity for employment throughout one's senior years. This is particularly true in the public sector, as Komiya very deftly shows. As part of an implicit wage package, government bureaucrats when they retire in their early fifties are taken care of by the *amakudari* process; namely, layers of government have been created largely driven by the need to create positions for retired government bureaucrats. This creates an unchecked waste of government spending as well as an increased opportunity for corruption. Given the demographic problems facing Japan, there seems no possible justification for this ever-expanding, and largely unaccountable, sector to continue to exist in the economy. Unfortunately, as Morishima, Komiya and several other authors clearly point out, politics in Japan is still largely 'village politics', more concerned with redistributing income to rural constituencies and political contributors than with governing the country. If then Japan is to avoid the fate predicted by Morishima, the political structure and government bureaucracy will need to change radically. Given vested interests, this seems difficult if not unlikely.[19] However, change via an increasingly disenchanted electorate, one which feels not only disappointed but also largely betrayed, remains a possibility. This would require an effective opposition to face the Liberal Democratic Party, an organization that at times seems on the verge of imploding, waiting only for an appropriate shove.

The third and last issue, budget balancing, is a more contentious problem, one that Komiya tries conscientiously to approach even-handedly. Given the acknowledged waste involved in government spending, it is hard to argue that such spending cannot be cut. But as the economy restructures and the population ages, greater welfare demands will also inevitably grow. If the business sector does restructure along the lines endorsed by Morishima, welfare provision no longer will remain largely an implicit responsibility of the private sector. Government must inevitably step in. The effect of this burden of added spending is difficult to estimate. Given Japan's rather impenetrable governmental accounts, it is somewhat foolhardy, to say the least, to distinguish exactly what the current budgetary problem is and how large it might become. Though there is a consensus behind some sort of cyclically balanced budget, the issue of when government spending can be cut back or taxes raised is not self-evident.[20]

Sheridan continues this discussion of Japan's long-range choices by providing a very interesting and useful analysis of the formation of Japan's business structure, or what she terms business culture. It is reminiscent in its acuity to Ronald Dore's (1986) book, *Flexible Rigidities*. Japan, forced to join the international community in the mid-nineteenth century, had only its labour force available as an abundant resource. Despite a lack of capital or technological ability, Japan was determined to catch up and, as we know, it did. To do so the Japanese made a virtue out of their constraints. An increasingly well-trained and highly motivated workforce, one willing to forgo immediate rewards, proved to be the engine which could drive Japanese expansion. Sheridan shows exactly how it was accomplished.[21] She points out that Japan in the past has always been able to respond to unanticipated economic shocks, such as the oil shocks in the 1970s, by simply squeezing their employees harder. The real break with past practices will come if such a strategy can no longer provide an effective solution to deal with current economic problems. Japan would be forced to change. What Sheridan terms 'a make-shift solution' would be shown to be largely a cul-de-sac.

Like others in this volume, she also recognizes that corporate reform means a necessary shift away from private to public provision of welfare. Previous corporate arrangements, like so much else in the Japanese economy, worked on the assumption of continuous and predictable growth. The 1990s showed just how dangerous economic institutions built on this assumption could prove.[22] Sheridan sees the need for a new business culture. Like Komiya, she disparages the assumption that it must be a carbon copy of that which characterizes the US.[23]

At this point we do run into a serious problem with the paper. In some ways Sheridan's analysis, or at least a good portion of its conclusions and implications, are more in tune with the early 1990s when the limitations of the Japanese economy were still not fully apparent. Besides the opening acknowledgement of the current recession, there is no other clear recognition of the relevant constraints on Japanese choice. Certainly, those choices must be limited by past decisions and by existing and future economic possibilities. Given the increasingly competitive nature of international markets and the possible inability of Japan to limit the encroachment of outside risk, the William Morris option suggested by Sheridan does not seem viable unless she is talking about William Morris the Hollywood agent rather than William Morris the turn of the century English artist and craftsman. Given the current situation, it is difficult to accept that the issue of quality, rather than quantity, of life will be decisive in an era when firms are struggling to stay afloat and employees are uncertain about their employment prospects. As opposed to the era of oil shocks, when adjustment demands also provided clear opportunities, there may be simply no room to question objectives. The debate may be sadly and narrowly limited to how even simple objectives may be reached. The sort of fundamental restructuring which would flow from Sheridan's analysis may simply prove to be uncompetitive and thus not viable.

THE SHORT RUN

The focus of the second half of this volume is on the immediate financial difficulties facing Japan and what general relationships and policy implications can be drawn from these events. This is true of the Yoshitomi paper, which acknowledges the central importance of the ailing financial sector for understanding the reasons behind Japan's economic disappointments. It is this sector which impedes Japan in its attempts to recover from a period of extended economic stagnation. Japanese banks have indeed been brought low: only a decade ago these same banks were expanding internationally and were assumed to be capable of steamrolling the rest of their international competitors with their vast pool of assets. Both British and US banks anticipated facing the same fate as once-proud British and US carmakers in the 1970s. This presumption best indicates how little the outside world knew about Japanese banks and perhaps how little Japanese banks knew about banking. The authors in this volume make this abundantly clear as they examine the banking problems that have plagued Japan and have prevented any sustained economic recovery.

Hutchison *et al.* try to understand the origin of the banking crisis. As these authors point out, too little work has been done to understand systematically what in particular causes these periodic débâcles. Ideally, a general model would allow banking authorities to recognize an incipient problem before it was fully realized; otherwise, supervision remains largely a process of depending on anecdotal evidence and using certain rules of thumb. The risk, however, of employing such general models is that what may work for the average country goes badly off-track when applied to a specific economy. Premature intervention is not without its risks and costs. As Eileen Mauskopf implies in her commentary, the problem lies in deciding whether the specifics of a given case are more important than generalized trends. What may be important for policy is not what banking crises have in common, but what differentiates them. However, what Hutchison *et al.* attempt does make an important contribution to policy work since it goes at least part of the way towards supplying banking supervisors with a checklist. Certain warning signs should not be allowed to pass unnoticed. The correct action may inevitably require the discretion and good sense of the policy-maker, a requirement that inevitably leaves many economists feeling uneasy. We can hope, however, to provide some sort of benchmark to be used by, and with which to judge the actions of, government banking authorities.

Although there are questions concerning the predictive ability of their model, what the authors do come up with makes intuitive sense. They oblige the reader by lining up and interrogating the usual suspects. What is unfortunate here is that, due to data limitations, one of the more likely culprits escapes the round-up. Real-estate prices would logically be one of the best leading indicators of asset inflation and of an overextended banking sector. Certainly in Japan, as well as in many other countries, the rush towards real-estate lending followed by the inevitable collapse of real-estate prices will dependably exacerbate the increasing fragility of any banking system. The companion of asset inflation, or perhaps the other leading indicator, is often financial deregulation. Deregulation combined with an often concurrent increased degree of competition sees financial institutions taking greater risks by expanding into new areas of operations, often areas where they lack proper experience. This is a recipe for almost any organization to overextend, leaving itself vulnerable to even small economic shocks. It has been all but inevitable that banking crises follow deregulation. This is important to keep in mind since the full costs of these various 'big bangs' have been inadequately examined. Deregulation itself isn't automatically suspect. It does, however, mean that quite extensive preparations need to be made, including more effective supervision and increased accountability through improved flows of information.

Hutchison *et al.* also provide a reason for Japan's extended, and at times seemingly irremediable, banking problems. As subsequent scandals revealed, the objectives of the supervisors merged too closely with those of the objects of supervision. The extent and length of any crisis may depend largely on the political leverage of the country's banking sector as well as those associated with that sector. In Japan's case, this was compounded by the perceived necessity to keep afloat the heavily indebted large contracting firms previously mentioned.

If then it is possible to have at least some feel for when banks may be slipping into irremediable difficulties, what should government supervisors do? This presents a somewhat intractable puzzle, as Jenny Corbett points out in her valuable contribution. Given the necessary information asymmetry, which is especially severe in the case of Japan, regulators will inevitably find it difficult to know how to proceed. Banks must be prevented from hiding their losses, a Japanese specialty, by simply rolling over loans that would best be foreclosed. On the other hand, a too restrictive approach would see viable firms starved of credit.

Regulators themselves lack credibility. The politics of the relationship, the unwillingness of governments to allow banks to fail, leads financial institutions to discount heavily any tough public stance, though it is unclear that taking hardline positions is necessarily productive. Policy prescriptions applied to banking sector rescues, while appearing authoritative, often conflict with sound theoretical analysis. Corbett highlights these contradictions very effectively. She provides a useful service by defining the conditions under which different policy prescriptions will be most effective. Unfortunately, it is far from a simple matter to determine which relevant conditions are prevalent. In the case of Japan, it does appear that regulators delayed for an inordinately long time, as though they were hoping that returned economic growth would make such issues moot. This was a fundamentally flawed approach since a damaged and inefficient financial sector meant that sustained growth would be difficult. At best, an economic resurgence would have succeeded in only temporarily subduing the urgency with which the banking sector needed to be repaired. Certainly the notions that:

- no one should get hurt;
- no banks should be seen to fail;
- management need take no responsibility for their past decisions,

did nothing to resolve the problem. In a larger sense, this points to a bigger issue facing Japan. Being able to estimate risk has become an essential skill in navigating the new financial markets. Japan has striven instead to make risk a factor of small consequence, effectively to shield its population by protecting and regulating key aspects of its economy. The Japanese quite naturally find that they lack these skills, leaving them ill prepared to live in a more risk-filled environment.

Japan's economic woes began when it assumed that it had found an infallible key to economic growth instead of an approach applicable to a specific set of economic circumstances. Facing some almost insurmountable difficulties, it now realizes that its previous illusion of superiority created an economic trap from which it has been ineffectually trying to flee in the 1990s. Will the Japanese overcome the challenge inherent in many of its long-range problems? To do so the country may need to adopt more of the individualism of liberal capitalism while at the same time preserving Japan's comparative advantage, the ability to cooperate and work efficiently as a group, which is based on mutual trust and loyalty. If anything, the pragmatism that has long characterized the Japanese may see them through. They have a long history of success under adversity and a stubborn refusal to accept defeat. Whether Japan will continue as an economic powerhouse remains debatable, but it will most probably continue to be a wealthy country with a relatively high standard of living, even if it finds sustained growth an elusive goal in the future. Whatever Japan's potential ultimately may be, it will best be achieved when its political, institutional and cultural structures are once again in sync and supportive of a vibrant and flexible economy.

NOTES

1. See Yoshitomi, Chapter 5 in this volume, for a precise recounting of these events.
2. As Masaru Yoshitomi makes clear in Chapter 5, the size of the proposed budget consolidation was considerable. The total tax increase of 9 trillion yen represented 1.8 per cent of GDP (5 trillion more from the increased consumption tax, 2 trillion from the end of a temporary income tax reduction, and 2 trillion in increased social security contributions). Public works spending was also sliced by 3 trillion yen or 0.6 per cent of GDP.
3. The extent of the Ministry's awareness is arguable given the inherent opaqueness of prevailing accounting standards. See Ito's discussion of Chapter 7 in this volume.
4. The quote often attributed to Goering is: 'Whenever I hear the word culture, I reach for my pistol.' For those who are idly curious, the actual author is a German playwright, Hanns Johst, who wrote the following lines in a 1933 play: 'Whenever I hear the word culture ... I release the safety-catch of my Browning.' How the misattribution occurred is left as a project for the insightful and curious reader.
5. Objectives themselves may vary. It would be hard to argue that in the post-war period Japanese firms were clearly profit maximizers. It would be simpler to demonstrate that the incentive structure provided to management encouraged the pursuit of market share and revenue growth even at the expense of profitability. In his

paper, Morishima argues that this reflects the long-standing Japanese imperative to catch up to western industrialized countries. Such behaviour is consistent with the Japanese aim of reducing risk and raising the prosperity of the country.

6. ' ... la forme d'une ville change plus vite, hélas! que le coeur d'un mortel' (Baudelaire 1954: 288).

7. 'If it's not broke, don't fix it' describes this particular mind set. The problem is that, except in hindsight, it is difficult, if not impossible, to distinguish between change for change's sake and attempts to anticipate the direction in which economic markets are moving.

8. The archetypal American entrepreneur was the risk-taker *par excellence*. This refusal to play it safe, and a certain willingness to shave margins experimentally close, gave the US a competitive edge in the nineteenth century. But it was the peculiar circumstance and origins of the country that provided a form of economic flexibility consistent with an individualistic culture. These circumstances proved conducive to a continued drive for economic efficiency. In some ways the early US was the embodiment of an Adam Smith-like society. Vast territories and a scattered population provided a blank slate in lieu of a structured economic environment. Flexibility grew out of an assumption of unlimited opportunity; namely, a given belief in the ability to start over emboldened individuals to undertake risky enterprises. A failure in one activity could later be counterbalanced by success in another. In this early society of independent producers, some of the efficiency to be gained by a strict division of labour was surrendered in order to achieve the versatility and flexibility provided by encouraging more well-rounded, jack-of-all trades: 'The American is often shipwrecked, but no other sailor crosses the sea as fast as he. Doing what others do but in less time, he can do it at less expense' (Toqueville 1967: 403).

9. Abernathy and Hayes (1980) are a good example of this type of literature, which flourished in the first half of the 1980s when the myth of Japanese invincibility was building. In contrast, as Eileen Mauskopf points out, the lack of accountability evidenced in its prevailing system of corporate governance is one of the engines driving Japan's financial collapse.

10. Keynes's *General Theory* can be understood as a particularly famous example of this rhetorical approach. For some economists, the worst fate of all is to be ignored. It is in effect part of their marketing plan at least to shock readers into attacking the views stated. Unless some sort of dialogue is initiated, the work itself achieves nothing. The Nobel Prize winner George Stigler gave up writing a monthly column in a business magazine when, despite his best efforts to be outrageous, not a single reader bothered to respond. He saw no reason to continue.

11. As Patrick points out in his reply, there is something definitely peculiar about this predicted Japanese collapse. Morishima does not expect economic security, comfort or well-being to vanish; he claims only that Japan will be incapable of sustaining a role as a major economic force in the world. In some sense, this should be no real cause for alarm; in fact, Morishima's vision of Japan in the year 2050 reflects a country that is no longer so painfully driven. It may in fact become a country less concerned with catching up, or with dominating, one where its citizens learn to relax and enjoy themselves.

12. Morishima remarked in his presentation that teachers who previously had started class with a Nazi salute during the war were now the same people who were expected to imbue young Japanese students with democratic principles.

13. It could be argued that, although politicians were known to be corrupt, Japanese in general believed that the country was held together by a well-educated and dedicated bureaucracy serving the interests of Japan as a whole. The Ministry of Finance scandals have certainly undercut that image. Morishima draws an interesting parallel with the rampant corruption evident in the Tokugawa era leading up to the Meiji Restoration. The spread of bribery and economic stagnation do not seem to be an entirely unusual coupling.

14. Debt-holders tend to be more interested in cash flow than in corporate profit. They

are heavily risk averse since they share only the downside of a corporation's fortunes. It was not then merely the focused drive to catch up with western nations that explained this continued emphasis on market share.

15. Many of the large construction firms are virtually insolvent. According to company reports for fiscal year 1997, three of the top five contractors posted heavy losses:

- Kajima   6.0 billion yen profit
- Shimizu   −45.0 billion yen loss
- Obayashi   10.8 billion yen profit
- Taisei   −112.3 billion yen loss
- Kumagai Gumi   +217.6 billion yen loss

They survive on continued public spending and the willingness of their bankers to roll over their loans. Bankruptcy would scuttle not only these firms but also their main banks. Needless to say, the flow of sizeable political contributions from these publicly minded construction giants would also dry up.

16. This is largely an impressionistic judgement based on an evaluation of the younger generation in Japan. Morishima finds them a particularly hopeless lot. This is the same group which Patrick admires and Sheridan suggests may be capable of bringing about a transformation of Japan's business culture.

17. The problem of an ageing population and a steadily dropping birthrate is now even plaguing China. The idea of a shortage in the numbers of available Chinese seems a contradiction in terms at the very least. However, years of a forced one-child policy now leave Chinese leaders wondering how the mass of an ageing population will be sufficiently supported by a dwindling number of Chinese children.

18. Okabe clearly points this out in his discussion of Komiya's paper.

19. One problem which blocks any serious change is that at least a portion of Japanese leadership (corporate, political and governmental) is not dissatisfied with a very slow-growing economy. They are still quite comfortable and are loath to surrender any of the advantages they now command.

20. I do think we need to dismiss the US as the prime mover behind Japan's budgetary problems. Komiya tends to take too seriously America's propensity to tell others what they should do and the effect such posturing has. Japan has shown over the years a distinct ability to acquiesce to requests without responding to them. Often the US serves as a stalking horse, allowing Japanese politicians to make an unpopular decision and then to turn around and blame it on the US.

We must remember that in the 1980s, at the height of Japan's economic success, the Japanese seemed quite willing to lecture the US on economic policy. Even Australian politicians, flushed with an unexpected level of economic success, feel fit these days to lecture the rest of the world on economic probity.

What does seem clear is that the economies of Japan and the US are inextricably linked. Any large-scale repatriation of Japanese funds out of the US would seriously crimp economic growth on either side of the Pacific. Both countries are deeply interested in the continuing viability of the Japanese economy despite whatever transient political grandstanding occurs.

21. Making a strength out of a limitation would continue to serve the Japanese. In the immediate post-war period, a devastated Japan lacked sufficient capital or road transport. Out of the necessity of dealing with these limitations came the celebrated *kanban* or 'just in time' inventory system. Required working capital was minimized. Locating supply firms close to the core-manufacturing firm reduced transport costs. Keeping inventory low also brought with it the associated benefit that the required lean production caused any production bottlenecks to become visible quickly. Correcting these inefficiencies, or continuous improvement, led to an internationally competitive manufacturing sector.

22. In a loosely parallel fashion, US welfare programmes instituted in the late 1960s and early 1970s also assumed the death of the business cycle. The oil shocks demon-

strated the real opportunity costs of such programmes, a cost which the electorate over the next few decades proved increasingly unwilling to pay.

23. While acknowledging the importance of innovation, risk-taking and an effective financial sector, Komiya thinks that Japan would be more successful if it made use of its traditional strengths. These include (see p. 104):

- a high level of education;
- a law-abiding public;
- a low crime rate;
- harmonious labour–management relations;
- sound macroeconomic policies;
- relatively equal income distribution.

REFERENCES

Abegglen, James C. and Geoffrey G. Stalk (1982), *Kaisha, the Japanese Corporation*, New York: Basic Books.

Abernathy, William J. and Robert H. Hayes (1980), 'Managing our way to economic decline', *Harvard Business Review*, July/August: 53–77.

Baudelaire, Charles (1954), 'Le cygne', in *Fleurs du Mal*, Fresno, CA: Academy Library Guild, 289.

Dore, Ronald (1986), *Flexible Rigidities*, London: Athlone Press.

Elliot, Thomas Stearns (1962), 'The love song of J. Alfred Prufrock', in *Collected Poems 1909–1962*, London: Faber & Faber, 13–18.

Ishihara, Shintaro (1976), 'A nation without morality', in *The Silent Power: Japan's Identity and World Role*, Tokyo: Simul.

Morishima, Michio (1982), *Why Has Japan 'Succeeded'?*, Cambridge: Cambridge University Press.

Noguchi, Yukio (1998), 'The 1940 system: Japan under the wartime economy', *American Economic Review Papers and Proceedings*, 88 (2): 404–8.

Toqueville, Alexis de (1967), *Democracy in America*, Garden City, NY: Anchor Books.

PART I

Future Directions

2. Why do I expect Japan to collapse?[1]

Michio Morishima

I

The Japanese have had a generous attitude towards various religions. In the past they have permitted a number of religious groups to be active simultaneously within the country. In modern Japan, Shintoism, Buddhism and Confucianism are available as major religious options. In addition to these, Christianity and other foreign religions have gained a following in recent times. The Japanese have been drawn equally to new religions formed only a generation or two ago. This vast multiplicity of choices shows both their tolerance and at the same time their indifference to spiritual life. Among these many choices, the one which perhaps appeals to most Japanese is Confucianism. As a religion, it is one of the most irreligious and worldly in the sense that it detaches itself from ceremonial occasions such as marriages and funerals and does not confront the problems of birth and death.

In the Tokugawa period (1603–1867) Confucianism was the moral backbone of the samurai class. From the Meiji Revolution to the defeat experienced in the Second World War, moral education at school was strictly along Confucianist lines. Nevertheless, it rarely had its own temples or churches. It was in the school classroom and the family sitting room that Confucian doctrines were taught to children. Those children whose parents were neither from the samurai class nor well educated had no place other than the classroom in which to learn Confucian ethics. Families of this background were more likely to find such education intrusive. These were the people who enthusiastically accepted the decision of the General Headquarters of the Occupation Forces (GHQ) to prohibit schools from engaging in this type of moral teaching after the Second World War. As a result, most Japanese in the 1990s have no particular respect for or knowledge of Confucianism. Contemporary Japan is now nearly devoid of the asceticism that once

25

inspired it. This is increasingly true as time goes by since memories of pre-war life are fading rapidly amongst Japanese families.

It is a well known fact that, after the war, the GHQ ordered the Japanese government to make a number of substantial changes, such as: enforcing the New Constitution; complete disarmament; dissolution of the *zaibatsu*; land reform; educational reform, and a number of others. Of all these reforms, the one that produced the most powerful effect in the long run was the switch from the old to the new education system. Those educated under the old system did not automatically approve of the newly educated young people. But while the former still dominated society, firms could enforce an initial Confucian type of training upon school leavers and university graduates who were accepted only provisionally as employees: failing these training courses caused appointments to be terminated. This selection programme, however, ceased to work well when most of those with an older style of education started to retire from their active posts and were of necessity replaced by those educated under the post-war system. Therefore, by the end of the 1980s, Japan had been transformed into a country with a very changed identity.

Associated with this change, the type of nationalism that had been another important factor in forming a distinct Japanese ethos had also received a deadly blow. In the middle of the sixth century, when Japan first imported Confucianism, China was a mighty and prosperous country. Korea was similarly advanced as well as being culturally superior to Japan. In such an environment the Japanese became self-consciously defensive about their perceived inferiority. Not unexpectedly, a reactive spirit of nationalism was already flourishing by the end of the seventh century. Nationalism was then conjoined to the recently imported Confucianism. The resulting militant ethos made the Japanese particularly materialistic, encouraging them in maintaining a keen interest in the richness of their secular life. They subsequently learned from their experiences in the Second World War just how dangerous virulent nationalism could be. But when it ended with a devastating defeat, many Japanese feared that a continued nationalistic ethos would inevitably bring a Hitler-like leader to power in the future. Today most Japanese people believe that they are free from any such danger in the foreseeable future: it appears that by dropping two nuclear bombs the US also devastated nationalism. Stripped of this underlying nationalistic fervour, the Japanese lost confidence in themselves and withdrew from any serious role in international affairs. Instead, they preferred to avoid the world of international power politics as much as possible. Protected by their American ally, they single-mindedly pursued their own material gain, ignoring all outside criticism no matter how severe.

In the 1990s Japan entered a new era in which the post-war generation clearly dominated the country for the first time. This changeover occurred just as Japan faced the stark necessity of converting an economy best characterized as capitalism from above (or state-guided capitalism) to one where capitalism from below (or competitive capitalism driven by the market) could dominate. How successful will they be in this very difficult undertaking? I shall set the focus of my investigation on a vision of Japan in the year 2050. Nevertheless, in the following analysis I shall not be concerned with the actual working of the Japanese economy or society in the future. I shall only list a number of convincing premonitions which I believe can lead us to a clear-cut image of the future of Japan. Based on these insights, the reader will join me in concluding that the future of the country is not very bright: Japan will not be able to remain in the top group of industrial countries; its international influence will become obscure and insignificant. Though there is a reasonable chance that Japan's manufactured output will remain internationally competitive, I must say that the dream of an age of Japan is now over.

II

The first fact which may be regarded as a premonition of this downfall is a sharp drop in the population.

Fact 1: A Sharply Declining Population

In 1980, when comparing 18 major countries, Japan had the lowest percentage of people aged 65 years and older. In 2010 Japan is expected to have the highest percentage of these people. Moreover, the replacement of the old generation by those newly born will be far from adequate. In fact, the indexed age of the population, the ratio of the population 65 years old and over to that less than 15 years old, will rise very rapidly in the first half of the next century; it was 96.6 in 1996 but is expected to be 118 in the year 2000, 196 in 2020 and 247 in 2050. In a rich country like Japan, married couples prefer stringent family planning. They have few if any children, the very children who would be destined to support a large number of old people. It is not surprising then to discover that population forecasts estimating trends in the next century required a downward revision in 1993 and again in 1997.

According to the most recent forecast, we can say that the Japanese population will decline from its current figure of 125 570 000 to an estimated 2050 figure of 100 496 000. If these figures are accepted, Japan will lose 20 per cent of its present population in the next 50 years. The decline will be enormous in the years between 2020 and 2050.

Moreover, any population forecast is inherently unstable downwards. Once a pessimistic forecast is announced, couples hesitate to have babies. They realize that these innocent infants will have an even heavier prospective responsibility than was previously imagined. This newly born generation will one day have to maintain an even larger number of unproductive seniors at a reasonable standard of living. This can only increase the guilt that couples often feel about bringing another child into the world. Deciding how many children to produce is naturally the most important and increasingly difficult decision potential parents can make. Where birth control is practised, population growth is no longer simply a natural phenomenon but the result of people's decision-making. This type of consumer behaviour is partly a matter of choice but also partly modified by custom. When the statistics are examined for any evidence of instability we find that, according to the forecast made in 1993, the Japanese population in the year 2050 which was to be 111.5 million was revised to 100.5 million in the 1997 forecast. The 1993 forecast has produced an apparent revision in family planning which amounts to a decrease in the 2050 population of 11 million. If this instability hypothesis is correct, even stricter birth control measures will be taken hereafter. The present forecast which indicates that the 2050 population will be only four-fifths of the actual 1996 population in retrospect may be seen to have been too optimistic.

III

In Confucianist countries, people's social class is determined by their educational achievements. The period of school education is not only a period of intellectual training but also one in which children are allocated to various social classes. This is true of western societies as well, to some extent, but it is particularly so for Confucianist countries. When higher education was rare, those who graduated from a university would be automatically recognized as members of the literati; but when higher education became universal, universities were classified into a number of different categories. Though the competition to enter a good university naturally intensified, this education race did not necessarily produce Confucianist graduates. In some cases it might have had quite an opposite effect by producing much more individualistic and self-centred Japanese. Such an ironic outcome is a consequence of Japan's defeat in the Second World War.

Fact 2: Occupation Resulted in a New Type of Education which Aimed at Creating a New Type of Japanese

As soon as the Occupation Forces came to Japan, their General Head-quarters (GHQ) ordered the Japanese government to change the aim of its education policy. The government introduced a new system of education in 1947 in order to replace the old one that had a strongly ultra-nationalistic bias. Children born in 1941 were the first generation who could climb the ladder provided by this new education system without experiencing any other contrasting experience.

We may then classify the Japanese people into three groups: (a) those born after 1940, who are called the 'post-war' generation; (b) those born before 1925 and who therefore completed their education before the end of the war, who are referred to as the 'pre-war' generation; and (c) those born between 1925 and 1940, who were transferred from the old to the new education system at some point in their educational development. This last group serves as a 'transitional' generation. The ages of the oldest segment of the post-war generation and those of the youngest of the pre-war are listed, for several selected years, in Table 2.1.

Table 2.1 The generational shift in Japan

| Year | Generation | |
	Pre-war	Post-war
1960	36	19
1970	46	29
1980	56	39
1990	66	49

We find that, while the pre-war generation dominated the world of business and politics in the 1960s and 1970s, it lost its power in the 1990s.[2] The 1980s were an intermediate period during which the pre-war generation was steadily replaced by the transitional group. We may say that power began to be further transferred to the post-war generation by the middle of the 1990s. It could have been predicted that this handover of power would be accompanied by social and possibly economic strains. The new education ordered by the GHQ was carried out with the intention of implanting American ideas in Japanese children. It differed greatly from the old education based on Confucianism which emphasized family values and loyalty to the nation. An early indication of the incompatibility of these approaches to education came in 1970 when the novelist Yukio Mishima committed suicide after failing to convince officers and soldiers that reviving the pre-war Japanese morality of loyalty and patriotism was both necessary and urgent. Mishima's act was performed abruptly in an hysterical and farcical way, but we should note that it occurred in one of the early transitional years when power could be expected to begin to move away from the pre-war generation to the post-war one. Mishima himself was one of the oldest members of the transitional group.

Moreover, it must be noted that the American or European values taught in Japanese schools after the war were of a dubious character. In its post-war Japanese version, individualism became no more than a solemn-looking encouragement of egoism. Liberalism was taught as a doctrine that could lead to anarchism. This state of confusion is not surprising since school teachers themselves had no proper understanding of these concepts. They had been, until the end of the war, experts in Japanese Confucianist education, teaching children selfless devotion to the Emperor as the guiding principle of the nation.

Japan became widely known as a country where politicians, government officers and businessmen worked well in collaboration with each other, at least until the beginning of the 1980s. However, since 1990 when the so-called economic 'bubble' burst, the imperturbable solidarity of these three professional groups fractured. The disclosure in the newspapers of countless wicked acts, such as bribes between businessmen and officials, insider trading, and dinner parties at unnecessarily expensive restaurants sponsored by local governments to entertain officials of the central government, became the norm. Such devastating blows to the previously established high level of work discipline seem to have been particularly closely related, in the case of those which occurred in the 'bubble period', to the fact that the active working lives of politicians, government officials and businessmen differ greatly from each other. When a new permanent Under-Secretary of a department (or Minister) is appointed, those government officials who are the same age as or older than the new appointee must retire. We may therefore say that most government officers are less than about 53 years old. In the business world, on the other hand, employees usually work until they are 58 years old. Some of them remain until, say, 63 years old as executives, whilst those who are selected as presidents, chairmen or honorary advisers work for their companies until they reach approximately 73 years of age. It is not exceptional for politicians to outlast their business bosses. Given these disparities, it follows that the early years of the 1990s were critical. By this time, all those serving as government officers were the educational product of the post-war approach, whilst many of the top managers of business firms were still from the pre-war or transitional generation. Moreover, there were still men with outdated ways of thinking in the political arena.

The Japanese political world today basically remains mired at the level of village politics. Men who possess the requisite political upbringing dominate it. At general elections, the political ideas of the candidates and even the parties they belong to are irrelevant to the voting decision. Politicians are assessed from the viewpoint of the benefits that they will deliver to the individual voter. Men of political pedigree thoroughly understand the mechanics of patronage by virtue of which they have built their fame as well as their fortune. However, their knowledge of political theory is weak and they are largely unfamiliar with economic reasoning. At best there prevails a traditional Confucianist ethic in village communities formed by political bosses and their hangers-on.

We must remember that, in addition to the political world, the world of business also remained largely unchanged. Most school leavers and university graduates found their places, of course, in the business world. In spite of the GHQ's best efforts during the post-war occupation, the mentality, social customs and power structure observed by most adult Japanese did not change much from those that had prevailed before and during the war. New graduates came to their new employers, and to their new communities in which they worked and lived, as strangers. They were considered to require re-education so that they would behave in an acceptable manner. Those whose manners and personal skills were found to be inappropriate lost their jobs. Retraining schemes of this kind worked well until the early years of the 1980s. By the middle of that decade these new recruits differed so markedly from their predecessors that they became known as the 'New Human Species' and were treated as odd members of society. In the latter part of the 1980s retraining itself became unsuccessful. The incoming group of trainers belonged to the same misfit generation and were deemed to be equally odd by the top managers of these firms.

It is not surprising that the New Education produced a significant number of confused youngsters. Despite this, no viable alternative existed. After a series of successively aggressive student movements in 1968 and 1969, many Japanese families began to send their children to

America to be educated there. Coincidentally, many Japanese companies expanded their overseas business at this time. These children,
most of whom naturally received their education in English, were
appointed to work at the foreign offices of such companies. Their unor-
thodox educational background proved initially to be a great advantage
in advancing their careers. Most of them achieved promising positions
as middle-level managers of influential companies in the early 1980s. In
this way Japan gained a group of employees who were clearly of good,
international quality. Unfortunately, they were but a small fraction of
the total workforce and, even though widely employed, they did not fit
in well with the upper, executive stratum of the pre-war generation.

The structure of Japan's workforce, however, was changing rapidly
during the 1980s. Until 1986, the business and political world was run
largely by people from the transitional and pre-war generations. By
1990 few of the pre-war generation remained as active executives. As
has already been pointed out, after 1994 Japanese society split into
three major sectors: the government departments, consisting of 'newly
educated' officers; the political world, still abiding by traditional rules
of behaviour; and the 'mixed' world of business, consisting of a top
executive class, still keeping to the Confucianist ethos, and an employee
class formed by the post-war education system.

It is clear that Japan is undergoing a great and rapid structural change
in this last decade of the twentieth century. In reaction to this distinctive
change, the business ethos of Japan will falter and break away from the
traditional Japanese way of thinking. It was, however, this base that
enabled it to unify politics, administration and business during Japan's
expansionary phase from 1950 to 1980. This cleft in Japanese society is
only transitory, but it may create some very long-lasting effects. We
may then observe the following.

Fact 3: The Post-war Japanese Educational Reform did not Agree with Durkheim's Stipulation Concerning the Proper Role of Education

The New Education was introduced immediately after the Second
World War with the intention of changing completely the ethos of the
Japanese and the character of their society. It was important, not only
for the occupying Americans but also for the Japanese themselves, to
remove all the jingoistic and ultra-nationalistic elements from the Old
Education enforced during the war. However, it is obvious that the
Old Education minus all these elements does not equal the New Edu-

cation, despite the usual tendency for the victor of a war to compel its own ideology on the defeated.

What I want to point out here is not this fact but another one that flows from it: any educational reform will produce devastating effects upon society unless it is coupled with an appropriate programme of social reform for the existing society. Usually, a drastic change in education is contrary to Durkheim's teaching in the sense that it does not necessarily accomplish the role that he proposed for education. According to him, the education of children aims at adapting them to the social environment within which they are expected to live.[3] For example, mother lionesses can successfully educate lion cubs to be lions only if the conventional practices of lion society remain unchanged. We can see that, if we do not change the workings and customs of an adult society, the effectiveness of any new educational system which we may introduce must be very limited. We are constrained to choose a conditional best from among those belonging to the traditional sphere of choice. In so far as the post-war educational reform was concerned, there was no intention, at least on the Japanese side, to change their adult world. When introducing educational reforms the GHQ, however, entirely disregarded existing Japanese conventions. These conventions were themselves the target the occupying forces wished to destroy. There was no possibility that children educated in the new way ordered by the GHQ could fit into the traditional society that the Japanese were determined to maintain.

Therefore, when the New Education was introduced, the Japanese should have been prepared to change their society to make it appropriate for their children, who would be products of the New Education. The Japanese, nevertheless, made no such effort. They rebuilt the country in a form that was as close to their pre-war empire as possible. In fact, as has been stated, boys and girls were re-educated after leaving school, before their employment was made permanent, so that they would support the traditional way of life in Japan. This was merely a temporizing policy, but the Japanese government did nothing concerning the revision or naturalization of the New Education after the GHQ had gone back home.

In fact, throughout the postwar period the Japanese did all they could in order to conserve the traditional character of their society. Naturally, those who stood up at general and local elections after the war were squires or celebrities representing their constituencies. They had no distinct political ideas apart from those candidates who were involved in the labour movement. Their mentality may be compared with that of British politicians before the time of Walpole. In fact, Japanese politics was and still is a kind of village politics that is mainly concerned with bringing back a share of benefits created by the central or local government to their constituencies. It is true that the political structure was westernized, especially in the Meiji period and just after the war, but native customs and conventions were still the most powerful factors in political decision-making. Elected representatives had no political theory, philosophy or ideology that they consistently adhered to, but these politicians were tough negotiators when it came to distributing benefits.

Nevertheless, it is true that there were politicians in the early post-war period, 1946–80, such as Shigeru Yoshida, Tanzan Ishibashi, Hayato Ikeda, Eisaku Sato, Takao Miki, Takeo Fukuda and Masayoshi Ohira, who were able or at least acceptable. All of these, other than Ishibashi and Miki, had experience as career government officials and only joined a political party at a later stage of their life before finally becoming prime minister. This domination of the political stage by ex-bureaucrats did not escape notice or criticism. True born party men successfully lobbied for more significant positions. During the ten-year period 1988–97, nine different prime ministers achieved office. Of them, only Kiichi Miyazawa started his career as a government official; all others were solely party men. Their individual performances were obviously and significantly worse than that of the prime ministers who had first had careers as government officials. After this dramatic change, the morality of Japanese political circles reverted to that of the pre-modern years. It deteriorated to the extent that Japan was finally degraded to a nation ruled by the sensibility and philosophy of village politicians.

The ethos of politicians in the 1980s may at best be said to have adhered to the lines of an essential Confucianism which emphasizes the six points first written down in a condensed version by Emperor Hongwu (1368–99) of the Ming dynasty of China. The emperor emphasized the following virtues:

1. filial piety;
2. concordance with neighbours;
3. respect for seniors;
4. responsibility for educating and disciplining one's own offspring;
5. contentment with one's given calling; and
6. abstinence from villainy.

The Imperial Rescript on Education issued by Emperor Meiji in 1890, which influenced the pre-war Japanese immensely, was clearly based on Hongwu's 'Six Instructions'. It is evident that, compared to Plato's philosophy, Confucian ethics is very primitive. It permits interpretations which are not necessarily consistent with the original text. For example, should one always agree with views held by neighbours? Therefore, many versions of vulgar Confucianism are possible. In recent years, politicians whom I would still call Confucianists have deteriorated into vulgar persons who are reduced to being mere hunters of benefits for their constituencies.

IV

As Hongwu's Six Articles state, Confucianism respects the virtues of inherited qualities, as points 1, 3 and 4 show. It encourages elitism and even, in the worst case, nepotism. It orientates an individual's behaviour towards taking an interest in the happiness and prosperity of the immediate larger group at hand. It does not emphasize an individual's achievement, and as far as Hongwu's Six Articles and Meiji's Imperial Rescripts are concerned, it has no clear universal principle for assessing an individual's achievements. It stands in opposition to an American style of education which produces self-centred children. In a Confucian society, individuals are not assessed in terms of their achievements only. There is, however, no rigorous principle of egalitarianism.

It is then obvious that, in the latter part of the 1980s and afterwards, Japanese party politicians increasingly found it difficult to deal with government officers who received a post-war American type of education. Individuals under that system are appraised according to their achievements performed on the basis of universalism and egalitarianism. Under these conditions the famous, or notorious, Japan Inc. could continue to function only with increasing difficulty. This cleft has turned out to be even more serious, because the business world has another cleft of a similar nature within itself: Confucian bosses versus employees who are products of the New Education. Such a divisive society is a natural sequel of the defeat of Japan in the Second World War. Disaster inevitably follows at some time in the future when a social malfunction results from an ideological inconsistency which exists between various groups and classes of society. In this case, the result has been much delayed but still arises from the American imposition of the New Education upon the defeated Japanese. We observe in addition:

Fact 4: An Absence of Elitism and Therefore an Absence of a Locomotive

The ratio of male applicants for university admission to the total number of males born in the same year reached 40 per cent by 1975. It kept at more or less the same level until 1996, though there was a bit of a slump in the late 1980s. For girls the figures were 12.5 per cent in 1975, reaching 24.6 per cent in 1996. If two-year colleges are included, the ratio for girls increases to 32.4 per cent in 1975 and 48.3 per cent in 1996. The admission ratio for two-year colleges was insignificant for boys throughout this period. It was always less than 2.3 per cent, except when it hit 2.6 per cent in 1975 and 2.4 per cent in 1976. All these figures show that Japan has been greatly influenced by, and become very similar to, America. Her higher education sector is the second largest in the world after the US.

Moreover, the New Education was implemented in the hope of avoiding particularism and ascription of any kind. The power of a pupil's memory was cultivated, but their ability to make value judgements withered. Although they became very able at memorizing everything just as it is, they were weak in reasoning, and, therefore, not good at decision-making. A high admission rate to universities results in a very noisy room if university entrance examinations become too easy. Students, as a consequence, have lost their pride in being university students. In Japan now, higher education is no longer a base for elitism. The spirit of *noblesse oblige* has ceased to prevail in any corner of Japanese society. This is crucially damaging to Japan because she is a Confucianist country, one which is structured in such a way that intellectuals need to play a leading role in sustaining the nation. There is a great danger that Japan will collapse from above, rather than from below.

Since the middle of the 1970s many Japanese students have gone to America for further study. Once they obtain a PhD, their chances of being appointed to teaching, research or managerial posts become much higher than if they had chosen to stay in Japan. Thus Japanese graduate schools are bypassed by able students. In this way, Japan increasingly entrusts the elite education of her best young people to American universities. This creates splits in society which have become both wider and deeper.

V

In the 1980s Japan's economy was faced with serious problems. First, her industrial regime, Japan Inc., was criticized by foreign competitors. Japan was warned that she would be isolated in the world of international trade if she stuck to that regime. Second, it was time for the Japanese to change their way of financing business enterprises. They needed to switch away from a dependence upon market loans, according to which enterprises borrow necessary funds from a bank, towards using an equity-financed system that allows money to be raised by issuing additional shares of stock. This was due to internal pressure, rather than to any particular external one. Entrepreneurs found equity financing much cheaper than loans. These problems were very difficult to handle neatly. In what follows, we shall see how they were dealt with in turn.

Fact 5: The Japanese Way of Business is Deadlocked

The idea of 'the Japanese system of economic administration' was formed and carried out after the war when the occupational forces dismantled the country's pre-war system. It was an especially crucial blow to Japan that all the major groups of *zaibatsu*, the natural basis for reconstructing the economy, were ordered to disband. These *zaibatsu* were the most important means by which the wartime government attempted to control the economy. The country needed to invent organizational alternatives which would efficiently utilize the able, young economic and technological administrators of either the government or the *zaibatsu* companies. However, these companies were divided into their component pieces. The government then pretended not to see that they were working in collaboration with one another. In order to make this possible, the companies which were split from the same *zaibatsu* companies helped each other via reciprocal share-holding. This cooperation in supporting each other's shares became a basis for natural cooperation in business matters. Although *zaibatsu* families were strictly removed from the business world, their businesses survived the postwar period by forming their own groups of giant enterprises with banks and comprehensive trading companies at the centre.

Such a grouping of enterprises is obviously a coalition and directly opposed to the spirit of fair competition. During this period of economic planning, Japanese government officials became proficient in handling an imperfectly competitive economy. They retained this structure as long as possible by deferring the introduction of a competitive mechanism, even at the cost of friction with those foreign countries which supported the idea of free competition. This implicit guardianship of major corporations produced benefits for politicians and government officials alike, as well as for the businessmen of those big enterprises. First, the big-business sector would clearly support a policy of segregating big from small and medium businesses. Politicians would naturally expect in return large reciprocal political donations. Also, for big enterprises it became very important to employ talented ex-government officials who could successfully influence government decisions. By this means, high officials of the central (or local) government could subsequently find good posts for themselves in the business world. At least for them the very early retirement age set for civil servants is no substantial disadvantage. Moreover, the maintenance of this coalition creates feeble politicians; they are merely country gentlemen without explicit knowledge of politics or economics, but they can hold on to their posts if they behave in the way their under-secretaries prescribe. Under-secretaries support politicians because they expect their bosses to look after them when they retire.

Such a trinity of politics, bureaucracy and business can provide a refuge for evil people. Bribes, insider dealings, conspiracies among key players and even crooked accounting are not necessarily exceptionally rare. Business morals have crumbled since the late 1980s. It is no exaggeration to say that the public prosecutor's office could, if it desired, discover a crime simply by examining the accounts of any big company. This trinity, which has become increasingly rotten, has now reached the last moments of its life, unless it is subjected to drastic modification.

This is a real-world description of the decade from 1987 to 1997. It may be considered as a premonition of what will happen in the early decades of the coming century. Once the moral values of a nation have broken down, restitution can be achieved only with great difficulty. Because the older generation will die soon, the ethical cleft existing in the present society will naturally be only partially filled. We cannot place our hopes on the coming generation: they have received only a feeble moral education and have been full participants in the collapse from which Japanese society must now recover. The generation that is just now entering school was born too late to help avert the coming crises. By the time they reach the gate which opens on to the adult world, the collapse will have occurred. We have, as a parallel to its business structure:

Fact 6: The Japanese Way of Finance which is Also at a Deadlock

During the war the government changed the banking system substantially to make it compatible with a planned type of economy. First, the excessive number of banks which existed at that time was reduced so that each prefecture had one, and only one, savings bank. Savings gathered at the prefecture level were sent to city banks, which allocated them to companies according to the production targets specified by the government. Where the savings were less than the amounts required, the gaps were filled by loans from the central bank to the city banks. Thus, during the war, industry was financed by means of loans from banks, while equity finance deteriorated. Stock exchanges had only a nominal existence or none at all during most of the years of the 1940s.

A particular bank (or sometimes banks) given the responsibility for financing a company was nominated as its main bank. This relationship was not legal but merely moral. It was sufficient to strongly encourage industry to pursue an ambitious plan of investment. After the war, when the reconstruction and expansion of the economy still remained its first priority, the government and the central bank were in favour of maintaining this wartime formula. Equity finance never flourished until the late 1970s. In those years, however, there emerged a disequilibrium between the lending–borrowing market and the market for equity finance. Japan already had huge, first-rate manufacturing companies which could raise money through the stock market at a price far cheaper than the market rate of interest.

The companies which obtained money in this way speculated in land. The price of land naturally increased, seeming to justify the speculation. Even small landowners borrowed money by offering their land to the bank as security for borrowing to buy another lot. A crazy spiral of land prices characterized the land market. The price of land, in terms of an index set at 100 in 1983, reached 350 in Tokyo and 250 in Osaka in 1988. Banks accumulated loan collateral in the form of land. A similar crazy and greedy attitude by the Japanese was observed at the start of the oil crisis: housewives rushed to shops and supermarkets to buy rolls of toilet paper as they had heard that they would become scarce due to the oil crisis. The Japanese tend to believe in a type of collective responsibility, namely that 'no one in particular can be labelled a bad person if all of us do it together at the same time'. This herd-like behaviour nurtures a strong tendency towards excessive price or asset inflation in Japan.

The price of land in the Tokyo area stopped rising in 1988 and remained stationary until 1991. However, it continued to increase sharply in other areas: in Osaka and Kyoto, for example, the peak reached 450 in 1991. Then it began to decline dramatically; it dipped almost to a level of 150 in both the Tokyo and Osaka areas by 1995. Those who had obtained loans by offering landed property as security were, for all practical purposes, bankrupt. The collateral for these bad loans, in the form of an enormous amount of land, remained in the hands of the banks. This sequence of events clearly describes a speculative economy. The Japan Inc. structure and main bank system, which filled the Japanese with pride, was also largely responsible for creating and ultimately sustaining the 'bubble'. The authorities could have stopped a further expansion of the 'bubble' at a relatively early stage in 1988 by raising the interest rate. It should have been raised, but it was kept low due to the pressure exerted by export industries.

In fact during the 'bubble' period, the Marshallian k was rising steadily, so it was only common sense to assume that serious inflation would eventually follow. Nevertheless, the authorities did not change the rate of interest; they preferred a further expansion of the economy to price stability. They were still fixated on economic growth and their understanding of the financial aspects of the economy was and is almost as poor as it was during the wartime planned economy.

This may be seen from a slightly different angle. There are two types of finance: (a) finance by means of loans; and (b) finance by selling financial commodities on competitive markets. In the former case lenders, usually banks, carefully examine the investment plans for which the borrowers want to obtain funds. The amounts banks lend depend on how well the borrowers can be trusted. In the latter case, either financial commodities such as bonds and stocks are sold in the relevant exchanges or new stocks are issued. In this latter case, however, newly issued stock in the 1950s and the 1960s had been distributed to the shareholders at face value, in proportion to the number of shares they already held. They could sell or buy an appropriate amount of the newly issued stock after they had obtained their own allotment. On the other hand, the company issuing new shares obtained only the face value of the shares issued, which may be appreciably less than the market value. None the less, it is true that until the late 1970s, when finance by means of issuing new shares at current prices become popular at last, financing by means of competitive markets was still weak in Japan. Switching from loan financing to equity markets was clearly observed in the early 1980s.

Changing technology also made such a switch more attractive. The last two decades of this century have been the age of electronics and computerization. Banks themselves benefited from the latter by greatly reducing their costs. The development of electronics enabled them to invent various new financial commodities. Old commodities became obsolete and were replaced by new ones. The financial markets became very competitive. Sitting in a London office, banks and security companies easily competed with the Tokyo market. The major weapons determining the outcome of this type of war are computer hardware and software. Japan so far has been good at exploiting the former territory, but weak in developing software programs. Moreover, reflecting its post-war history in which Japan relied lightly on equity markets and mainly on loan-based finance, Japan has fallen far behind the Anglo-Saxon countries in producing skilful dealers. This failure has led to a lack of financial innovation, and hence she was unable to assume leadership when competing in the financial revolution. Japan has so far been content to be a follower, or even a follower of followers. This has produced a number of serious results. First, the main bank system became almost useless, because non-financial companies could finance themselves through bond and equity markets, rather than by obtaining loans from their main banks.

Second, effective use of their computing resources should have allowed companies and banks to examine their investment programmes more precisely, allowing risks to be reduced considerably. Banks could have offered financial services more cheaply. Inevitably this should have led to a realization that the mutual holding of shares was an expensive means of conserving the current managers in power. By using stock exchanges more effectively, a better way of managing enterprises would have become available. Consequently, the leverage that banks could exert within enterprise groups subsequently declined. In a crisis such as occurred during the 1991 'bubble', companies found themselves with insufficiently large cash flows to justify holding other companies' shares. Therefore, they were forced to sell. A tit-for-tat process commenced, and the mutual share-holding system necessarily collapsed.

Countries with financial organizations which were advanced in software programming could gain an advantage over Japanese organizations. With the opening up and general deregulation of financial markets in many foreign countries, Japanese financial firms found themselves unable to compete at an international level. Furthermore, it became increasingly difficult for parent companies to control subsidiaries effectively because the latter could now acquire additional funds by offering new shares on the stock exchanges. In this way the financial revolution resulted not only in the collapse of the Japanese type of financial system but also in the demise of the Japan Inc. type of industrial structure based on self-contained groups of enterprises.

In the same way as the steam engine completely changed the mode of production during the industrial revolution, so the electronics revolution that is now under way will bring about an entirely different mode of finance. This change in financial structure will give rise to a further change in the industrial and commercial systems. When the 'bubble' inevitably burst, this emerging process accelerated. In consequence of this financial revolution, the permanent employment convention will eventually become very difficult to maintain. Long-run contracts and obligations between subsidiaries and their parent company will be cancelled. The usefulness of the main bank system will disappear and, therefore, it is unlikely to be maintained. In order for the Japanese economy to survive it must become more competitive. Those sectors which most benefited from the coalition of interests under the regime of Japan Inc. will lose their strength. Japan in this way has to envisage a transition period from the existing form of capitalism from above to the sort of capitalism from below that correctly could be labelled a true neoclassical revolution. This is inevitable, because otherwise Japan will either be internationally isolated or be left far behind in the ongoing march of advanced countries.

VI

The Japanese economy is now in the middle of an important transformation period. The journalists say that it is the Japanese version of a financial big bang; I reckon it is far more comprehensive. Japan has now to transform her idiosyncratic state capitalism into a new institutional structure where the neoclassical competitive mechanism can prevail. This deserves to be specially mentioned as:

Fact 7: A Transition from State-guided Capitalism to Market-driven Capitalism

What I have said above is evidence that the economic regime established after the Meiji Revolution, that is, capitalism from above, survived with some modifications throughout the four decades which followed the 1945 surrender to the Allied Forces, but it began to collapse by the beginning of the 1990s. Throughout those years, except for a few selected ones during which liberalism was enhanced, a powerful government sector provided the economy's principal support. This was mainly because democratic power was still very weak in Japan. None the less, the post-war economy at last has begun to show signs of giving way to a system of competitive capitalism, not because the necessary democratic power has developed at a grass roots level within the present regime, but because it has become impossible for state capitalism to survive. The current system has rotted away at its core, spreading decay into every corner of society.

Moreover, as has been pointed out, those educated after the war, though they believe in individualism and liberalism, were not educated well enough. They lack sufficient moral courage, readily accept nepotism and are even willing to threaten other parties if this convinces them to surrender to their proposals. They neither bravely nor coolly accept the outcome of competition. These characteristics of the new post-war generation which contributed to the collapse of state capitalism will not provide a base for competitive capitalism. An underlying moral strength, corresponding to the Protestant ethic lauded by Max Weber as the essential element in the rise of western capitalism (from below), cannot be discerned among the present-day Japanese.

In my previous book,[4] I pointed out that there are three kinds of religion: (a) the rational one which justifies the ruling political forces; (b) the rational religion whose objective is to emancipate the ruled individuals; (c) the mystical religion. In Japan, Confucianism has served as a category (a) religion. Category (b) religions are all weak, whilst Shintoism, a type (c) religion, mainly serves the ruler but also provides some benefits for the ruled. The New Education introduced after the war should be classified as being based on a philosophy which characterizes a class (b) religion. Its principle of competition, however, was reinterpreted in Japan, especially in the post-war period, as one which encourages people to do their best in catching up with and overtaking the advanced countries of the West materialistically. It fitted the Japanese perfectly because they need a doctrine that serves as a vehicle for self-justification. Secular material life has predominated, allowing nationalism to be kept at a distance. Unfortunately, the Japanese have become obsessed by this perceived need to catch up. As a consequence, they are still compelled by their own greed to engage persistently in profit-reducing sales.

This commonly held attitude seems to be responsible, at least in part, for the present crisis. Having missed opportunity after opportunity to correct this persistent imbalance, it is quite probable that the post-war generation could be forced in the near future to consider asking the remaining nationalists for their support. Already strident voices are beginning to be heard among a subset of journalists, as well as in some corners of the political world. A number of academics are in sympathy with them, and others are too weak to oppose their arguments.

However, it is inconceivable, as far as I am concerned, that any significant number of Japanese, motivated by nationalist ideology, would rouse themselves to sustained action in the foreseeable future.

It is difficult to expect capitalism from below to succeed after the collapse of the present state-guided regime. In the same way as Catholicism may be said to prevail only among clergymen, laymen being left unaffected by its precepts, the principles of Confucianism influenced, for the most part, only the minority samurai class in the Tokugawa period, the rest of the population being left to enjoy their own material lives.

We can now observe many cultural features that Japan's present society has in common with those that dominated the latter half of the Tokugawa period, but especially the way in which people generally lead their lives. The Tokugawa economy was at a peak in the Genroku period, 1688–1704. It subsequently declined and the Japanese economy never really recovered until the outbreak of the Meiji Revolution, 1867–8. During this extended period, the Japanese ethos, which was noted for its industry and faithfulness, died out. Instead, people indulged in transitory pleasures.

At the time of the Meiji Revolution, the Japanese were lucky as they had a clear list of things they had to accomplish. They had first to establish a nation state. By gathering information from senior nations, it was easy to construct a programme for building a New Japan. In the case of the present crisis, however, no similar navigational chart is available. Though everything necessary for the construction of a progressive economic nation has already been accomplished, Japan still lacks a sufficient number of capable, motivated people who possess such qualities as courage, fairness and honesty. They do not necessarily all have to be great and outstanding, but most of them must fulfil the requirements mentioned above. How could Japan develop a sufficient number of such people? This is a matter that largely depends upon education. We already know that the post-war New Education failed to produce the type of people we must have now. It is much more difficult to produce a multitude of people who can shoulder the burden required for the formation of capitalism from below than to get a small number of great men who can work to create a nation-state. The future of Japan will depend upon the quality of the mass of the Japanese people, not a small elite capable of excelling. If that quality is low, the Japanese will be forced to accept that their ranking among the industrialized nations will fall sharply.

Let us now point out how difficult it is to transform an economy based on state capitalism, or capitalism from above, to competitive

capitalism, or capitalism from below. They are different in man
some of the most fundamental points of contrast between the
follows. As has been stated, these two types of economies r
porate funds differently. In the case of state capitalism, the stock market
is not usually well developed. Since firms normally borrow money from
banks, the most important quality for entrepreneurs to have is trust-
worthiness. The personal relationships between entrepreneurs and their
bankers are the greatest asset that they can cultivate. To establish a
good relationship they meet each other not only in their offices but also
in high-class restaurants, theatres and golf clubs, often accompanied
by geisha-girls. Of course, excessive entertainment should be regarded
fundamentally as no different from bribery.

Moreover, under the old system, those firms which retain and accumulate profits are considered, other things being equal, as healthy
companies by their bankers. If dividends are low, then the price of their
shares is also low. But this is not a matter of concern for the owners of
the firms. It is more important that they have a good relationship
with the banking sector, especially their main banks.

Circumstances are totally different under competitive capitalism,
where firms raise funds by issuing stocks. Since newly issued stocks are
sold at their current prices, the firms obtain a larger sum of money if
prices are higher; therefore the owners of firms want to keep them as
high as possible. A maximum flow of dividends becomes a firm's policy
in such an economy. Consequently, the amount of profit retained within
the firm is minimized.

Thus the managerial principles guiding contrasting types of economic
firms are entirely different. At the transition point from one type of
economy to the other, managers have to change their own character.
However, Japanese businessmen have not responded quickly. They continue to behave as if they are still in an economy characterized by state
capitalism. Due to this maladjustment, their firms have performed very
poorly in an increasingly competitive world. Many of them have, moreover, been accused of criminal acts.

VII

Lastly, there are big differences in disposition between those Japanese
who took leading positions during the period from 1945 to 1980 and
those who became dominant figures after 1985. These differences were
more or less taken for granted when we discussed the previous facts. In
many ways these distinguishing characteristics have not been sufficiently

incorporated into the prevailing economic analysis of Japan's current problems. Not only in this regard but also for other matters, these differences in disposition have not been explicitly stated, but even more to the point, these differences have not been taken sufficiently into account.

The new Japanese are the products of the defeat Japan experienced in the Second World War, as I have repeatedly stated. I emphasize that Japan has risen and fallen accordingly as the old Japanese have been replaced by the new. But this replacement has taken time; in the interim the proportion of the old and the new has been fluctuating from a reasonably good mixture to an unworkable one. When Japan was composed of an efficient mixture of the old and the new, it was once said that the twenty-first century would be the age of Japan. Contrary to what was once believed, in the future when the old Japanese have totally vanished and the century has become genuinely new, there is no possibility that an improved mixture will revive these hopes. Needless to say, there are variations among the new Japanese. Although I do not think they greatly differentiate among themselves, we must consider the possibility that the right-wingers or ultra-nationalists may be able to engineer a revival. In addition, we must also point out that there is a chance of anarchism, nihilism and decadence in the coming years.

Fact 8: An Ideological Crisis – a Possible Right-wing Reconversion

A society like the one which characterized post-war Japan, divided into two distinct generation groups having entirely different experiences, is constructed in a rather complex fashion. On the one hand, there are people who are aware that they acted as assailants during wartime, and on the other, those who think of themselves as having sufferered after the war. The former group mainly consists of those who are now over 70 years old, while the latter are those under 60 years old. Between them there is a group holding mixed feelings.

Each of the two groups is further subdivided into two subgroups. In the first group there is a right-wing subgroup believing that the assaults they committed were justified, while the left-wing subgroup is ashamed of the nation's conduct in that period. The second group is also similarly divided into right-wing and left-wing subgroups. Its right-wingers are unhappy with and humiliated by the surrender that Japan had to accept, while left-wingers consider that the post-war treatment of their country by the occupation forces was fair. They appreciate that Japan has recovered her status as a democratic country. The transitional generation, stretching from wartime through the post-war period, lack any experience of battle but vividly remember the shameful surrender. As a result, the ratio of right-wingers to left-wingers may be, I guess, surprisingly high in this transitional generation.

I assume from the comments observed in newspapers and magazines that the ratio of right-wingers in the transitional generation is higher than that in the pre-war generation and that this in turn is higher than the post-war percentage. I may, therefore, conjecture that the years between the late 1990s and the early 2000s are those that will be most dangerous from the viewpoint of a possible right-wing revolution. I nevertheless believe that this period will most probably pass calmly. In the first quarter of the next century, Japan will consist largely of un-dynamic people motivated by the principle of peace at any price. Not one of them will be inclined to raise a protesting voice in response to international aggression. They are simply hedonistic, mammonistic and self-indulgent. They have no sense of duty, no religion, no love for their motherland and no element of ascription. Japan will be a country where people's work ethics lack a decisive character since their model for proper behaviour, neoclassical economic textbooks, discusses none.

It is not surprising, however, that we can point to a similar spiritually depressed society that occurred earlier in modern Japanese history. After the Genroku period, almost all clans observed that the population of the capital towns of those feudal clans was declining. It is true that the clan economies suffered greatly, but most of them survived for more than 150 years after the end of the Genroku period in 1704 until the Meiji Revolution. During these years an intellectual class emerged in the capital town of every clan. The culture that flourished in the early years of the Tokugawa era and that had recorded its peak in the Genroku period started to be propagated from big towns to minor ones. In the end, it spread even to the provinces and villages.

This is the kind of stationary equilibrium which Japan achieved under her policy of seclusionism. If no 'black ships' had come to Japan to ask for the opening of her ports to foreign trade at the end of the Tokugawa era, this equilibrium would have been maintained. The royalists would not have appeared: even if there had been some, they would not have obtained sufficient popularity. In the present crisis too, if Japan could close the country she would settle once again into an equilibrium, even if a rather low one. She would in this way avoid any right-wing revolu-tion. I judge that the Japanese would be satisfied with this state, as those in the late Tokugawa period were, because of their political enervation.

From this premonition of a crisis, one may conclude, as some opinion leaders do, that Japan urgently needs patriotic politicians and businessmen. However, it would be difficult and dangerous to try to obtain such people in a short period of time by converting existing people into that requisite type. Even though we may get a number of them, they are insufficient to build the sort of capitalism from below that we now want to establish. We could only succeed in reviving capitalism from above at best. But even this is very difficult to achieve, because that type of capitalism has now been shown to be rotten and unworkable in Japan.

We may then ask what type of religion is able to provide the necessary ethos which would promote a neoclassical competitive system. Max Weber says Protestantism is a solution. Another solution may be Confucianism. Both of them are mainly rational religions but the former is more philosophical and sacred than the latter, which is concrete and secular and can hardly be said to be concerned with God, the soul or other supernatural beings. The Japanese, who are by nature irreligious, became even more irreligious after the war, because it was prohibited by order of the occupation forces to provide any religious education in schools. As a consequence, the spiritual bases of those secular work ethics that motivate workers, capitalists and entrepreneurs in neoclassical competition have faded away. The contemporary Japanese are bereft of a proper moral background necessary for 'neoclassicalism', or the 'spirit of capitalism', to employ Max Weber's usage. It is then almost certain that Japan will not recover from this present crisis.

Fact 9: Moral Decadence

According to Vilfredo Pareto's theory of residues, there are six fundamental residues:

1. the instinct for new combinations;
2. group persistence;
3. the need to show one's sentiments by outward actions;
4. sentiments related to sociability;
5. integrity of the individual and the appurtenances he or she relies on;
6. integrity of the species – sex.[5]

The first residue may alternatively be referred to as the propensity to innovate, while the second is concerned with people's social considerations. From the point of view of these two residues, the Weberian problem of the spirit of capitalism may be restated as an attempt to examine under which religious background a people's instinct to innovate is stimulated. That is to say, using Pareto's terminology, Weber sees that residue 1, resulting in innovation, is stimulated when residue 2 prevails among an aggregate of individuals who share the people's Protestantism sentiment. On the other hand, Schumpeter's problem of transition from capitalism to socialism discusses how the residue of innovation will lose strength and be replaced by the residue of group persistence.[6] What remains unspecified is how a decline of residue 1 stimulates 2. We may thus see Schumpeter's problem as being a reversed Weberian one. Alternatively, we may say that in the former case residues 1 and 2 act as substitutes, while in the latter case they behave as complements.

However, the problem of Japan, which I am dealing with, cannot be seen strictly from this Paretian angle, which emphasizes a circulation of economic regimes. This is because present-day Japan does not have a sufficient amount of both residues 1 and 2. The problem occurs in the absence or almost total absence of both these residues. Turning our eyes to the remaining residues 3–6, the Japanese still have a moderate amount of sentiments 3 and 4 as individuals, but these are now very weak when expressed at a national level or in an international context. As a result, the Japanese cannot rely on these residues in trying to escape from this present depressed phase of its economic history. In this way we are led to view residues 5 and 6 as the key elements in any examination of contemporary Japanese sentiments.

The integrity of the individual and the conservation of the nation or society are dealt with in residues 5 and 6, respectively. Money and other assets are a means of accomplishing the former, so the strong desire for riches that characterizes the present-day Japanese shows that their residue 5 is still strong. On the other hand, thanks to the development of birth control techniques, the motive of preserving the nation is now completely separated from erotomaniac pleasure. The contemporary Japanese are very weak in the former, as our first fact showed, while their lust of the flesh is easily provoked. It is true that in most advanced countries similar phenomena are observed, but it is said that sexual morals are very lax in Japan, as *Newsweek* (December 1996) points out. In fact, high school girls readily prostitute themselves for their own sexual enjoyment. This shows how strong residues 5 and 6 are among Japanese teenagers. Given this initial allocation of residues, developing healthy work ethics that sustain neoclassical competitive economies is difficult.

No ethics which emphasize loyalty to the employer or the company are qualifiable, because workers in such economies should be free to move from one firm to another. The loyalty that workers should respect and obey is more abstract. The educational atmosphere of contemporary Japan is entirely out of tune and sterile when it comes to promoting a sense of obligation or responsibility to something abstract or transcendental. The Japanese are educated to be too materialistic. There is no religious environment. No serious discussion is held in the family, none at school. Since they are educated to be materialistic or utilitarian, they have no interest in talking about ethical values, idealistic matters or social obligations even as abstract exercises.

Computerization, mechanization and robotization have been carried out in various industries. As I have observed from their utilization in banks and other financial companies, workers' and managers' lives in their offices have been very much simplified. No judgement is needed, work is done by computers or other kinds of machines, and the workers have to adapt only the rhythm of their work to the movement of the machines. They are then not allowed their own choice of movement. They all carry out a simplified task over and over again. And finally, they are alienated from and do not talk to each other. They themselves become just another kind of machine.

Then, when they return home, they sit in front of the TV set and select a channel by pushing buttons in a more or less random way. This is mainly because all channels air similar programmes. (TV companies construct their schedules so as to gain maximum ratings. Since the solution to this programming problem is unique, all channels broadcast almost the same kinds of programme.) Their family lives after dinner are more or less similar, and again alienated by machines from other members of the family. They scarcely talk to each other. Where each family is like this, the economy has virtually no reason to expect either charismatic entrepreneurs or charismatic politicians to develop. Corresponding to the mode of production realized in the age of computerization and mechanization, we have this type of family life as an element of the superstructure of society. Based on this Marxian relationship, Japan has to find an ethos that can play the role of encouraging a robust spirit of capitalism from below to flourish. It is extremely difficult for the Japanese – especially for the many Japanese who have already lost a strong desire to do so – to reform their economy drastically so as to remove bribery, conspiracy, blackmail and so on in order to establish an economy based on fair competition.

VIII

We may further point out that international relations are included among the most disheartening elements.

Fact 10: An Unfavourable External Environment

During the post-war years Japan entered into an alliance with the US. If there is still a need to maintain a security agreement with America, the Asian countries as a whole, rather than a single country such as Japan or China, should enter into such a treaty with the US. The US would then not need to feel very unhappy about the Asian countries forming a single economic community, which will be explained later. The security agreement between Japan and the US was originally formed mainly for the purpose of defence against the USSR. By it Japan gained great economic benefits during the Korean and the Vietnamese wars. After the collapse of the USSR, the alliance shifted its target to China. Most contemporary Japanese believe that if trouble arises in the East Asian region, Japan would wage war against China on the side of the US. But I am unable to subscribe to this view.

When Japan invaded China in 1937, the US kept away from the trouble, at least initially for some years, during which time both Japan and China tried to drag the US into the war on their respective sides. Since Japan was winning the war, she could offer the US better conditions than China could. Nevertheless, China persuaded the US to be its ally because it offered an argument that was more persuasive than Japan's. The Chinese have characters and personalities with which western people, particularly Anglo-Americans, are more at home than those peculiar to the Japanese. Since there is now no serious military threat in the Far East, the US will rationally calculate the advantages to be gained between two options: (a) an alliance with Japan targeting China; and (b) an alliance with China that isolates Japan. If the leaders of the US adopt the view that Japan will decline drastically in the world ranking of nations, while China will come up considerably in the first quarter of the coming century, the US may very likely choose option (b), rather than option (a) which they are now actually pursuing. American leaders will soon realize that socialism with Chinese characteristics is no more than a kind of capitalism from above. They will come to believe that they can collaborate with China in the same way as they did with Japan when its economy could also be characterized as capitalism from above, that is, during the period 1950–90. It would be senseless to form an alliance with a weak, debilitated Japan against a powerful China.

The US could realize, at a much cheaper cost, her aim of Pax Americana in the region of East Asia by choosing the Chinese option.

If this speculation turns out to be correct, Japan's position in East Asia will decline to the present level of Taiwan and South Korea. The US base on Okinawa would then become the means for attacking Japan in an emergency. Of course, Japanese politicians will want to avoid this, but I do not expect that they have the capacity, as I have speculated already. If this happens, many of the Japanese would be angry at this act of 'treachery' by the Americans, but no one would be able to stop the progress of the newly formed US–China locomotive. Japan would be unable to escape from this ruinous position and would stay there for a very long while.

In this sense it may be regarded as a long-run equilibrium position. The Japanese would settle and remain there for a few centuries. This is the final outcome flowing from her stupid decision to wage war against the US, Britain, China, Holland and many others in 1941. When the war ceased, it was said among the Japanese that their country would be reduced to a position no better than that of the Asian countries which Japan had invaded. It is true that America did not implement this policy directly and immediately. But it is also true that the sequence of political, social and economic events which occurred after the war eventually did lead her to the position which she would have been prepared to accept when she surrendered to the Allied Forces.

Of course, there will be many people dissatisfied with this low equilibrium position. There will be a number of occasional right-wing movements. But they will not be strong enough to shock Japan into escaping from such a trap. This is because the then dominant US–China alliance will work at a sufficiently effective level so that Japan will be left helpless, however heavily she arms herself. This is also because the position she will settle at will not be so miserable as might be conceived. The industrial technology that Japan now commands is extremely advanced and broad. It is unbelievable that every one of her industries would deteriorate. On the other hand, we would be wise to discount an overly optimistic view, because it is difficult for a nation that is unsuccessful in maintaining a competitive economy to retain at the same time a fair number of prosperous industries. I expect that this future long-run equilibrium may be compared with the Tokugawa era, which followed Japan's defeats in the two Korean wars, 1592 and 1597. Life was quiet and materialistically not too bad, but the people's positive contribution to the rest of the world was far below the one that they make now.

However, it is almost certain that the population of Japan will decrease drastically in the coming few decades. It is also true, none the less, that the country has enough houses and office buildings suitable for the present population and for the present level of economic activity. Japan will necessarily suffer from a huge excess supply of houses and buildings throughout this age of long-run depressed equilibrium. A vast multitude of people could potentially come into Japan from various poor places in Asia, because life in Japan would still be very attractive and comfortable to them even though it would be considered unsatisfactory according to Japanese standards. Then, naturally, Japan would become a multiracial country. This could easily happen because, though many Japanese believe that they are a people of a pure race, they have been very mixed in the past, mainly with the Koreans and especially at the beginning of their history. This would be a process of *aufhebung* for Japan into a more open, cosmopolitan country.

As a plan for avoiding an expected big Japanese downfall, I proposed in December 1995 the idea of forming a North-East Asian Economic Community consisting of China, Japan, North and South Koreas and Taiwan.[7] It is not surprising that it was entirely neglected by politicians and opinion leaders in Japan, because many Japanese still feel uncomfortable about the Chinese and the Koreans, though there are also groups who are pro-Chinese and pro-Korean. This Japanese prejudice against the people of these two nations differs little from that widely held in the first decade of the twentieth century, when the Ch'ing and Li dynasties of China and Korea were finally collapsing. They looked down on these two nations, generally speaking, although there were some who were enthusiastically sympathetic.

I nevertheless believe an improvement would be possible. There are many small and medium-sized businesses in the western part of Japan which are keen to have a close relationship with China and Korea. The Tokyo government is too pro-American or pro-western and neglects or does not emphasize properly Japanese interests in Asia. This biased representation of Japan's real interests spreads all over the country and permeates large and small enterprises alike. If the Tokyo government could be brave enough to establish a co-government based in Osaka or Fukuoka to deal with Asian matters, then Japan can, even at this late moment, greatly change its future course.

This would be an enormous organizational innovation, providing many new opportunities for small and medium-sized enterprises. Big business too would find new frontiers. Moreover, it is most important to recognize that if future history develops in this way, there would then be no need for an alliance with the US by either China or Japan. As a result, Japan would be able to evade the worst scenario described above. All three nations, especially the US, could reduce defence costs enormously. Okinawa would at last be free from the obligation to offer air and naval bases to the US. (If there were a need to maintain a security agreement with America, the Community as a whole, rather than a single country such as Japan or China, would enter into a treaty with the US, as I have said before.) The US may not end up feeling too displeased about the formation by Asian countries of a single Community. After the recent serious financial crises in various parts of the region, Asia no longer serves simply as a treasure house for the US. Instead, Asia may turn out to be a heavy burden. Dormant resources in China could be activated, even if Japan only maintained its present level of technology. Other member countries of the Community could obtain more or less similar benefits. If however, this Community fails to coalesce, then this Pareto-optimal state will elude the Asian states due to their intractable and mutual suspicion of one another.

In spite of this trump card, the true cause of the Japanese collapse remains. The people, like the Romans in the age of their decline, are enervated, epicurean and undisciplined, and lack true leadership. It has already been said that as long as they remain so, Japan must follow the path trodden by the Romans. Their ability to operate a neoclassical, market-driven economy will be extremely poor. In any case, a significant educational reform is necessary, one which teaches children the essence and true meaning of individualism and liberalism.

However, it takes a very long time, more or less of the order of 40 or 50 years, to obtain qualified people this way. Before the productive life of these people is reached, Japan will experience a very long slump as it did after the Genroku period. She can and must bear it. During this era of stagnation she will become widely recognized as belonging to a certain class of nations regarded as being much lower than the one to which she now belongs. We may, however, expect that she will at last succeed in establishing democracy. In this way, Japan will complete the time-intensive task necessary to transform her current state capitalism into a neoclassical, competitive one. Finally, it must be added that the member countries of the North-East Asian Community are physically and culturally similar; so those Japanese involved in the tasks related to this Community would work more freely in this historically familiar atmosphere. They would adapt themselves appropriately to the prevailing circumstances. Therefore, as I have said already, they would learn work ethics by doing business with their colleagues in the Community. If the Japanese could settle into such a state of affairs, they would not be very unhappy. An internationally insignificant country with a reasonably high standard of living: this is my image of Japan in the midst of the twenty-first century.

NOTES

1. On 5 April 1997 I received a letter from Professor Craig Freedman asking me whether I, as the author of *Why Has Japan Succeeded?* (1982), might be able to appraise Japan's status in the next century. The conference he organized is entitled 'Why Did Japan Stumble?', but I shall talk about a collapse of Japan rather than a mere stumble, because I found myself becoming very pessimistic as soon as I began writing this thesis.
2. Note that my previous book, *Why Has Japan Succeeded?*, published by Cambridge University Press, appeared in 1981, when the pre-war generation was still powerful in Japanese society. But towards the end of the 1980s the hegemony handed over control to the post-war generation, as symbolized by the fact that Toshiki Kaifu, a university graduate according to the new education system, was elected Prime Minister for the first time in 1989.
3. Emil Durkheim, *Iducation et Sociologie*, Felix Alcan, 1922.
4. Morishima, *Why Has Japan Succeeded?*, pp. 194–5.
5. Pareto, *The Mind and Society*, vol. II, London: Jonathan Cape, 1935.
6. J.A. Schumpeter, *Capitalism, Socialism and Democracy*, London: George Allen & Unwin, 1943.
7. M. Morishima, *Nihon no Sentaku* (An Option for Japan) Iwanami-Shoten, 1995.

RUMINATION ON MORISHIMA

Hugh Patrick[1]

> *I believe that man*
> *will not merely endure:*
> *he will prevail.*
> William Faulkner

Michio Morishima is an eminent economic theorist and also an amateur cultural and intellectual historian of Japan. This is evident in his paper 'Why Do I Expect Japan to Collapse?', which is the focus of the discussion here.

The paper is most appropriately understood in the context of its intellectual heritage, Morishima's stimulating and controversial 1982 book, *Why Has Japan 'Succeeded'?*. The book informs us about a number of major themes alluded to but, due to a lack of space, not developed in the paper. The paper asks where Japan is likely to be in 2050, and why. As the contrasting titles suggest, Morishima seems to see a less shining future for Japan than he once did. His style is sometimes exaggerated, his terminology sometimes apocalyptic.

Morishima's paper is rich, dense, multifaceted and full of ideas – many insightful, some superficial, and some not deserving consideration. He likes to make provocatively extravagant statements.

He put *'Succeeded'* in the book title in quotation marks. I wonder why he did not put Collapse in the title of the paper in similar quotation marks. After all, his definition of collapse turns out not to be a collapse at all. The final words in the paper are: 'An internationally insignificant country with a reasonably high level of living standard: this is my image of Japan in the midst of the twenty-first century.' I interpret this to mean that Morishima, like many Japanese, is ambitious: he wants Japan in 2050 to be an internationally significant country with a high standard of living. And, if my expectations are correct, it will be. His use of 'collapse' really refers to what he sees as happening to the values and moral basis of Japanese society, and hence to its economy. This is the paper's principal concern.

The moral basis of capitalism, including what motivates the human behaviour that makes capitalism work, is an issue of central importance both for economics and for philosophy. Few economists are willing, or feel able, to explore the nature, causes, effects and implications of the ethical system on which capitalism is based. This was the task Morishima boldly set himself in his book, in particular to explain both the difference between Japanese and western capitalism and the moral, ethical and religious foundations of Japanese capitalism. Because each country has its own history, culture and system of values, Morishima (1982: 201, fn 1) quite appropriately says 'it is erroneous to assume unconditionally that one can construct an economic model in the abstract and apply the logic of the model to the realities of a country'.[2]

Morishima is to be lauded for his bravery and boldness as an economist in addressing the value system requisites of different patterns or forms of capitalism. My impression is that there is now a considerable literature by economists, sociologists and others on this key theme. However, I do not know that literature, and Morishima's only references are to Weber, Durkheim and Pareto – all writing before 1920 – so I have the impression he does not know it either. In his defence, it can be said that he is addressing the specific topic of the moral basis of Japanese capitalism. Although in many ways concerned with the same issues, he does not mention the *Nihonjinron* literature, nicely defined by Dore (1991: 57) as 'the analysis of what it is to be a Japanese'. This literature flourished particularly in the 1980s, exploring and asserting Japanese specialness, even uniqueness. Nor does Morishima seem to be aware of the seminal, if complex, interdisciplinary analysis of polymorphic liberalism of another economic theorist, Yasusuke Murakami (1996) and the book edited by Yamamura (1997) of critical essays evaluating Murakami's contributions. (For an earlier essay on his views on the relationships between economy and culture, see Murakami and Rohlen 1992.)

Religion

Morishima uses the terms religion, morality, ethics and ideology more or less interchangeably. Although ideology is not a word much used in these texts, it was central in the title of his Marshall Lectures – 'Ideology and Economics' – which formed the basis of the book. He identifies 'three kinds of religion: (a) the rational one which justifies the ruling political forces; (b) the rational religion whose objective is to emancipate the ruled individuals; (c) the mystical' (p. 43; also see Morishima 1982: 154, 194–5). In this schema, he identifies Shintoism as (c), and Confucianism as (a).

The book discusses Buddhism, Shintoism and Confucianism in Japan; in the paper Morishima primarily refers to Confucianism. This is not surprising since he is particularly influenced by Weber's concept of the Protestant ethic as a rational basis for western capitalism, and he sees the variant of Confucianism that developed in Japan as its counterpart for Japanese capitalism.

I am puzzled by Morishima's use of the term religion, especially because he refers to Confucianism as a secular religion capable of making an analytical, rational judgement of the realities of life (Morishima 1982: 198). I certainly do not deny his view that capitalism may have a spiritual as well as a moral or an ethical basis – though that spiritual element remains opaque to me. At any rate, at the risk of simplification, I use the term 'moral' here to encompass ethical concepts and religions. What we are considering is the value system that underlies capitalism and, in particular, the relationship between changes in Japanese capitalism and changes in the Japanese value system. More about this later.

Morishima is apparently enthralled by the Japanese version of Confucianism as a rational system of ethical principles and as an ideology that permeated and mobilized Japan's elite, providing the moral basis for capitalism from above (state-led capitalism). The central tenets of Japanese Confucianism included: strong hierarchic family relationships; loyalty to superiors and, ultimately, to the nation; emphasis on education to produce the 'good man'; frugality; and the support of a military elite which, inevitably, was interested in western technology and science (unlike its more bureaucratic counterpart in Confucian China). But there were negatives as well: unquestioning obedience to authority; elitism; acceptance of an extremely bureaucratic set of personal and social relationships which was group-orientated and anti-individualistic; potentially fanatical nationalism; and a vulnerability to moral capture by the military, as occurred in the 1930s. These themes are developed in his book. His paper contrasts Confucianism with the newer value system he sees as a requisite for a neoclassical type of competitive capitalism (capitalism from below), but which he perceives as developing only slowly and weakly.

The vast multiplicity of religions in Japan today – Buddhism, Shintoism, Confucianism, Christianity, the new religions – demonstrate, he claims, Japanese 'tolerance and at the same time their indifference to spiritual life. Among these many choices, the one which perhaps appeals to most Japanese is Confucianism. As a religion, it is one of the most irreligious and worldly' (p. 25). My reaction in reading this was twofold. First, I do not know how to measure the importance of religion in the lives of people but, at the very least, I see religious ceremonies regularly entering Japanese lives, especially at the times of marriage and death. Second, most Japanese probably do not know what Confucianism means. However, on reflection one could argue that many Confucian values – importance of family, acceptance of and respect for hierarchy, the central role of education for economic and social advancement, rationality, emphasis on this world – have deeply permeated Japan and are accepted by most Japanese today.

Morishima's 'Premonitions'[3]

Morishima's argument involves what he lists as ten premonitions. Basically they are sweeping pronouncements, statements generally not supported by social-scientific evidence or more than casual empiricism. While each premonition is quite clearly labelled, the ensuing discussion touches on a wide and occasionally disparate set of themes. Morishima's premonitions lead him to conclude that Japan's future, at least for the next 50 years, is not bright. The discussion is fascinating and provocative, but by no means convincing.

There is considerable overlap in the discussion of these premonitions, so my discussion is generally on the themes rather than the specific premonitions. That said, I will specifically consider three premonitions: population decline; a possible ideological crisis; and an unfavourable external environment.

Central themes
Four central themes emerge from his premonitions. First, Japan's state-led capitalism (capitalism from above), which began in the early Meiji era, is now at a dead end and increasingly discredited. It is essential and inevitable that Japan shift to a neoclassical, market-based, competitive type of capitalism (capitalism from below). If it does not, Japan will lose international competitiveness or become internationally isolated.

Second, the performance of an economy is dependent on the specifics of the underlying value system, which shapes human behaviour. Japan's former value system was Confucian and nationalist; it supported capitalism from above. However, this value system was rejected in the post-war educational system, which was imposed by the US occupation and essentially this system has continued since then.

Third, the value system required to support competitive capitalism is based on the best attributes of individualism and liberalism. However, while Japan's post-war education system has been based on these principles, its teaching has been at best superficial, at worst destructive. Individualism and especially liberalism have not been embedded sufficiently deeply to have created a new strong value system in Japan's post-war generation (to Morishima, those born after 1940 and thus schooled after the war).

Fourth, the values of the post-war generation are very different from those of the pre-war generation (those born before 1925) and even from those of the transition generation (those born between 1925 and 1940). The values of the post-war generation are weak, even perverse.

The education system has failed to produce the type of person Japan's new competitive capitalism must have in numbers that are far more substantial than the total it needed to establish an elite-based capitalism. Japan requires 'capable, motivated people who possess such qualities as courage, fairness and honesty' (p. 44). Rather, the system has created people who, in the first quarter of the twenty-first century, will be 'undynamic people motivated by the principle of peace at any price.... They are simply hedonistic, mammonistic and self-indulgent. They have no sense of duty, no religion, no love for their motherland and no element of ascription' (p. 47). They are materialistic and greedy, nothing more. They will lack the creative, entrepreneurial spirit necessary to drive a successful system of capitalism from below. 'The people, like the Romans in the age of their decline, are enervated, epicurean and undisciplined, and lack true leadership' (p. 54). Japanese 'are educated to be too materialistic. There is no religious environment... [T]hey have no interest in talking about ethical values, idealistic matters or social obligations even as abstract exercises' (p. 50).

Thus, according to Morishima, because of the lack of an adequate value system the Japanese economy will perform poorly over the next 50 years. The requisite human will to achieve successful capitalism from below will not be there, and the education system, which has not successfully embedded a requisite new value system, is at fault. Morishima does not directly identify the causal mechanisms whereby Japanese values drive its economic performance, such as their effects on choices between saving and consumption, work and leisure, and so forth. I interpret Morishima as saying that Japan's inadequate value system will make it incapable of developing the conceptual break-throughs that result in major innovations, and that not enough Japanese will have the 'entrepreneurial spirit' to commercialize innovations, whether created at home or abroad.

Population
Population decline is the first premonition Morishima lists. It is empirically based on the 1997 demographic projections that Japan's population will decline some 20 per cent by 2050, to about 100 million, which was the population in the mid-1960s. Morishima asserts that the decline may be even greater. What surprised me is that he did not then go on to argue that the absolute decline in the labour force, combined with a

decreasing household saving rate by an aged population, would mean that the labour and capital inputs needed to achieve GDP growth would be insufficient. Aggregate growth might be close to zero even though per capita growth would continue. Perhaps this was too obvious. In any case, to Morishima, the lack of appropriate values, not population decline, is the fundamental cause of Japan's future downturn.

Population estimates are the source of a major internal contradiction in Morishima's analysis. Having said that the population will decline, he asserts (premonition 10) that 'a vast multitude of people could potentially come into Japan from various poor places in Asia . . . Then, naturally, Japan would become a multiracial country' and 'a more open, cosmopolitan country' (p. 53). If this indeed happens, and goes smoothly, then this new, different Japan could thrive and do well, not collapse at all. However, Morishima treats this idea as a throw-away, without developing its full, complex implications.

My optimism about Japan's future, at least relative to Morishima's, is not based on such a profound transformation of what we mean by Japan as massive immigration would imply. Japan is unlikely to become an Australia, Canada or United States. If Japan does change into a multiracial or multiethnic society, then Morishima's analysis and my presumptions later in this paper are irrelevant. However, like him, I consider this a low-probability scenario.

Possible ideological crisis
Morishima raises the spectre of 'an ideological crisis – a possible right-wing reconversion' during the period in which the transition generation (born between 1925 and 1940) are in power (premonition 8, p. 46). What this might entail is not discussed. The 'right wing' apparently comprises those 'unhappy with and humiliated by the surrender' (ibid.). He assumes that the ratio of right-wingers is highest in the transition generation, next highest in the pre-war generation, and lowest in the post-war generation. I find that surprising since my sense is that the transition generation is by far the most pacifistic. In any case, Morishima sensibly judges that any right-wing resurgence will probably end calmly.

'An unfavourable external environment'
The last source of Japan's collapse, according to Morishima (premonition 10, p. 51), is that the United States, rationally assessing the respective power trajectory of Japan and China, will shift from an alliance with Japan that targets China to an alliance with China that isolates Japan. 'If this speculation turns out to be correct, Japan's posi-

tion in East Asia will decline to the present level of Taiwan and South Korea' (p. 52). To avoid this, Morishima proposes the establishment of a North-East Asian Economic Community comprising China, Japan, North Korea, South Korea and Taiwan. This would obviate the need for a US alliance with either China or Japan, and permit all to reduce defence expenditures. Moreover, Japan's small and medium enterprises, especially those in the western part of the country, would benefit from such close relationships. However, even with such a Community, Japan's decline is not prevented since 'the true cause of the Japanese collapse remains' (p. 54).

The End of Japan's State-led Capitalism

The thesis – that Japan's state-led capitalism is coming to an end and inevitably will be replaced by a neoclassical-type competitive capitalism – is compelling, although I do not agree with all of Morishima's analysis. He asserts that one important cause of the collapse of capitalism from above is its pervasive corruption, as reflected in the extravagant entertainment of central government bureaucrats and politicians by businessmen and local government officials. I regard this more as a symptom than as a major cause. Such entertainment is nothing new in Japanese culture; it goes back hundreds of years, certainly during the Tokugawa and medieval eras, and probably to the beginning of Japan's recorded history. What is new is a publicly expressed morality that deems such behaviour unacceptable. Today the media are stressing the need for accountability and decision-making that is independent, not based on bribery. Actually, the *dango* system of government purchase contracts and kick-backs to politicians, a major mechanism for the financing of Japanese politics, is substantively much more important.

I see the breakdown of capitalism from above – the weakening of the iron triangle of collusion among political leaders, central government bureaucrats and big business – as due to a complex mixture of domestic and international forces. The sheer growth of the economy, including achieving the widely held goal of 'catching up with the West', has engendered the forces of competition, and made many post-war economic institutions outmoded. Domestically, the coming to an end of the 1955 Liberal Democratic Party regime of one-party dominance and the struggles throughout the 1990s to create a new political party system based on one or multiple opposition parties with real power presage transition to (hopefully) a more balanced, competitive, democratic political system. This struggle and the erosion of faith in the bureaucracy have contributed to the economic problems Japan currently faces.

Probably more important economically has been the increasing trade and financial integration of the world economy and of Japan in it, which makes competitive markets necessary. Japan's process of removing barriers to trade, finance, foreign direct investment and other international economic transactions is taking a long time, but it is irreversible and inevitable unless the world environment changes dramatically. The long-run benefits of international competition, despite the shorter-run costs of adjustment, mean that a retreat to Tokugawa-style isolation – an idea Morishima flirts with – would simply be too costly for Japanese economic well-being.

I do not accept Morishima's analysis or views on a number of smaller issues, although they are not central to his basic argument. There is not space to consider them all. None the less, the following example is illustrative.

Morishima thinks that because Japanese firms in a competitive financial system will raise funds in the stock market rather than through bank loans, they will have to pay out a high proportion of their profits as dividends to keep stock prices high, thereby depleting internal sources of finance (p. 45). This ignores the reality of corporate finance markets. Large companies will substitute commercial paper for short-term bank loans and bonds for long-term loans. I agree that Japanese managers will have to change their behaviour by placing a far greater emphasis on profits and profitability (return on equity). While the traditional post-war financial system is indeed at a dead end (premonition 6, p. 39), the reforms, consolidations and implementation of financial deregulation policies currently under way are likely to result in a competitive, market-based financial system by the first decade of the twenty-first century.

My Presumptions

Morishima's boldness provides me with a licence to sketch my own presumptions (not premonitions) about Japan in the year 2050. As he argues in his book, small differences can be the cutting edge of substantially different results: Weber's Protestantism versus Catholicism, Morishima's Japanese versus Chinese Confucianism. Similarly, modest differences between Morishima and myself result in quite different prognostications for Japan in 2050. This reflects the fact that the range of possible outcomes, domestic and international, widens exponentially as the time horizon expands. (For an interesting scenario experiment, looking to the year 2020, see Nakamae 1998.) Certainly, previous 50-year segments of Japanese and world history – from 1850 to 1900,

1900 to 1950, 1950 to the present – are indicative of how dramatically circumstances can, and probably will, change in unexpected ways.

My view of Japan's long-run future is more optimistic than Morishima's, though admittedly supported by no more evidence than his view. It stems from two sources: my understanding of Japanese modern economic development since the Meiji period, particularly after the Second World War; and my perceptions about the nature, values and characteristics of the post-war generation of Japanese.

Morishima interprets Japanese modern economic development and growth from the Meiji Restoration until the 1980s as the result of state-led and elite-led capitalism: capitalism from above. Government policy certainly has been important and supportive, but in my view the real source of Japanese development and growth has been the myriads of entrepreneurs and workers in smaller-scale enterprises. They have provided the major source of output and employment throughout the modern period. (For a more extended discussion, see Patrick and Rosovsky 1976: ch. 1.) Big business has been very visible and typically close to government, but its share of GDP produced has always been smaller than in the United States or Europe.

Meiji Japan's industrialization was built on the labour-intensive silk spinning and cotton textile industries, neither close to, and certainly not led by, the government. Until 1930, more than 50 per cent of Japanese factory workers were female. Japan's post-war economic system, founded to some extent on Noguchi's '1940 economic system', has indeed involved much more government involvement, interference and regulation than the pre-1930s economy. (For a recent explication, see Noguchi 1998.) However, the assessment of the role of the government, and particularly of its industrial policy, has been debated vigorously. Most economists reject the state-led development and Japan Inc. models of Chalmers Johnson and others. Industrial policy had its successes and its failures; two major industries, automobiles and consumer electronics, never benefited especially from government support.

In my view, the rise of big-business managerial capitalism in post-war Japan has been more significant than the leadership and support of the government. Top management has become a new elite. Professional management has successfully insulated itself from outside corporate control by ensuring that a majority of the company's shares have been held by friendly corporations, epitomized by *keiretsu* cross-shareholdings and by internal boards of directors. Thus it has become self-perpetuating. Management has somewhat insulated itself from labour markets through the permanent employment system and from financial markets by bank loans. Firms have been insulated from competition in output markets by government regulation, which persists in many service sectors.

All this is changing, Morishima and I agree. Market-based competitive capitalism and its benefits have intruded on Japanese managerial capitalism from abroad. Manufacturing has led the way: not only because Japan's import barriers were removed. Opportunities for exports to global markets have led to globally competitive Japanese firms. The costs of insulated labour and financial markets now outweigh their benefits.

Does this mean that managerial capitalism will come to an end? I doubt it. It is the wave of the future (indeed, it is already here) not only in Japan but in virtually all advanced industrial nations. Dore terms this corporate capitalism, which he sees as embodying group-orientated values and principles relative to individualism. He contends that 'the middle-class elite of the future is going to be a corporate elite rather than an individualistic one' (Dore 1991: 114).

Japanese managers simply have been more successful than most, particularly those in the United States, in creating a system that maintains their corporate control. This does not have to be incompatible with efficient, market-based competition. Toyota and Sony are prime examples. However, in order to stay in power under competitive capitalism, managers will indeed have to become much more responsive to the stock market and, accordingly, will have to attach a far higher priority than in the past to return on equity.

Thus, I differ from Morishima in that, in my view, modern Japanese economic development has always combined capitalism from above and capitalism from below. Market-based competition has been the central feature of most industries dominated by smaller enterprises and wherever entry has been easy. The Japanese have always been entrepreneurial, eager to make profits and to have control over their own lives by owning their own businesses. Market pressures and deregulation are forcing an increasing range of industries dominated by large firms to adjust to competitive capitalism as well, but without (at least so far) having to give up the essence of managerial capitalism – namely, management control.

Like Morishima, I see the market-based competitive capitalist model as becoming predominant over the next 20 years or so, in that big enterprises also will become increasingly subject to the dictates of the market. Unlike Morishima, I see this as a continuous process, and one that will proceed reasonably smoothly and successfully.

Post-war Values

The major difference between Morishima and myself is our quite different interpretation of the value system of the post-war generation of
Japanese. His fulminations do not describe the Japanese post-war generation that I know. We are both treading in areas where neither of us
really knows very much, I suspect. We need the help of scholars of
contemporary Japanese religion, society and culture.

It is my perception of what motivates, and will motivate, Japanese
economic behaviour that leads me to argue that 'Japan will prevail'.

The value system of the post-war generation has changed in important
respects: it is more individualistic, less ideological, perhaps more secular.
But I see far greater continuity in values than Morishima does. Like
its forebears, the post-war generation is pragmatic, flexible, realistic,
ambitious, this-worldly. It values education, and not simply because it
is the route to economic and social success. The dynamism, vigour
and entrepreneurial spirit that has long characterized small businesses
persists: it is quintessentially Japanese (and whether or not it has a
strong Confucian basis, which I doubt, is not really relevant).

Is the post-war generation more greedy and materialistic than past
generations? I doubt it. Is it less so? That too, is difficult to judge. The
fact that the Japanese save more than before the Second World War
need not reflect a lessening of materialism. It probably is due rather to
a lifetime consumption horizon in which, compared to the past, Japanese
can expect to live longer and have the affluence that makes it easier to
accumulate assets prior to retirement.

Most Japanese have rejected militarism and ideological nationalism
– values that prevailed in earlier times. The Emperor is not very
important and is primarily a symbol of state. However, I suspect the
post-war generation is less committed to pacifism than the transition
generation. (I wonder to what degree the Japanese would pursue a
policy of peace at any price if the country's national security were to
be directly threatened.)

Like people everywhere, younger Japanese are preoccupied mainly
with their own lives and their own domestic environment. Yet they are
becoming increasingly internationalist through foreign travel, media
coverage of foreign events, and enhanced awareness that Japan is deeply
integrated into the world economy. Awareness of others leads to an
awareness of self. Even as they become more individualistic, the creation
of the Japanese version of the US Peace Corps and the rise in humani-
tarian and human rights-orientated non-governmental organizations
(NGOs) indicate a communitarian commitment by many younger

Japanese. The Japanese today have a healthy, not a destructive, nationalism.

What has brought about these changes in values? Certainly, education is an important ingredient; at the least, it no longer inculcates the pre-war nationalistic Emperor-orientated ideology. I do not know how deeply it embeds the values of individualism and liberalism, and neither I suspect does Morishima. But values are learned mainly at home and from peers, not just in school. And there have been a number of social forces affecting families such as urbanization, the rise of the nuclear relative to the extended family, and affluence itself. For the first time in Japanese history a generation has been brought up in an environment where abject poverty has been essentially eradicated and a reasonably high standard of living is the norm. The bottom 20 per cent of the Japanese population have close to the highest standard of living of the bottom 20 per cent of any country in the world; only the Scandinavian countries may do better. For the overwhelming part, they have jobs, places to live, adequate food, access to good education and medical care, and live in safe environments.

Young Japanese are far more willing to take occupational risks than their parents, to leave a decent job in order to take a position at a different company. It is not necessarily because the post-war generation is inherently greater risk-takers: affluence lowers the costs of occupational risks. None the less, labour market imperfections, especially for the large-firm managerial elite, remain an important barrier to the establishment of new, high-tech, venture capital firms. The key problems inhibiting venture capital in Japan, unlike the United States, are the lack of good job opportunities for those whose new firms fail, and the lack of financier expertise to evaluate new projects, not the lack of funding itself.

Morishima asserts that a value system based on individualism and liberalism is an essential requisite for successful performance in market-based competitive capitalism, without further explanation. I can visualize a wide range of individualistic and liberal behaviour that is compatible with market-based competitive capitalism. After all, most markets – even within competitive environments – are not spot or one-shot markets; they are markets in which the benefits of repeat business are substantial. Every economy is part of a larger social and political system, incorporating communitarian as well as individualistic elements. Dore (1991) nicely discusses four types of individualism: anti-authoritarian and anti-statist; self-reliance and self-fulfilment; self-sufficiency, which he terms 'emotional ungroupishness'; and self-seeking, self-enrichment, pursuit of pleasure. Each has a different impact on economic performance.

The Implications

As the Japanese become more individualistic and embrace liberalism – which implies some convergence of Japanese and western values – will the Japanese somehow become 'less Japanese'? By no means. Japanese values and Japanese society have changed tremendously over the past 50, 100, 200 years. Yet – thanks to education, affluence and television – the Japanese population is far more homogeneous than it was 100 or 200 years ago, and at the same time more pluralistic. Murakami's (1982) 'new middle mass' embodies 80–90 per cent of the Japanese population.

My impression is that, while most Japanese cannot readily define what it means to be Japanese, they are aware both of its meaning and of the distinctiveness of being Japanese. I do not think that awareness will change much in the coming 50 years, even as the definition of being Japanese becomes more international and individualistic.

In my judgement, the value system of the post-war generation is sufficiently strong and supportive of market-based competitive capitalism that it will be a beneficial, not an inhibiting, influence as Morishima believes.

If that is the case, how do I visualize the position of the Japanese economy in 2050? I see no reason to reject the standard projections that aggregate GDP will grow slowly at best, or even decline. (See, for example, Kosai *et al.* 1998; Feldman 1996.) The decrease in labour inputs, despite greater and more efficient utilization of women and older workers, will more or less offset the rate of technological change (total factor productivity) and continued capital deepening. On a per capita basis, Japan's GDP and standard of living none the less will be substantially higher.

Japan will continue to be a member of the leading advanced nations, probably in a relative position not so different from today's Western European nations, though further behind the aggregate GDP of the United States. The reasons are demographic. Western Europe, like Japan, has low fertility rates, so only if European countries pursue an active immigration policy will their GDP grow significantly. Even so, none is likely in 2050 to have a population as large as Japan's. Assuming that the United States continues to maintain its immigration policies, its aggregate GDP should grow more rapidly.

While Japan will not, contrary to Morishima, be an insignificant country in 2050, all of today's advanced countries (the OECD members) will be relatively less significant. As newly developing countries with large populations succeed in growing more rapidly than the OECD nations, they will become more important players on the world scene. China, India, Brazil, and even Indonesia, come immediately to mind. As Russia achieves economic growth and political stability, it will regain significance. However, should the European Union become a true United States of Europe, then it and the United States of America would be the two dominant global players.

In the non-economic international arena, since the Second World War Japan has consciously remained relatively inconspicuous. Unless the world military-security environment turns sharply for the worse, I see no reason for Japan to alter its stance as a peace-loving nation of only limited military capability. However, it would be overly optimistic to believe that world perceptions of power will change so much that this will particularly enhance Japan's international status.

Still, Japan might choose to become even more significant than its projected absolute and relative economic and market size dictate. There are two globally important areas in which Japan could make major contributions with a minimum of controversy: science and the environment. Japan could construct a world leadership role for itself by contributing substantially to the world's pool of scientific knowledge. Over the next 50 years it would need to invest heavily (and successfully) in basic, as well as applied, scientific research. Japan could also decide to become the world environmental leader, developing and providing technology, focusing a strong foreign aid programme on environmental protection, perhaps even taking the leadership in facilitating international agreements and protocols. Each, and indeed both, of these are certainly within Japanese capabilities – intellectually, financially and morally – and both are compatible with (though not compelled by) market-based, competitive capitalism.

Conclusion

The Japanese today lack the clear vision provided by a desired long-run growth path, unlike the leaders in the early Meiji era and unlike both leaders and the general public following the loss of the Second World War. Japan has now 'caught up with the West' in technology and standard of living and has rejected military catch-up. It no longer has the benefit of being a follower. But none of the leading nations has a clear vision of its desired future 50 years hence.

Japan today is indeed among the leading nations of the world, respected for its economic and technological prowess. However, although the Japanese want global acceptance and status, they have not evidenced much desire for global leadership. Japan, unlike the United States, does not have an ideology – a set of its own values – which it wants the rest of the world to adopt. I see little reason why these modest ambitions will change greatly in the next 50 years so long as the international environment is peaceful and supportive.

What will Japan be like in 2050? Its standard of living (per capita income) will be of the order of 50 per cent higher than today. With a population of 100 million, it will continue to be among the world's largest economies and societies. I certainly do not visualize Japan as being less significant than it is today. In short, unlike Morishima, I expect the Japanese and Japan to prevail over the next 50 years, just as they have over the past 150.

Notes

1. I have benefited from comments on an initial draft by Robin Landis and especially by Larry Meissner.
2. To convey Morishima's meaning, I quote him extensively. When from the paper, the citation is simply the page number of this volume. I have used the 1984 English paperback edition of his 1982 book, which contains a brief but illuminating Postscript.
3. *Editor's note*: In the draft version of his paper, Morishima referred to a set of premonitions. In his final version he refers to these as facts.

References

Dore, Ronald P. (1991), *Will the 21st Century Be the Age of Individualism?*, Tokyo: Simul Press.
Feldman, Robert Alan (1996), 'The golden goose and the silver fox: productivity, aging, and Japan's economic future', *Japanese Economic/Market Analysis*, 12 June, Tokyo: Salomon Brothers.
Kosai, Yutaka, Jun Saito and Naohiro Yashiro (1998), 'Declining population and sustained economic growth: can they coexist?', *American Economic Review Papers and Proceedings*, 88 (2): 412.
Morishima, Michio (1982), *Why Has Japan 'Succeeded'?*, Cambridge: Cambridge University Press. Citations in this paper are to the 1984 paperback edition, Cambridge: Cambridge University Press.
Morishima, Michio (1998), 'Why do I expect Japan to collapse?', paper presented at the Macquarie University conference, Sydney, 21 August.
Murakami, Yasusuke (1982), 'The age of new middle mass politics: the case of Japan', *Journal of Japanese Studies* 8 (1): 29–73.
Murakami, Yasusuke (1996), *An Anticlassical Political-Economic Analysis*, Stanford, CA: Stanford University Press.
Murakami, Yasusuke and Thomas R. Rohlen (1992), 'Socio-exchange aspects of the Japanese political economy: culture, efficiency, and change', in Shumpei Kumon and Henry Rosovsky, eds, *Cultural and Social Dynamics*, vol. 3 of

The Political Economy of Japan, Yasusuke Murakami and Hugh T. Patrick, general eds, Stanford, CA: Stanford University Press.

Nakamae International Economic Research (1998), *Scenarios for the Future of Japan*, http://www.gbn.org/scenarios/japan

Noguchi, Yukio (1998), 'The 1940 system: Japan under the wartime economy', *American Economic Review Papers and Proceedings*, 88 (2): 404.

Patrick, Hugh and Henry Rosovsky, eds (1976), *Asia's New Giant: How the Japanese Economy Works*, Washington, DC.: Brookings Institution.

Yamamura, Kozo, ed. (1997), *A Vision of a New Liberalism? Critical Essays on Murakami's Anticlassical Analysis*, Stanford, CA: Stanford University Press.

REPLY TO PATRICK

Michio Morishima

In various places Professor Patrick misunderstands me. For example, he says that I flirt with the idea of a retreat to Tokugawa-style *isolation*. I have never even hinted that there is the faintest prospect that Japan would be tempted to choose international isolation in 2050. I mentioned Tokugawa Japan in order to emphasize that the Japanese standard of living will be fairly high in spite of their international insignificance in 2050, as it was in the Tokugawa era.

I ignore hereafter all such points and confine myself to replying only to his comments on my prognostication for Japan in 2050.

I have pointed out that the Japanese economy consists of two tiers. On the upper tier, the triangle of politicians, bureaucrats and businessmen has been rotten for at least the last ten years. On the lower tier, firms have not yet introduced any incentive scheme that encourages employees to work harder and more effectively. They do not even try to do so. In fact, most companies do not usually provide any extra bonuses to those who have made an exceptional contribution to the business. These employees are only awarded a certificate of merit. Moreover, it is still very difficult for a worker to move from one company to another.

Thus the upper tier is rotten, while the lower tier has not yet been offered a set of appropriate incentives that could spur competitive behaviour. Lacking any change in this situation, the present rotten capitalism from above will not be transformed to a healthy capitalism from below. My own prognostication necessarily follows from this analysis.

Patrick regards 'the myriads of entrepreneurs and workers in smaller-scale enterprises' as the principal members composing the potential core of a market-driven capitalism (or capitalism from below). This he contrasts to the state-guided capitalism (or capitalism from above) which he essentially equates to 'the big-business managerial capitalism' supported by the iron triangle formed from the common interests of political leaders, bureaucrats and managers of big businesses. But he fails completely to refer to the fact that this triangle has become entirely rotten. Patrick also ignores the fact that many small businesses are so rigidly structured that competitive mechanisms are inoperative in various markets, particularly those involving skilled workers and managers. Adopting Patrick's approach leads quite naturally to his optimistic conclusion that Japan will prevail in the next century. At the same time it obviously contradicts a mountain of press reports telling us, *ad nauseam* every single morning, how deeply rotten the iron triangle has become.

3. Declining population, the size of the government and the burden of public debt: some economic policy issues in Japan[1]

Ryutaro Komiya

INTRODUCTION: AN OVERVIEW OF RECENT MACROECONOMIC DEVELOPMENTS

Japan's economic growth rate in the 1990s has been very low, compared both to its own rate in previous decades and to that of other major industrial countries. There were some signs of recovery in 1996, but the economy went into another recession in 1997–8: the unemployment rate reached 3.9 per cent in March and 4.1 per cent in April 1998, the highest on record since 1953.

In the prolonged depression of the 1990s, there have been two opposing views among Japanese economists as to what macroeconomic policies the government should pursue. On the one hand, there are orthodox Keynesians such as Hisao Kanamori, Hiroshi Yoshikawa and many others in favour of expansionary fiscal policies. For example, Yoshikawa (1998) states that the main cause of the long depression is a shortage of aggregate demand, aggravated by an anti-Keynesian fiscal policy. According to Yoshikawa, this was especially evident in the 1997 fiscal year when the government cut expenditure and introduced a tax increase (including increases in social security taxes) totalling 8 trillion yen. Increased taxes worked to depress consumers' demand. He proposes that the government continue with expansionary financial policies as long as depressed economic conditions persist.

On the other hand, a group of economists, who might be called 'non-Keynesians', are sceptical of the merit of orthodox Keynesian fiscal policy. They are more or less influenced by the 'new classical macro-economics' which seems to dominate economics in the United States. Toshihiro Ihori (1998) writes, for example, that under the current circumstances neither government investment nor tax reduction will have much effect on aggregate demand expansion as long as the public continues to increase savings instead of consumption. The Japanese persist in doing so despite having sufficient income and even though they are not subject to liquidity contraints. The key to conquering the present depression, he writes, is not a simple demand expansion policy but extensive reforms including deregulations, privatization and tax reduction. These would raise the unemployment rate and cause more bankruptcies in the short term, but he believes that it will be difficult for the Japanese economy to regain strength without going through such an ordeal.

Public opinion and government policy have been wavering between countercyclical (expansionary) fiscal policy, on the one hand, and structural reforms on the other. In 1996, when there were some signs of recovery, the pendulum swung to structural reforms: the government enacted the Fiscal Structural Reform Act, cut expenditures, raised taxes and embarked upon fiscal and administrative reforms.

It should come as no surprise that such policies slowed down business conditions. When the governments of the United Kingdom and New Zealand undertook extensive reform programmes, their economies went into recession and recorded very low, even negative rates of growth for a few years.[2] It was after going through a difficult period of reforms and adjustments that the citizens of these countries began to enjoy the fruits of these reforms, such as higher efficiency in the various sectors of the economy, lower rates of inflation and unemployment, and surpluses in the government budget as well as in the current account balance.

The general public in Japan has been impatient, however, and as business conditions deteriorated in 1997 the pendulum began to swing towards expansionary fiscal policies in the second half of that year.

Major factors responsible for Japan's worsening business conditions in 1997 and 1998 are, perhaps, not only fiscal retrenchment, but also a series of currency crises in East Asian countries which broke out in the summer of 1997, and a 'credit crunch' (*kashi-shiburi*) phenomenon which became serious from the autumn of 1997. The last one is an unfortunate and yet unresolved legacy left over from the so-called 'bubble economy' which characterized the years between 1986 and 1990 in Japan.

By the spring of 1998 as business conditions slowed down further, public opinion swung definitely to expansionary fiscal policy. In addition, the United States government also put strong pressure on the Japanese government to undertake expansionary fiscal policy. After some hesitation and resistance, Prime Minister Ryutaro Hashimoto changed his budgetary stance in early 1998 by, say, 120 degrees, if not by a full 180 degrees. Moreover, the Obuchi cabinet, inaugurated after the defeat of the ruling Liberal Democratic Party in the upper house election of July 1998, decided both to expand government expenditure and to reduce tax substantially, largely disregarding the Fiscal Structural Reform Act.

It is beyond the competence of the author to give a definitive answer to the question of whether countercyclical fiscal policy or structural reforms should be given priority in Japan at present. In this paper I should like instead to focus on three issues which I have chosen as being among the most important when evaluating the above question in a long-term perspective. These issues are: (a) the declining population and the measures to cope with it; (b) the call for a smaller government; and (c) the burden of public debt.

DECLINING POPULATION

The declining birth rate, the ageing population and the decline in population expected in the near future are serious demographic problems common to most advanced industrial and East European countries today. The special feature of Japan in this regard is that these demographic changes are happening very rapidly. For example, it took 70 years for the proportion of those who are 65 years and older in the total population to increase from 7 per cent to 14 per cent in the United States and 85 years in Sweden, but it took only 24 years in Japan.

Also, in Japan the general public, and even specialists in areas directly affected, were not sufficiently aware that the drastic demographic changes would take place so soon. The government's official estimates of Japan's future population, compiled and published once every five years, have been adjusted downward each time they have been published in the last 20 years (see Figure 3.1). I would say that the average Japanese has realized the seriousness of the problem only in the last two or three years.[3] Hence the concepts people have about Japan's future society have yet to fully incorporate all the expected demographic changes. Consequently, Japan's various social welfare systems have not yet been adjusted to fit the changed conditions that will prevail in the near future.

Why are these demographic changes so rapid in Japan? As a society becomes richer and women's social and economic status improves, more women receive higher education and have jobs after graduation. Both men and women get married at a later age than before; they have fewer

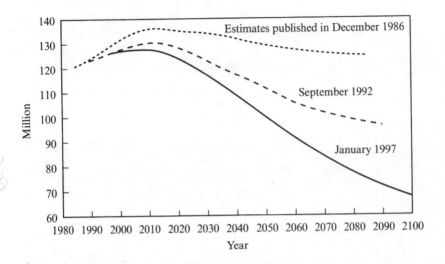

Source: Medium value estimates given by Institute of Population Problems, Ministry of Welfare, *Estimates of Japan's Future Population*, various years

Figure 3.1   Japan's total population in the future

children, as children become more expensive in terms both of the relevant opportunity cost and of the explicit extra costs of education and housing. Another factor may be the development of financial institutions for saving and a widespread social security system. In former times the best way for people to prepare for their retirement was to have enough children to support them in old age. As financial institutions and social security systems develop, however, the incentive to have children is weakened.

Facts About Japan's Future Population[4]

Both the rise in per capita income and the improvement in women's social and economic status have been very rapid in post-war Japan when compared to other countries. Demographic changes also have been, and will continue to be, very fast. The average number of children a woman bears during her lifetime, estimated under certain assumptions, is called the 'total fertility rate'. If this rate is 2.1, the size of the population will be maintained over the long run. In Japan the total fertility rate was above 2.0 until 1973 but declined rapidly thereafter, down to 1.8 in the early 1980s and then hovering somewhere around 1.42 to 1.50 between the years 1992 and 1996. It dropped again to 1.39 in 1997, an alarmingly low level, about the lowest among the OECD countries, with the exception only of Germany, Italy and Spain.

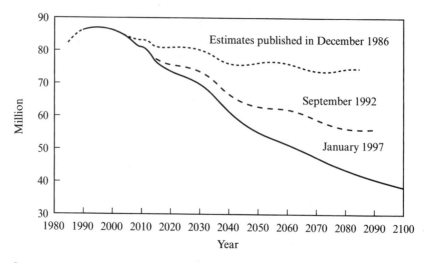

Source: As Figure 3.1

Figure 3.2   Japan's working-age population in the future

According to the government's official 'medium value' estimate, Japan's population will peak in the year 2007 and decline thereafter until it reaches 67 million in 2100, which is about half the present size (Figure 3.1.) Japan's working-age population, those between 15 and 64 years old, had already peaked in 1995 and will become half the peak size by 2080 (Figure 3.2). These estimates are based upon the assumption, however, that the total fertility rate will recover soon to 1.6 from its present lower level, an assumption which is criticized by some as being too optimistic.

According to an estimate by Yashiro *et al.* (1995, part 2, ch. 1, the 'standard' case), Japan's real GDP will begin to decline after the year 2010, although per capita GDP will continue to rise after that year. The annual rate of increase in per capita GDP between 2010 and 2020 however, will be, only 0.2 per cent (again, the 'standard' case), partly because of the decline in the ratio of the working-age population to the total population.[5] In 1995, when the yen–dollar exchange rate reached a record high, Japan's per capita GDP converted at the market exchange rate was 48.6 per cent higher than that of the United States, which was the third highest among major countries, after Switzerland and Luxembourg. Japan's share of the world's GDP was then roughly estimated to be somewhere between 15 per cent and 18 per cent. This is the highest share Japan has ever recorded, and it will never be surpassed in the future. Japan will be a 'dwindling giant' economy in the twenty-first century.

Burden on the Future Generations: a Parable of an Island Community

The smallness of a country's population is not a serious disadvantage generally speaking, unless the country aims to be a big power in world politics. What is economically most important for the welfare of the citizens of a country is per capita income. Small countries such as Switzerland and the Scandinavian countries have been very prosperous, enjoying the highest per capita incomes in the world. A rapidly declining population, however, creates great social difficulties.

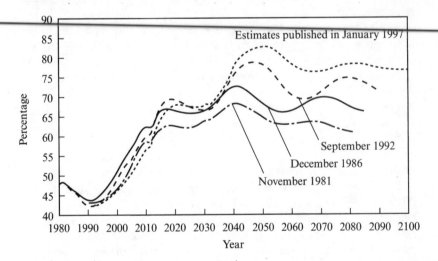

Note: The dependent population index is defined as the ratio of dependent population (those aged above 65 and below 14) to those of working age.

Figure 3.3   Japan's dependent population index

The effect on working people of supporting elders and youngsters as the dependent population index rises (see Figure 3.3) is more or less the same whether we are analysing a highly complicated society such as Japan or an imaginary small community on an isolated island. Think, for example, of the nearly extinct community on Easter Island off Chile, which left mysterious '*moai*'. Considering the problem from a macroeconomic perspective, in either society those of working age must bear the cost of living for the elderly as well as their medical and long-term nursing-care (*kaigo*). Assuming that other conditions are the same, when the dependent population index rises, the average living standard of the population is bound to decline, since the total output declines, on the one hand, and the costs of medical and related care for the elderly rise, on the other hand. This is inevitable because consumer goods cannot be stored for more than a few years, and the average lives of most capital goods are in the range of only 10–20 years. Also many of the structures built by public investment may become useless after, say, 30 years or even less. Public finance in general will face difficulties, since there are substantial economies of scale in providing 'public goods'. Difficulties in public finance will be acute in local communities where population declines rapidly.

Some economists seem to think that a shift of public pension financing from a 'pay-as-you-go' to a 'full-funding' approach will lower the burden of future generations. However, if one looks at the problem from a macroeconomic perspective, such a shift does little to change the true burden.[6]

Perhaps the only major difference between contemporary Japan and the imaginary island community in this regard is that the former has international economic relations with other economies of the world and can accumulate financial assets and investments overseas.[7] Another difference may be that the present working-age population of Japan can invest in human capital, such as knowledge, education and social reforms, which can contribute to the productivity of their posterity.

Babies born this year and later will reach working age after the year 2013 and will graduate from college after the year 2020. To cope with this decline in the labour force in the coming 10–20 years, measures to raise what is called the 'labour force participation ratio' could be pursued. But one of the most valuable – perhaps *the* most valuable – legacies the present generation can leave to their children and to future generations (including those who are 40–50 years of age at present) is simply more children. Social reforms to raise the birth rate are accordingly the most valuable form of government action.

Measures to Raise the Birth Rate

Because of the reaction of the public to the slogan and policy of 'bear and raise more children' (*umeyo fuyaseyo*) during the militarist era, the

Japanese government has so far largely refrained from pursuing active policies to raise the birth rate. Measures to raise birth rates in most European countries do not seem to have had substantial effects. But as the concepts and norms of Japanese people about the family and offspring are still quite different from those in countries with a European tradition,[8] some measures to raise the birth rate may work. I think the Japanese government should try whatever measures are likely to be effective in raising the birth rate. Although I am not a specialist in this area, I dare to propose the following four measures.

(a) Reduction in working hours

In 1985 the average working hours in a year for paid employees in the manufacturing sector were 2 166 in Japan, much longer than the 1 890 hours worked in the United Kingdom, the 1 680 hours in Germany, or the approximately 1 400 hours in Sweden. By 1995 the average working hours in Japan were reduced to 1 972 hours, which is shorter than the 2 163 hours in the United States or the 2 002 hours in Canada.[9] It can no longer be said, therefore, that Japanese working hours are the longest among the industrial countries. But these figures are concerned with the manufacturing sector alone. Under Japan's present working customs, it is not unusual for people working in offices in Tokyo, Osaka and other large cities to work until 8 o'clock or 10 o'clock in the evening, sometimes without being paid. Officers in their twenties to forties in the government offices in Kasumigaseki and elsewhere often work until 10 o'clock or even midnight and on weekends. The working customs in large banks, trading companies and other corporations are more or less similar.

Such working customs were formed in the old days when, in large cities, only the husband worked and the wife was a full-time housewife, devoting herself to housework and childcare. Then, women worked outside the household only during their teens and early twenties before they married. Japan's present working customs are not well suited to family life in a modern, urban society in which both men and women have regular jobs outside the home. I think the present customs should be radically changed so that both husband and wife can arrive home by 6 or 7 o'clock, which is normal in industrial countries other than Japan. It would contribute to young men and women getting married younger and having more children than at present.[10]

Many Japanese tend to think that such phenomena as fewer people getting married, people getting married at older ages, or married couples having no or few children are all matters primarily concerning women. But I think this is basically wrong. Women cannot get married unless

men also do so. Moreover, in today's society, unless husbands as well
as wives go home earlier and share the housework and childcare, the
birth rate will not rise.[11]

Generally speaking, the length of the working day should be decided
by employers, labour unions and individual employees, subject to labour
laws. But the long working hours in some sectors of present-day Japan
apparently have undesirable social effects, or what are called 'external
diseconomies' in economics, such as a low birth rate and increased
juvenile delinquency. The latter problem may partly be due to the
absence of a father at home, caused by his long working hours. I believe
that the government should do – and can do – something to reduce
these long working hours.[12]

(b) Reinstatement after childbirth

I agree fully with all those people who believe that the government
should help expand the facilities and services of day nurseries, extend
maternity and childcare leave, and otherwise help working mothers –
and fathers – to have and take care of children.[13] In addition to what
many people propose, I would like to suggest the following to encourage
women to get married and have children.

In the 1930s and both during and immediately after the Second World
War, many Japanese men who were employed on a so-called 'life-time'
commitment basis by private companies, schools or the government
were drafted into the army, served in the army, and/or were detained
in Siberia for two, three or even five or six years. After coming back
from the army or Siberia many of them were reinstated in their former
posts.

I wonder whether it would be possible to develop some such reinstatement practice for women who have babies and take care of them for
two, three or possibly up to five years. At present, many women,
especially those who are career- or profession-orientated, hesitate to
get married, to have children, and/or to have more than one (or two)
children, because they are afraid of losing not just income for a period
of time but also their 'career' status in the 'life-time' employment
system. The above-mentioned pre-war employment practice suggests
that a pause in employment for a few years could be compatible with
Japan's traditional 'life-time' employment practice.[14]

(c) Tax reduction for housing

The above two are concerned with work and employment customs
which are matters dealt with in contracts between private parties. Yet
I believe the government can do something to promote a change in

customs and practices in desirable directions if the public comes to understand fully the need to increase Japan's population. My third and fourth proposals are directly concerned with government decisions. According to a number of questionnaire surveys, the high costs of housing and education are among the most frequently cited reasons why young couples have no or few children. Subsidization of housing for those who have children through a substantial income tax deduction to cover the cost of additional space for their children may work to raise the birth rate. A similar tax deduction could be considered for the cost of educating children.

It is important for the above to be done through deductions in personal income taxes, because both the provision of housing and the financing of housing loans by the government or public corporations tends to be inefficient. These give rise to an unnecessary and wasteful expansion of the public sector (see pp. 84–98 below).

(d) Bonuses under the public pension programme to parents for raising children

My fourth proposal concerns the insurance premium required by the public pension programme. One of the most serious difficulties resulting from the declining birth rate and the diminishing working-age population is concerned with the possible breakdown of the public pension programme. To maintain old-age benefits (payment of pensions) at a reasonably high level commensurate with the living standard of the working-age population, the insurance premium paid by the latter under Japan's present pension programme, which is based upon a mixture of 'pay-as-you-go' and 'full-funding' approaches, would become very high: as much as 35–40 per cent of monthly wages. People who know about the present state of Japan's public pension programme are afraid that it could break down in the not-too-distant future.

Whether or not to get married, to have children, and how many to have are, in principle, decisions to be left to individuals without any interference from the state. In the case of the public pension programme based upon a pay-as-you-go approach, however, there is an aspect which economists label 'external economies' that should not be ignored. When a couple gives birth to a child, he or she will become, after 18–22 years, one of the payers of the insurance premium – and one of those tax-payers – who support the payment of old-age pensions. From society's point of view, having children contributes to the financing of future public pension obligations. This may be considered to be the 'external economies' effect of having children under the public pension programme. Nowadays people are having fewer children than in former times, partly or even primarily because it is financially quite costly to do so. The public pension premium scheme should take into account the facts that; first, having children contributes to the future financing of the public pension programme; second, nowadays having children is financially quite costly; and third, the low birth rate is a serious 'macroeconomic' problem for contemporary Japan.

I propose that this 'external economies' aspect of having children be taken into account in the public pension programme. For example, couples giving birth to children and raising them may be given special bonuses in the form of reduced public pension premiums while they are raising children. Bonuses may be continued until the children begin earning incomes and paying pension premiums themselves. The total amount of bonuses given to a couple should be more or less equal to the costs of having, raising and educating children and largely proportional to the number of children.[15]

These bonuses might ordinarily be dealt with in the personal income tax system, but with the recent increase in the level of basic exemptions in income tax, there are now a large number of employees and self-employed people who do not pay any income tax or pay only a small amount, whereas almost everybody of working age is supposed to pay a public pension insurance premium.[16]

THE CALL FOR SMALLER GOVERNMENT

The issue I wish to address next is whether Japan's government, or public sector, is 'too big'. As with most other industrial countries, the weight of the government in the Japanese national economy has been rising steadily in recent years. As far as we can see from the national accounts statistics, the share of government expenditure in GDP doubled in 35 years from 16.9 per cent in 1960 to 34.6 per cent in 1995.

The rise in the share of government expenditure as a percentage of GDP is largely the result of increased social security benefits, not government final consumption. The latter's share in GDP has been largely flat over the past 20 years. The role of the government in providing social security benefits and services in Japan today does not seem to me excessive. Since the population is ageing further and at the same time the family system which supports the elderly is weakening, I would expect to see an increasing need for social security related government expenditure.

When an international comparison is made of the share taken by government expenditure in GDP among major countries, Japan's total government expenditure does not appear particularly large. Yet the share of government investment (gross fixed capital formation of general government) as a percentage of GDP for Japan is remarkably high compared to other major countries (Table 3.1).

Table 3.1 *General government^a gross fixed capital formation as a percentage of nominal GDP (%)*

	1971–75	1976–80	1981–85	1986–90	1991–95
United States	3.7	3.4	3.4	3.5	3.2
Japan	5.3	5.9	5.4	5.0	6.0
Germany	3.9	3.3	2.6	2.3	2.6
France	3.5	3.1	3.2	3.2	3.3
Italy	2.9	2.9	3.7	3.5	2.7
United Kingdom	4.8	3.1	1.9	1.8	1.9
Canada	3.6	2.9	2.6	2.4	2.3
Australia	4.5	4.0	2.8	2.5	2.1
Belgium	3.1	2.8	2.9	1.6	1.4
Denmark	n.a.	n.a.	2.4	2.1	2.0
Netherlands	n.a.	n.a.	2.9	2.6	2.7
Spain	2.6	2.1	n.a.	3.9	4.1
Sweden	5.0	4.2	3.6	2.9	3.1

Note: ^{a} General government means central and local governments, excluding government enterprises.

Source: OECD, *National Accounts*, various years

According to my general impression, the ratio of the number of public employees to total population is not particularly high in Japan, at least as far as the central government – which I call 'the first layer' of the government sector – is concerned. It is true, however, that a meaningful international comparison in this regard is quite difficult.

In my view, what is 'too big' about the government or public sector of Japan is, first, government investment, and, second, what I call the third and fourth layers of the public sector. The size of Japan's public sector has tended to become excessively large, partly because of the employment practice of the public sector which is called *amakudari* in popular Japanese. The word is a colloquial expression that refers to the employment after their retirement, of former officials of government ministries, agencies or public corporations, by public and private cor-

Future directions

porations that are related in some way to those ministries, agencies or public corporations. The word carries a sarcastic or even biting nuance, so that it is not openly used by those who are directly concerned.[17] The practice of *amakudari* is closely related to Japanese employment customs such as *shushin-koyo* (the life-time commitment or long-term employment) and *nenko-joretsu* (promotion according to seniority), which have deep roots in Japanese work ethics.

Roughly speaking, a typical 'career' officer in a ministry of the central government enters the ministry at about 22 years of age, immediately after graduating from a university and after passing a highly competitive entrance examination. He or she works there for 25 to 35 years as a 'state employee'. After retiring from the ministry, the former state employee (*taikan*), works as an 'OB' (old boy, ex-official) of the ministry

Table 3.2 General government financial balances surplus (+) or deficit (–) as a percentage of nominal GDP (%)

	1981–85	1986–90	1991–95	1996
United States	–3.0	–2.5	–3.1	–1.6
	(–3.0)	(–3.2)	(–4.0)	(–2.5)
Japan	–2.8	1.3	–0.6	–4.4
	(–5.6)	(–1.9)	(–3.9)	(–7.3)
Germany	–2.5	–1.5	–3.1	–3.8
France	–2.7	–1.8	–4.4	–4.2
Italy	–11.6	–10.9	–9.7	–6.7
United Kingdom	–3.0	–0.7	–5.8	–4.4
Canada	–5.5	–3.7	–6.1	–1.8
Australia	–2.2	–0.1	–3.3	–1.4
Belgium	–10.8	–7.2	–6.1	–3.4
Denmark	–5.9	0.9	–2.8	–1.6
Ireland	–11.6	–5.6	–2.3	–0.9
Netherlands	–5.4	–5.1	–3.5	–2.4
New Zealand	n.a.	–4.8	–0.5	3.1
Spain	–5.0	–3.6	–5.5	–4.5
Sweden	–4.8	3.2	–7.8	–3.6

Note: Figures in parentheses for the United States and Japan are financial balances of general government excluding social security funds. For other countries the balance of the social security funds is unimportant.

Source: OECD, *Economic Outlook*, various years

in an *amakudari* post or several of them arranged by the ministry, until reaching the age of 70 or so.[18]

The practice of *amakudari* has given rise to the emergence and growth of a large number of what might be called 'government–industry complexes', explained below. They have multiplied and proliferated over the 50 years since the end of the Second World War, and have become, in my view, a heavy burden on both tax-payers and the private sector.

Another conspicuous feature of Japan's government sector in recent years, which stands out when making an international comparison, is its sizeable deficits (Table 3.2). As a result of large continuing government deficits, Japan's ratio of outstanding government debt to GDP has risen sharply in recent years. Most recently, Japan's ratio has become one of the highest among OECD countries (Table 3.3). Will it prove to be a heavy burden on Japanese citizens and their posterity?

Table 3.3 General government gross financial liabilities as a percentage of nominal GDP (%)

	1980	1985	1990	1995	1996
United States	37.0	49.5	55.5	63.4	63.9
Japan	51.2	67.0	65.1	80.6	86.4
Germany	31.1	42.8	45.5	62.2	64.9
France	30.9	38.6	40.2	60.7	63.0
Italy	58.1	82.3	104.5	124.7	125.2
United Kingdom	54.0	58.9	39.3	60.0	61.3
Canada	44.0	64.1	72.5	100.5	100.3
Australia	n.a.	n.a.	21.3	43.4	43.8
Belgium	78.2	122.1	129.7	133.5	130.1
Denmark	44.7	76.6	68.0	76.9	74.8
Ireland	72.7	104.6	96.3	84.9	76.5
Netherlands	46.9	71.7	78.8	79.5	78.5
Spain	18.3	50.8	50.3	70.7	74.6
Sweden	44.3	66.7	44.3	80.3	79.8

Source: As Table 3.2. These figures are for general government including social security funds.

In this section I shall discuss the first two of the above three problems: namely (a) government investment and (b) government–industry complexes. The problem of the burden of public debt, which is closely related to the issue of the bigness or smallness of the public sector, is dealt with in the next section.

Government Investment

The reason the ratio of government investment to GDP is remarkably high in Japan when compared with other countries (Table 3.1) is, in my view, and perhaps in the view of many others, because the political power exercised by politicians and government officials, especially those connected to the construction industry, is disproportionately strong in acquiring budgetary appropriations for government investment *vis-à-vis* the power of the tax-payers who bear the cost of actual government investment. Unfortunately, there also has been strong pressure from the United States to expand the Japanese government investment even more.

Politicians – including prefectural governors and mayors – gain the support of their local constituency by building roads, bridges, ports, dikes, convention halls and other infrastructure projects, partly or even primarily because it benefits local contractors and expands local employment. Tax reduction is not such an attractive proposition for election campaigns held in provincial constituencies, since a majority of those voters do not pay income tax. Politicians are also highly successful at raising election campaign funds from construction companies. Government officials can increase their budgets as well as the numbers of *amakudari* posts which they can obtain after they retire from the government. Not only is *amakudari* of high officials from the central government to top management posts of large construction companies common, but also numerous high- and medium-level officers in prefectural governments obtain *amakudari* posts in local construction companies. Construction companies of all sizes of course, benefit from government investment.

Unlike products sold by private firms, the output of government investment is not subject to evaluation through the market mechanism. Unfortunately, in Japan most government investment projects are not even subject to a serious cost–benefit analysis, either before appropriations occur or after completion. Examples can easily be found of wasteful large-scale government investment projects such as:

- the reclamation of Hachiro-gata and Nakanoumi;
- the dikes of Nagaragawa and Ariake-kai – apart from their environmental diseconomies;
- the three routes which connect the main island and Shikoku,

consisting in all of 19 giant bridges: only one of these routes, at most, is economically justifiable;

- the 'deficit' local lines of the now dissolved Japan National Railways;
- little-travelled but expensive highways;
- little-used seaports, airports and publicly run hotels;
- recreational facilities visited by few guests.

For example, in his recent book *Waste of Money by Government Officials*, Shoji Sumitya (1998), a former Vice-Minister of Transportation, writes that a substantial percentage of public investment in large-scale commercial seaport facilities all over Japan is, among other things, a waste. Since he was not only once the top official in the Ministry of Transportation but also is an expert on seaports and marine transportation, his arguments are persuasive.

Some of those who are opposed to reducing government investment argue that Japan's government investment at present cannot be said to be excessive simply on the basis of an international comparison (Table 3.1), since certain public facilities are still apparently inadequate in Japan. They assert that, for example, such ratios as the proportion of paved roads and of population with water supply or proper drainage are still low in Japan when compared with some European countries. But such an argument is not convincing to me. Japan's very high level of government investment (as a proportion of GDP) has continued for at least 25 years (Table 3.1). 'Investment' is 'capital formation', and annual investment adds up to fixed capital (assets, facilities, structures and so on) if properly carried out. Japan's high level of government investment, as shown in Table 3.1, should have meant that by now the country would be equipped with a much higher level of public capital than other industrial countries, after spending a much higher proportion of GDP on government investment for the last 25 years. If it is not, Japan's annual investment up to the present must have been carried out improperly and must not have added sufficiently to fixed capital.

I would propose that Japan's government investment ratio (as a percentage of GDP) should be reduced to the average for the OECD countries, which is about 2.5 per cent, or at least no more than 3 per cent, that is half the present level. It should be possible to improve water supply, drainage, waste disposal and other public facilities steadily within this limit.[19]

US Pressure on Japan's Public Investment

One of the factors behind Japan's exceedingly high level of government investment is the United States government's strong pressure on the Japanese government to induce the latter to expand domestic aggregate demand by making 'unproductive' investment.

In a series of negotiations from 1989 to 1990, called the US–Japan Structural Impediments Initiative (SII), the United States requested Japan to expand government investment and to raise its ratio to GDP to 10 per cent. This was an 'unusual' request, to say the least. Japan's government investment ratio to GDP has been much higher than other countries' for many years (see Table 3.1). Initially the Japanese negotiators resisted this pressure, perhaps weakly, by pointing out that this ratio was already very high by international standards, and that such a request, one that is directly related to the budgetary process, clearly interfered with Japan's domestic affairs. In 1990, after the United States repeated its requests and after difficult negotiations, an agreement on 'The Public Investment 10–Year Plan' was reached. Japan would spend 430 trillion yen (an amount as large as Japan's GDP in 1990) over the ten years (1991–2000) on public investment. Since then, although the total amount in the Public Investment Basic Plan and the number of years covered by it have been revised twice – upward in 1994 and downward in 1997 – the Japanese government has remained committed to a very high level of public investment.

The 'theory' or reasoning behind the above 'unusual' request of the United States is, conceivably, the following:

- Japan's large current account surplus – for simplicity, hereafter called the trade surplus – is detrimental to the United States' interest as well as undesirable to the stability of the world economy.
- Japan's trade surplus is caused by Japan's large domestic saving, which exceeds domestic investment. In order to reduce Japan's surplus its domestic investment needs to be increased.
- An increase in Japan's private investment in plant and equipment would expand productive capacity and/or strengthen the 'international competitiveness' of Japanese industries, resulting in a larger Japanese trade surplus and/or a threat to US industries.
- It is in the interest of the United States to request Japan to expand government investment, which is 'unproductive' in the sense that it does not add to productive capacity nor strengthen 'competitiveness'.

Of these, the first point is entirely wrong and unacceptable to me, and so is the third and necessarily the subsequent conclusion or fourth point.[20] No reputable textbook of economics or international economics written by an American economist, or by any other economist, states that a country's bilateral or overall trade surplus is in conflict with the interest of any trade partner or with global economic welfare. Rather, they say the opposite, namely that free multilateral trade and free international capital movement are beneficial to all countries participating in a world trading system in which various countries have trade surpluses and deficits, sometimes persistently.

No clause in international agreements such as GATT, WTO or IMF requires its signatories to balance trade or current account receipts and payments, or to limit the size of their trade or current account surpluses. If a large trade deficit is unacceptable to a country, then that country itself should endeavour to improve its balance of payments by using policy measures acceptable under international agreements. This is the request the United States has always made of countries through the IMF – at least, of countries other than the United States itself – when they have run into payment difficulties.[21]

If aggregate demand throughout the world economy is deemed stagnant, some general expansionary measures, rather than the expansion of a particular country's wasteful public investment, is called for. For example, a new SDR allocation should be considered. But the United States has been generally opposed to a new SDR allocation as being inflationary.

It angers me that the United States government made such an unusual request of Japan, and particularly that the Japanese government did not flatly refuse the request from the beginning. Such a request was made, I think, because of the misperception that after the collapse of the Soviet Union the United States' number one enemy was Japan's large trade surpluses.[22]

The Four Layers of the Public Sector and Proliferating Government–Industry Complexes

It is useful, I think, to distinguish four layers of the government, or public sector, in Japan. What I call the first layer is the central government (state) proper, and explicitly 'state employees' as opposed to all public employees. Its size does not appear to me to be 'too big' based on international comparisons. The second layer is local government, that is, prefectures, cities, towns and villages, and 'local public employees'. The number of the latter may be somewhat too high. When an important official in the New Zealand government lectured in Japan on New Zealand's experience of administrative and fiscal reforms, he commented that the number of employees of Tomakomai City in Hokkaido which he happened to visit was about double that of a city with the same population in New Zealand.

As I have already said, I think the size of the government or public sector in Japan does not appear much 'too big' to me as far as its first and second layers are concerned. What is 'too big' is its third and fourth layers, in my view. The third layer is composed, first, of all sorts of public corporations (*kodan*, koko, jigyodan, kikin, *shinko-kai*, and so on) set up, approved and/or financed by the central government. Some of them are well-known organizations such as the Japan Highway Corporation, the Japan Development Bank, the Japan Export-Import Bank and JETRO (the Japan Export and Trade Research Organization), but many of them are not so well known. They are numerous, altogether about 90 counting only those called *tokusyu hojin*, and there are many other types as well. Their classification and legal status are quite complicated and difficult to understand. Very few existed in the early postwar years, but their number increased sharply through the 1960s and into the 1980s, although more recently the government has been trying to reduce this total. Most of them had a good enough reason to be established initially, but there are quite a few which appear to have outlived their social functions or become too large. They tend to expand and multiply by themselves, and once established it is very difficult politically to dissolve them or curtail their size even when they become unnecessary or redundant.

The second organizational category of the third layer is: (a) public corporations under local governments, called *chiho kosha*; and (b) local public enterprises (*chiho koei kigyo*) such as public utilities, railways, hospitals and so on, run by local governments. *Chiho kosha* are sometimes called the 'third sector', because they are usually set up as joint stock companies with capital invested partly by a local government and partly by the private sector. Each of them performs a certain public sector function, receiving subsidies and borrowing funds from the local government. While the number of 'local public employees' has not changed much recently, both the number of *chiho kosha* and the number of their employees are still increasing fairly rapidly: the former by 13.3 per cent and the latter by 17.9 per cent between the years 1993 and 1996.[23] As Japan's working-age population has already begun to decline, it should be obvious that the total number of *chiho kosha* employees cannot continue to increase indefinitely. *Chiho kosha* do not publish financial statements; a lack of transparency is as much a problem as their relentless proliferation.

What I call the fourth layer is composed of intermediate entities between the public sector and the purely private sector. On the one hand, they supply goods and services to the first, second and third layers, are assigned to perform certain administrative functions, receive some subsidies and/or are strictly regulated by the government (the first and second layers). On the other hand, they accept *amakudari* of government officials, and provide campaign funds for politicians.

The organizational form of the fourth layer entities is either a joint stock company or a *koeki hojin* (foundation or corporation for the purpose of public interest). *Koeki hojin* are set up in principle by private initiative – but sometimes in practice by officials – and are approved and supervised by government ministries, agencies and prefectures. They are non-profit organizations in principle, but in fact some of them earn profits – sometimes enormous profits – and pay corporate income taxes. Hence some of their top posts could be an attractive destination for *amakudari* officials.[24]

The US Military–Industry Complex and Japan's Government–Industry Complexes

In 1961, in his speech at the end of his second term, US President Dwight Eisenhower pointed out the threat posed by what he called the military–industry complex. He warned that generals from the US armed forces, who were very familiar with the inside workings of the military, tended to be hired by the munition industries as executives when they retired from military service. He said that an interest group which he called 'the military–industry complex' was being formed and was working to excessively expand defence expenditures in the United States. It seems to me that in Japan today 'government–industry complexes', similar to those President Eisenhower called the military–industry complex, are developing.

In present-day Japan a large number of government officials are hired on retirement from the government to fill the top posts of what I call the third and fourth layers of the public sector. This is what I have described as the *amakudari* process. Both government officials and their counterparts in the third and fourth layers work to expand budget appropriations and loans from government financial institutions to their respective fields, and to increase both government procurement and posts for *amakudari* officials. Thus a 'symbiotic structure' is being formed between government and industry, which sometimes involves politicians as well.

The American military–industry complex about which President Eisenhower warned the nation was just one, or at the most three, involving the army, navy and air force. In Japan unfortunately there are many large and small complexes involving all sorts of entities in the first, second and third layers of the public sector. A notable example is the above-mentioned coalition of politicians, government officials and construction companies which works to expand government investment at the central and prefectural levels. I shall give a few examples in the following subsection.

The Case of the Japan Highway Corporation

The Japan Highway Corporation (JH) is one of the largest *tokusyu hojin* in the third layer of the public sector, and runs a nationwide highway network. According to Naoki Inose (1997), a journalist, it could be called the second Japan National Railways (JNR). JNR was dissolved and privatized in 1987 after accumulating a huge debt.[25] The highways run by the JH are all toll-roads; but the toll revenues do not cover costs and the JH receives subsidies from the government, the amount of which has increased sharply in recent years. It borrows very heavily from the government under the *zaisei toyushi* (fiscal lending and investment) programme. Whether it can repay the debt depends on the amount of subsidies it receives in the future.

The JH's highway network is still expanding, and as it builds new roads in remote, sparsely populated parts of Japan, its 'real deficit' – deficits excluding subsidies – to be covered by subsidies from the government are bound to increase. This is the reason why Inose calls the JH the second JNR. The JH adopts a 'pool system' in determining the tolls of newly built roads, and the amount of 'real deficit' – or surplus – on each road is not published.

The JH has 66 'affiliated' or 'under-the-wing' joint stock companies, the stocks of which are mostly owned by a *zaidan hojin* (one type of *koeki hojin*) called Doro Shisetsu Kyokai (Road Facilities Association: DS for short in the following). It was established by OBs (old boys) from the JH, that is, those who had worked for a long time at the JH, and is supervised by the Ministry of Construction. These affiliated companies are engaged in all sorts of work related to the JH, such as running service facilities and parking areas on the JH's highways, leasing space to restaurants, shops and gasoline stations, collecting tolls, patrolling and maintaining roads.

The present situation of the JH and its affiliates as a whole looks appalling to Inose, since:

- the parent, the JH, is running deficits 'in real terms', once government subsidies are excluded, indicating that it is investing beyond an economically justifiable level. No official of the JH or the Ministry of Construction appears to be worrying about the future of this second JNR or 'a JNR without rails';
- while the parent is in deficit, all the affiliates under the wing of the JH, which are private joint stock companies, earn profits, presumably after paying high salaries to their *amakudari* executives and employees;
- affiliates earn profits because they operate in their respective monopolized territories where other private companies cannot enter to compete with them. Thus one of the reasons for the JH's deficit is mandatory procurement at higher prices from its own protected affiliates while leasing its land and facilities to these affiliates at below market prices;
- there are constant flows of *amakudari* officials from government ministries (mostly from the Ministry of Construction) to the JH, and from the JH to the DS and to its affiliates;
- none of these affiliates or the DS itself is subjected to any auditing of its accounts or to administrative inspection by the government; none publishes financial statements;
- there is no readily available information about them, except through private investigation by journalists like Inose.

Inose (1997) examines in detail two other large public corporations (*tokushu hojin*) besides JH: namely, the Water Resource Corporation and the Housing and Urban Land Corporation. The situations of these two are revealed to be more or less similar to the JH: public investment beyond an economically justifiable level; heavy borrowing of government funds; deficits covered by subsidies from the government; a large number of protected affiliates organized as private joint stock companies all earning profits; a constant flow of *amakudari* officials; and an almost complete lack of transparency.[26]

Examples of Smaller Government–Industry Complexes

These three public corporations and their affiliates are examples of relatively large government–industry complexes. In daily newspapers and magazines we encounter from time to time examples of smaller government–industry complexes. Here just three are cited, but one can easily find many similar examples:

- Recently it was reported that thirteen executives of six companies specializing in the maintenance and service of traffic signals and their control systems for the police departments of ten prefectures were arrested on suspicion of tax evasion.[27] What attracted my attention was not the tax evasion incident itself, but the report that, first, the servicing contracts between the police departments of the prefectural governments and the companies were all concluded bilaterally without going through any bidding process; and that, second, altogether ten police OBs were *amakudari* executives of the six companies.[28]

- A second example is a story I found in a magazine. From the proceeds of 'national' (apart from prefectural) horse racing, 10 per cent goes to the Treasury and 15 per cent to the promoter, the Japan Central Horse-racing Agency (JRA), one of the largest public corporations. According to columnist Takashi Higaki, since its establishment in 1954 the JRA has built up a family of 49 affiliates as destinations for *amakudari* OBs from the Ministry of Agriculture, Forestry and Fishery and the JRA. These 49 affiliates also employ horse-racing reporters after they retire from newspaper companies, he writes, and therefore 'it is common knowledge in this field that criticisms of the JRA are restrained'.[29]

- According to a recent item in a newspaper, there are many associations related to the securities business. There are 22, counting only those located in Tokyo. They are financed primarily by membership fees collected from their members, which are securities companies. The total cost of supporting these associations is a substantial burden on the securities business, especially now that it has run into a severe depression. Some leaders of the securities business talk about reforms, but nobody is bold enough to hang a bell on the neck of this particularly burdensome cat. Who is the cat? The 68 directors of these 22 associations are OBs from the Ministry of Finance or the Bank of Japan who came to their posts through *amakudari*.[30]

Need for Reform

Eschewing any further details characterizing the political economy of these government–industry complexes and *amakudari*, I would like to make a few points.

Japan's public sector, especially its government investment and its third and fourth layers, have become 'too big' over the past 30 or 40 years. The phenomena of government–industry complexes and *amakudari* have been the catalysts in this process. When I became a member of the Faculty of Economics at the University of Tokyo in 1955, the numbers of incumbent faculty members and professors *emeriti* were 27 and three, respectively. The retirement age at the University of Tokyo has been unchanged at 60 – the lowest among Japanese universities – and professors *emeriti* are nominated from among those who have served as professors for more than 15 years. The numbers are now 58 and no fewer than 36, respectively. The size of the faculty has more than doubled, while the number of OBs (professors *emeriti*) has increased by twelve times. The primary factor behind the change is undoubtedly the expansion of the average life span of the Japanese from 65.7 years in 1955 to 80.3 at present. The situation in government ministries is more or less similar. There are far more OBs (ex-officials) relative to incumbent 'career' – and 'non-career' – officials nowadays than 40 years ago.

The difference between universities and government ministries, however, is that while universities do not arrange post-retirement jobs for professors, ministries provide *amakudari* posts for their OBs. This is partly because 'career officials' retire earlier than professors – in their late forties and mid-fifties. As a result, ministries and other public sector organizations must create enough posts for them. Thus the third and fourth layers of the public sector have expanded and government–industry complexes have multiplied.

There are inherent pressures to expand the bureaucracy in most countries, whereas counteracting forces to restrict the public sector to within a reasonable limit are particularly weak in Japan.

It is now imperative to reverse the tide and get rid of the unnecessary burden of a large number of government–industry complexes. Now that Japan's working-age population has already begun to decline, it is important that the present generation dissolve and liquidate all the government–industry complexes, thereby making the public sector much slimmer for future generations.

How to deal with *amakudari* is a very difficult problem. On the one hand, the bureaucracy has always had an inherent incentive to expand. Straightforward prohibition or strict regulation of *amakudari* would be necessary to stop the expansion and proliferation of government–industry complexes. On the other hand, a new attractive life-cycle pattern for competent bureaucrats which does not depend on *amakudari* arrangements must be designed to attract young able people into the public sector. Otherwise it would become inefficient and stagnate, and would be unable to perform its key economic and social functions.

THE BURDEN OF PUBLIC DEBT

Japan's ratio of government deficit to GDP has been rising rapidly in recent years, and is now at a significantly high level when compared to other OECD countries (Table 3.2).

Whereas the members of the European Union, now in the process of monetary unification, have agreed recently to reduce the ratio of their government deficits to GDP to less than 3 per cent, Japan's ratio is forecast to rise to as high as 8 per cent in 1998.[31] Even if Japan were located in Europe it would still fail to be admitted to the European Monetary Union for some time to come. With a high level of borrowing each year, outstanding debt accumulates rapidly. Japan's ratio of general government liabilities to GDP at the end of the 1998 fiscal year is estimated at 120.7,[32] one of the highest figures among OECD countries (Table 3.3).

Does this high level of borrowing and huge governmental debt represent a heavy burden on Japan's citizens and its posterity? Whether a country's public debt is a burden on its citizens and posterity is unfortunately one of the unresolved theoretical issues in macroeconomics. Keynesian and non-Keynesian theorists have opposing views on this, although there are a variety of views among non-Keynesians themselves. I have looked into a number of textbooks dealing with either macroeconomics or public finance, but have found no clear exposition of the present state of academic understanding on this issue. I have given up, for the time being, trying to discover whether Keynesian theory, new classical macroeconomics or one of the others is the most comprehensible to me. Keynesians seem to pay little attention to the fact that expectations and hence the behaviour of the public are much affected by what the government does. Under the present conditions in Japan, it seems to me that the impact on private consumption of tax reductions financed by 'deficit bonds' is likely to be small, if there is any at all. This is because people have become pessimistic about the future, given that they have a government which is rapidly accumulating debt during a prolonged recessionary period. On the other hand, the new classical school assumes that the economy is more or less in what Keynesians call a state of full employment and that people are highly rational (they have full knowledge of the economy and its future as well as of economics). Both of these positions seem unrealistic to me. Below, I shall make a few points which I think are relevant when answering questions concerning the public debt burden.

Four Aspects of the Burden of Public Debt

The issue of the burden of public debt can best be presented as a question of what happens to a national economy when its government reduces taxes and finances the revenue loss by issuing public bonds.[33] There are at least four aspects of the question to be considered:

- Assuming that income (GDP) in the country remains unchanged, does the public raise its level of consumption? If the answer is 'yes', the level of investment will decline, and posterity will inherit a lower level of 'real capital', and hence a lower level of GDP. This effect is called the crowding-out effect on investment.
- If the public spends more on consumption, GDP may go up, and the subsequent rise in GDP may increase savings sufficiently to compensate, or more than compensate, the initial loss of savings.
- When public bonds are issued they are bought by members of the current working-age population. When the bonds are redeemed, say 20 or 30 years later, most of those holding these public bonds will have retired. Tax revenues necessary to redeem public bonds will then be collected primarily from those who are working rather than from the retired. Thus to some extent, outstanding government debt constitutes a burden on future generations, even if the level of 'real capital' in the country has not been affected by issuing public bonds.
- Most macroeconomics and public finance textbooks deal with the issue of the burden of public debt in a closed model without any international linkages. But to consider the issue in today's context, it is necessary to pay attention to its international aspects. In an international economy, when a country's government issues public bonds it is likely to result in a larger deficit, or a smaller surplus, in its balance of international payments (current account). This means that, in today's world of free international capital movements, the government is borrowing partly from its own citizens and partly from foreigners; or the government might be borrowing entirely from foreigners. To the extent that a government borrows from foreigners and its citizens must redeem those bonds, public debt is clearly a burden on its citizens.

Barro's Neutrality Theorem

Whether a country's public debt is a burden on its citizens and on its posterity is closely related to the question of whether a tax reduction financed by issuing public bonds is effective in expanding aggregate demand. According to Robert Barro's (1974) neutrality theorem using a macroeconomic model under certain simplified assumptions, the answer to the above two questions is very simple: they are both 'no'. These answers hold in an open-economy model also, since the citizens in the world of Barro's theorem are so rational that they offset what their governments do by increasing their saving as much as the government dissaves.

By pointing out the extent to which the assumptions of Barro's theorem do not apply to the real world – say, the present Japanese economy – one could derive results which deviate from Barro's clear-cut but simple answers. In the real world, generally speaking, perhaps a tax reduction financed by issuing public bonds would increase aggregate demand to some extent, worsen the current account balance, and leave some burden, perhaps smaller than the total amount of debt, on future generations.

Declining Population and the Burden

In many popular and textbook discussions of the burden of public debt, the size of the country's population is assumed to be either a given constant or steadily increasing. This is not appropriate in Japan today. As explained above (pp. 76–84), not only will the size of the population begin to decline soon, but real GDP is also expected to decline, starting sometime between the years 2010 and 2020, according to some estimates. When such probable changes in both population and GDP are taken into account, the burden of public debt on posterity should be thought of as heavier than otherwise projected.

An International Perspective: the Mundell–Fleming Theory

Keynesians tend to dismiss the burden of public debt on future generations as being small. For example, in discussing what fiscal policy the Japanese government should take at present, Keynesian-orientated economists Masayuki Ohtaki (1997) and Hiroshi Yoshikawa (1998) argue that the burden of public bonds is relatively insignificant by assuming, explicitly or implicitly, that Japan's national bonds are all 'domestic bonds' held by Japanese citizens and that when they are redeemed by tax revenues in the future both those who will pay taxes and those who will receive the redemptions will be Japanese citizens.[34] Hence, according to them, outstanding public debt is not much of a burden on either the country's citizens or its posterity, except that interest payments may pose some problems. I think this is a closed-model argument, lacking an international perspective, which must invalidate it for modern Japan. Such an argument is basically wrong, even if we use a crude Keynesian macroeconomics model.[35]

The Mundell–Fleming theory is concerned with the determination of income (GDP), the balance of payments on current account and the exchange rate in an open economy. It is a very Keynesian – or even crudely Keynesian – macroeconomic theory, being a straightforward extension of the so-called ISLM theory of an open economy. According to the Mundell–Fleming theory, an expansionary fiscal policy in a world of floating exchange rates and free international capital mobility has a direct, negative effect on the current account balance, an increase in the current account deficit or a decrease in the surplus. In a simplified open-economy macroeconomic model, fiscal expenditure crowds out the current account surplus, not domestic investment. This means that when a country's government undertakes an expansionary fiscal policy, by expanding government expenditure or reducing taxes, the country is borrowing a large part of its funds from abroad.[36]

If asked whether I believe in the Mundell–Fleming theory I would give a qualified 'yes'. When 'Reaganomics' was adopted in the United States, it gave rise to twin deficits: the budget and trade deficits. West Germany's current account balance had a large surplus before the East–West unification,[37] which drastically turned into a deficit from 1991 as the government budget deficit increased sharply after unification. In Japan, too, large changes in the government budget deficits were a crucial factor behind the unprecedented rise in the current account surplus from 1982 to 1986 as well as its sharp decline from 1991 to 1996.

Thus, from an international perspective, when a country's government reduces taxes and borrows funds by issuing public bonds in a world of free international capital movement, one should envisage the government as borrowing funds from a worldwide capital market, which includes its own domestic capital market, or reducing its supply of funds thereto. Hence, in this situation, borrowing by the government constitutes a burden on its citizens and on their posterity.[38]

Credit Rating and the Burden

Another international aspect of the burden of public debt is concerned
with the credit rating of government bonds in the international capital
market. It was reported recently that a representative of Moody's Investors Service, a US credit rating service company, expressed the view
that the company may reconsider its rating of Japanese government
bonds unless the conditions of the Japanese economy improve and the
budget deficit is reduced.[39] Although I have little knowledge of the credit
rating business, I understand that generally a heavily indebted government is given a low rating and must subsequently pay a higher rate of
interest in the international capital market. The citizens and financial
institutions of such a country may diversify their portfolios away from
holding the bonds of their own government. If Japan's ratio of public
debt to GDP continues to rise, such a possibility should not be ruled
out. If that happens, the rise in interest rates on Japan's public bonds
would be an obvious additional burden on Japanese citizens.

For this reason, I found it unjust that the United States Secretary of
the Treasury, Robert E. Rubin, repeatedly requested Japan, even though
informally, to reduce taxes 'permanently' in order to expand domestic
demand.[40] The news that Japanese government bonds might be 'down-
graded' was reported at about the same time as he was repeating this
request. I thought it was outrageous. It is an unjust interference in
Japan's domestic affairs. Decision-making on fiscal policy goes through
a delicate political-economy process in any country. Foreign governments and their officials who take no responsibility for the consequences
should strictly refrain from interfering in the process, however desirable
a certain policy is from their viewpoint.[41] Moreover, according to theoretical thinking recently developed in the United States, a tax reduction
financed by a bond issue is not considered to be very effective in
expanding aggregate demand: if Barro's neutrality theorem holds, the
effect is nil. Apparently, Secretary Rubin's economics is many years
behind recent developments in macroeconomics.

Coming back to the question at the beginning of this section, that is,
whether the present high level of borrowing by the Japanese government is a heavy burden on its citizens and their posterity, my answer is
definitely 'yes'. Its rapid reduction should be given top priority.

I am not advocating here that the government maintain a balanced
budget at all times. Fiscal policies may be used for countercyclical
purposes. An unbalanced budget in a particular year may be acceptable
if budget deficits in recession years and surpluses in boom years more
or less cancel each other out over a cycle. In Japan, the financial balance

of 'general government', excluding social security funds, has been in deficit ever since 1976. One cannot say that Japan's budget deficits are a part of 'countercyclical' policies.

Although the United States government has also been running budget deficits for many years, even it will have a surplus in 1998. Moreover, the size of US budget deficits has generally been much smaller than Japan's in terms of its percentage of GDP. Hence government's outstanding financial liabilities, again as a percentage of GDP, have also been much smaller in the United States than in Japan. Persistent annual budget deficits which are not required to be offset by surpluses in other years tend to lead to a lack of fiscal discipline, a 'waste of money by government officials' (Sumitya 1998) and an unrestrained expansion of the public sector.

CONCLUDING REMARKS: OVERCOMING PESSIMISM

In recent times, the prolonged depression, an increasing awareness of the consequences of a declining population and the realization that the Japanese economy and society now need extensive reforms have made many well-informed Japanese quite pessimistic about Japan's future.

I share the view that Japanese society has now reached an important turning point after about 50 years of highly successful economic growth and social reforms following Japan's defeat in the Second World War. Undoubtedly, many of the social institutions developed during the high-growth period of the 1950s and the 1960s have ceased to be consistent with today's conditions and needs. I think, however, that the Japanese need not be pessimistic about the future, especially as far as economic conditions are concerned.

From an economic point of view, what is needed for a country's citizens to be prosperous and happy in today's world is a high and steadily rising per capita income. The absolute size of its population or GDP matters little for the well-being of a country's citizens. Fifty years ago, Japan's income level was very low, about one-tenth the level of that of the United States and lower than that of any West European and some Latin American countries. Now that Japan has risen to the top income group, per capita income cannot be expected to increase as rapidly as it has done in the last 50 years. I think, however, that it would not be difficult for Japan to remain in the top income group if it could achieve a number of necessary economic and social reforms.

When discussing measures to revitalize the Japanese economy, some economists and journalists have compared a stagnant Japan with a booming United States, and paid much attention to such features of the United States as Silicon Valley, venture businesses and venture capital firms, NASDAQ (the National Association of Securities Dealers Automated Quotation system), and the collaboration between scientists in universities and entrepreneurs. I would not say that these are unimportant as factors contributing to economic prosperity. Social institutions which enable risk-taking by ingenious and ambitious people are certainly important, and so are 'high-tech' industries, and 'big industries' where economies of scale matter most: steel some time ago, more recently automobiles and jumbo aircraft.

Yet we should look at some small – in terms of population – European countries such as Switzerland and the Scandinavian countries, which do not have much in the way of US characteristics but have attained a very high income level for their people and an overall level of economic prosperity. We should consider carefully why these countries are prosperous and are respected by the international community. I think that, more important than some of the factors mentioned above in achieving a high income level for the whole population of a country, are such factors as a high level of education, a law-abiding public, a low crime rate, harmonious labour–management relations and sound macroeconomic policies. At least as important is a relatively equal income distribution and the spread of education which facilitates building a national consensus on major social and economic issues. The development of new, sophisticated technologies is of course important, but the propagation of such new technologies and the use of already known best practices by the majority of the population are also important.[42]

The rate of increase in Japan's per capita income in the first half of the twenty-first century will be much lower than in the last half of the twentieth century. During the latter period Japan travelled from almost the bottom income level among industrialized countries to the top. Looking back, it was part of a long catching-up process which dates from the beginning of the Meiji period. Now that Japan has reached the top-runner group in the race up the ladder of economic prosperity, it cannot hope that its per capita income will grow as fast as it did in the past or at a rate much higher than others in this top group.

But reflecting on how the Japanese people overcame the devastation immediately after the Second World War and all the vicissitudes they underwent thereafter to reach its present state, I am rather optimistic. I am confident that Japan will remain among the most prosperous countries of the world in the next half-century. The present and next generations of Japanese people will be bold enough, as were the

Japanese of one generation ago, to undertake whatever economic and social reforms are necessary to achieve that objective.

NOTES

1. This chapter is based on a paper presented at the Conference 'Why Did Japan Stumble: Causes and Cures' at Macquarie University, Sydney, 20 and 21 August 1998. The author thanks for their assistance and comments the members of the staff, especially Y. Hosoya, Y. Maeda and Y. Mizukoshi, of the Institute of International Trade and Industry, MITI, where the author serves as an adviser. He is grateful also to a number of colleagues and friends, including K. Iwata, M. Kanno, R. Murata, N. Takayama, N. Yashiro and H. Yoshikawa for providing information and offering comments on an earlier draft. The views expressed in this paper are the personal ones of the author and should not be taken as those of the organizations to which the author is affiliated.
2. The United Kingdom recorded a negative rate for growth in GDP in 1980, 1981, 1991 and 1992, while New Zealand did so in 1989 and 1991.
3. Public discussion about the reform of the public pension system in 1994 and thereafter and the introduction of the long-term nursing-care insurance (*kaigo-hoken*) system in 1997 contributed to the realization by most Japanese that little time remained to cope with the problems arising from drastic demographic changes. In particular, talk about the possibility of a breakdown of the public pension programme, the rise in the pension premiums, the lowering of pension benefits, the raising of the age at which the pension benefit begins to be paid from 60 to 65, and a discussion of the high cost of long-term nursing care for disabled elders, all made the general public aware of the urgent problems Japan faces in the near future, resulting from *koreika* (the ageing of population) and from *shoshika* (fewer children being born). These words now widely in use, especially the latter, are not even listed in many current dictionaries. Thus public perceptions of the shape society will take in the near future are changing rapidly. It is not surprising that the behaviour of the public is also changing rapidly. From a macroeconomic point of view perhaps the most important of such behavioural changes is a higher propensity to save.
4. This part owes much to Ogura *et al.* (1991), Yashiro *et al.* (1995), Ato (1996), Yashiro (1997a), and Yashiro (1997b).
5. See also Kosai *et al.* (1998).
6. If Robert Barro's neutrality theorem (Barro, 1974) concerning the burden of public debt holds, then such a pension reform will have no effect at all on this burden.
7. This possibility is precluded if the Japanese government and the public at large take the advice of the famous (notorious?) Maekawa Report (1986) seriously. It said, essentially, that having a current account surplus is a vice, which means international capital movement is undesirable. If a country accumulates public pension funds abroad, they are subject to exchange-rate risks. Also, OECD countries have demographic problems more or less similar to Japan's. Hence taken as a whole, Japan can not rely much on other OECD countries as places in which to accumulate public pension funds.
8. The value Japanese people attach to the family is still very high. For example, extramarital births are still rare, compared with 30–50 per cent in some European countries (although I do not know recent statistics on this).
9. Bank of Japan (International Department) (1996). Data on annual working hours were not provided in its 1997 edition.
10. Having worked in the Ministry of International Trade and Industry for ten years, I felt that young single officers were working so long that they did not have time to date with a girl- or boy-friend and fall in love. When a few years ago the Ministry

drafted a plan to revitalize the Japanese economy, I thought that one of the things the government could do was to prohibit government employees from working in their offices after, say, 5:30 p.m. and instead let them go home.

11. In the United States, where the total fertility rate even among whites is still close to 2.0, I understand most office workers go home immediately after 5 or 6 o'clock, and have dinner with their family, if they have one.

12. For example, at present it often costs less to employ a smaller number of employees than necessary and have them work overtime frequently, because the overtime wage rate is relatively low in Japan. Also, many social insurance charges and other fringe benefits do not increase with overtime work as they do with the number of employees. Unfortunately, under present Japanese employment customs, it is often difficult for an employee to decline his or her employer's (or supervisor's) request to work overtime.

13. It is important, I think, that the costs of such services or leaves be borne as much as possible by the government, which represents the whole society, and not by individual employers. This is because, if the latter is required to bear such costs, women of childbearing and nursing age will be discriminated against in employment.

14. The proposal here is not intended to encourage women to discontinue their work (employment) during their childbearing and nursing period, but to expand the menu of possibilities available for women, especially career-orientated ones.

15. The idea of charging differentiated insurance premiums based upon the number of children of the insured under the public pension programme was first proposed by Noriyuki Takayama (1996), to my knowledge. I thought about a similar idea and talked about it in my classroom. Then a student who was studying the public pension programme told me that she had come across such an idea somewhere, and later gave me the reference. Takayama told me in a private conversation that the idea of differentiating public pension insurance premiums according to the number of dependent children of the insured was discussed in Germany.

16. Those who have no children may object to the above proposal, and argue that they are already bearing much of the cost of bringing up other's children through income and other taxes which finance expenditure on primary and other education as well as on public health. But public expenditure on education and on child welfare was made even in the days when the birth rate was still sufficiently high. The reasons for doing so are, perhaps, external economies generated by education and public health as well as the issue of human rights. They are different from the reason for the above proposal, which is to raise the birth rate.

17. The original meaning of the word is 'descent from heaven'. It might be translated as 'post-civil-service employment', but the crucial factor in *amakudari* is that the employment is arranged by the personnel office of the ministry or equivalent employer.

18. The so-called 'non-career' officials retire from ministries at a somewhat older age, and work in posts arranged by ministries until the age of 65 or so. There are employment customs somewhat similar to *amakudari* in the private sector. Namely, an executive who has worked for a long time in a large bank or some other large corporation often moves to a high-salary post in another corporation which has close relationships with the former, under arrangements made between the former and the latter. But generally speaking, such practices do not harm society nor cause inequity, since both the former and the latter, as well as the arrangements between them, are governed, or at least constrained, by the principle of profitability.

19. Government investment in Table 3.1 covers only investment in the 'general government' sector and not investment in the 'government enterprises' sector in the System of National Accounts (SNA) statistics. Many of the wasteful large-scale investment projects cited in the text, such as the dikes of Nagaragawa and Ariake-kai, the 19 bridges between the main island and Shikoku, and the little-travelled highways of the Japan Highway Corporation (see pp. 88–9), have been undertaken by public corporations which belong to the 'government enterprises' sector, and hence their

investment expenditures are not included in the figures in Table 3.1. The purchase costs of land used for government investment, which are very high in Japan relative to those in other countries, are not included either, since Table 3.1 is on a national income statistics (SNA) basis.

20. For a more detailed exposition of this argument below, see Komiya (1994).

21. Some American economists and political scientists accept the economic logic of my argument in the text, but argue that Japan's large and rising trade surpluses, overall and especially bilateral with the United States, tend to cause a rise in protectionism in the United States and must therefore be reduced. I do not agree with this kind of argument, since such moves toward protectionism caused by trade imbalances are based largely upon superstition and partly upon the self-interest of vested interest groups. Consider anti-Semitism in Nazi Germany in the 1930s or the 'yellow peril' argument in Europe in the early twentieth century. When the public believes in a superstition that Jews or Japan's surpluses are harmful to their society or the world and follow demagogues motivated by localized self-interest, it is the duty of social scientists and politicians to explode these superstitions rather than to take them for granted.

22. Another factor behind the high level of government investment in Japan is the institution of 'construction bonds'. Under Japanese fiscal laws, financing government consumption expenditure is generally prohibited, but capital expenditure may be financed by bonds. Although in a recession year the government legislated a special law to legalize the issue of government bonds to finance consumption expenditure, the government budgetary policy for countercyclical purposes has tended to expand public works and other government investment.

23. This is according to Chiiki Seisaku Kenkyu-kai (1997). Figures quoted are for those *chiho kosha* in which the capital share of local governments is more than 25 per cent.

24. Counting those under the jurisdiction of 22 ministries and agencies of the central government, there were 7 318 *koeki hojin* in 1996. There were others under local governments.

25. The debt which the JNR left now amounts to 28 trillion yen, more than 5 per cent of Japan's GDP in 1997. How to dispose of this debt still remains a difficult political problem.

26. See also Takeuchi (1997). The JH has not refuted the severe and detailed criticisms by Inose and others, to my knowledge. The cabinet meeting decision on 26 December 1997 ordered the JH to improve its operation along the lines suggested by Inose, albeit in a lukewarm way. Hence, it appears that what Inose wrote about the JH was not far from the truth.

27. *Asahi Shimbun*, 14 and 15 April 1998.

28. I said to a few friends that one could comment 'And you too, Police!' (instead of Brutus) on this incident. Some of them told me then that I knew little about the police, and that the police are quite eager to secure *amakudari* posts in many areas.

29. *Ekonomisuto*, 25 November 1997.

30. *Nihon Keizai Shimbun*, 18 January 1998.

31. This is an estimate of the ratio of general government's (central and local governments, excluding social security funds) budget balance to GDP for the 1998 fiscal year, provided by the Japan Centre for Economic Research (1998: 56–7). This figure excludes from the deficit the transfers, which are planned to take place this year, of the debt of the dissolved Japan National Railways and the debt of the National Forestry Special Account to the General Account of the government. If these transfers were included in the deficit, the ratio in question rises to 13.1 per cent.

32. The figure quoted in the text is an estimate of the ratio of the liabilities owed by central and local governments to GDP at the end of the 1998 fiscal year, after the transfers of the debt mentioned in the previous footnote (ibid.: 56).

33. An increase in government expenditure financed by issuing public bonds may be

considered as a combination involving (a) an increase in government expenditure financed by a tax increase, and (b) a tax reduction financed by issuing public bonds.

34. Even so, there is an intergenerational distribution problem, described above, apart from the international aspect discussed below.

35. The Keynesian argument that lowering wage levels does not help to increase employment is also a closed-economy argument, not valid in a highly competitive open economy. For example, one of the main reasons why Japanese airline companies have been losing competitiveness and market share in international aviation services is their high real wages. Their wage levels were pushed up during the period of strict regulation and near-monopoly, and are now much higher than the wage levels of airline companies in neighbouring countries, including the United States. The labour unions of the Japanese airline companies have priced themselves out of the market, so to speak. If labour costs of Japanese airline companies are lowered, they could acquire, at least to some extent, a larger market share and expand employment.

36. Apparently the citizens in the Mundell–Fleming theory are not rational in the sense of Barro's neutrality theorem. New classical economist such as R. Barro would say that citizens are rational and clever enough to offset what the government does by saving as much as the government dissaves, and that nothing will happen, therefore, in the balance of payments or elsewhere. For the Mundell–Fleming theory, see any standard textbook of international economics or international macroeconomics.

37. Before unification, East Germany was nearly a closed economy as far as international capital movements are concerned and its current account was nearly balanced.

38. Since Japan is a capital-exporting country, its current account balance remains in surplus. Even when the government borrows heavily, the surplus is only reduced. The government budget deficit reduces national saving and the country's net wealth, unless the deficit is exactly matched by domestic investment, including investment in human capital, which contributes sufficiently to national wealth. The fact that a government budget deficit results in an increase in the current account deficit, or a decrease in the surplus, probably implies that the assumptions of Barro's neutrality theorem are not valid.

39. *Nihon Keizai Shimbun*, 18 April 1998.

40. For example, *Nihon Keizai Shimbun*, 23 March and 15 April 1998.

41. Here again, I was angry at the Japanese government for not making a protest to Secretary Rubin for his intrusion into Japan's domestic affairs, about which he knew so little.

42. Consider, for example, the content of economics courses taught at a large number of universities in Japan. Some teachers still teach the economics of ten or even twenty years ago. Moreover, as J.M. Keynes pointed out in the last pages of his *General Theory*, economic philosophy which politicians and policy-makers believe in and practise is often what they learned many years ago when they were 25–30 years old (see Komiya, 1996).

REFERENCES

Ato, Makoto (ed.) (1996), *Population Problems of Industrialized Countries* [in Japanese], Tokyo: University of Tokyo Press.

Bank of Japan (International Department) (annual), *Comparative Economic and Financial Statistics*, Tokyo: Bank of Japan.

Barro, Robert J. (1974), 'Are government bonds net wealth?', *Journal of Political Economy*, 82: 1095–119.

Chiiki Seisaku Kenkyu-kai (study group on regional policies) (1997), *A Latest Survey of Chiho Kosha* [in Japanese], Tokyo: Gyosei.

Ihori, Toshihiro (1998), 'Deregulation rather than demand expansion' [in Japanese], *Nihon Keizai Shimbun*, 30 April.

Inose, Naoki (1997), *A Study of the State of Japan* [in Japanese], Tokyo: Bungei Shunju.

Japan Centre for Economic Research (1998), *Quarterly Economic Forecasts*, no. 100, March.

Komiya, Ryutaro (1994), *Economics of Trade Surpluses and Deficits* [in Japanese], Tokyo: Toyo Keizai Shimpo-sha.

Komiya, Ryutaro (1996), 'J.M. Keynes and economic policy in Japan: looking through achievements of Korekiyo Takahashi, Tanzan Ishibashi and Kamek-ichi Takahashi', in Hisao Kanamori (ed.), *Is Keynes Really Dead?* [in Japanese], Tokyo: Nihon Keizai Shimbun-sha.

Kosai, Yutaka, Jun Saito and Naohiro Yashiro (1998), 'Declining population and sustained economic growth: can they coexist?', *AEA Papers and Proceedings*, May, pp. 412–17.

Ogura, Seiritsu and Makoto Kawamura (1991), *Forecast of Japan's Population up to the Year 2020* [in Japanese], JCER Discussion Paper no. 16, Tokyo: Japan Centre for Economic Research, April.

Ohtaki, Masayuki (1997), 'Business cycles and Keynesian economics' [in Japanese], *Nihon Keizai Shimbun*, 22–31 December.

Sumitya, Shoji (1998), *Waste of Money by Government Officials* [in Japanese], Tokyo: Yomiuri Shimbun-sha.

Takayama, Noriyuki (1996), 'Directions of reform of the public pension system' [in Japanese], *Rodo Keizai Jumpo*, no. 1565, August, 4–8.

Takeuchi, Yasushi (1997), 'Parasites on super-highways' [in Japanese], in Miyamoto, Ikuo (ed.), *The Secrets of Public Corporations* (special issue of *Takarajima*, no. 336), Takarajima-sha.

Yashiro, Naohiro (1997a), 'Changes in the composition of population and the Japanese economy', in R. Komiya, M. Sase and M. Eto (eds), *The Japanese Economy Towards the 21st Century* [in Japanese], Tokyo: Toyo Keizai Shimpo-sha.

Yashiro, Naohiro (1997b), *Economic Analysis of Japan's Ageing Society* [in Japanese], Economic Analysis, No. 15.

Yashiro, Naohiro and Japan Centre for Economic Research (eds) (1995), *The Japanese Economy in the Year 2020* [in Japanese], Tokyo: Nihon Keizai Shimbun-sha.

Yoshikawa, Hiroshi (1998), 'The tasks for the Japanese economy in transition' [in Japanese], *Nihon Keizai Shimbun*, 19–30 January.

COMMENT ON KOMIYA

Mitsuaki Okabe

Professor Komiya's paper provides first an overview of recent macro-economic policy debates in Japan, and thereafter discusses three important, but somewhat separate, issues facing Japan: the expected decline of population, the assessment of the real size of the Japanese government sector, and the burden of public debt.

The paper has all the charm found in his preceding papers. It is, first of all, very clearly, and moreover interestingly, written, a rare trait in a scholarly paper. Second, it utilizes suitable economic logic to its full extent, and demonstrates that powerful arguments can be made even without resorting to mathematical equations or sophisticated statistical analysis. Third, the paper extends to the relevant policy-orientated arguments and the political economy aspects of these issues. Fourth, the paper not only provides new insights into the issues but also includes several provocative elements. Given this last factor, one might think that it would be easy to provide critical comments; but not necessarily so, since the author is always very careful in phrasing and wording. Knowing that this kind of risk exists for the discussant, I shall try, first, to show how the three main issues in the paper are to be observed, and then raise some issues.

The Difference of the Time Horizon of the Three Issues

Although the three issues are undoubtedly very important ones, they are very different in terms of their economic time horizon. This means that the policy menu for each issue, as well as applicable analytical tools, naturally varies substantially.

Very roughly speaking, the issue of an expected population decline is one which extends 'super'-long-term, namely 20–30 or even 50 years. The size of government relates to the long term (say, ten years) or the medium term (say, five years). The burden of public debt can be an issue involving either long-term, medium-term, or short-term considerations (see Table 3.4). For each of the three, the author provides his policy recommendation with varying degrees of concreteness. For declining population, he strongly proposes raising the birth rate, which can certainly be one of the super-long-term policies. For reducing the 'real' size of the government sector, he recommends reforming the contractual basis of a bureaucrat's employment. This is consistent with the time span of the policy objective. For the issue of reducing the burden

Table 3.4 Main issues and related policy discussions in Professor Komiya's paper

Issues	The nature of the issue			Policies discussed or relevant related issue
	Super-long-term	Long- or medium-term	Short-term	
Expected decline of population	+			Raising birth rate***
Government size		+		Reforming bureaucrats' employment system**
Burden of debt			+	• Deficit reduction**(*) • Barro's debt neutrality proposition** • Mundell–Fleming propositions*

Notes:
* *Short-term*
** *Long- or medium-term*
*** *Super-long-term*

of public debt, he discusses such issues as Barro's neutrality theorem (a long- or medium-term issue) and the Mundell–Fleming proposition (of a decidedly short-term nature), and consequently asserts that deficit reduction should be a top priority.

Therefore, the nature of the issues in terms of both the time horizon and policy recommendations, as well as the appropriate analytical tools, seem in general to be mutually compatible. But in one important point the author's arguments seem to involve some problems, to which I now turn.

Demographic Issues

Professor Komiya's key argument for the first issue is two-fold: first, he claims that the expected decline in population beginning around the year 2010, due to the low birth rate, is a 'serious "macroeconomic" problem for contemporary Japan' (p. 84). He concludes that we should try whatever measure would be effective in raising the birth rate (p. 81). This intuitively understandable and straightforward policy recommendation would certainly address the issue. But what seems to be more important to me is that, although it is a policy option, it is only one of several options. Since the policy objective extends over the super-long-term, what is predetermined or considered as given may be changeable by public policies or owing to other factors; that is, we have more policy parameters in this kind of extremely long time span than in the usual long or medium term. Let me cite a few examples.

First, 'working age', which is assumed to be between 15 and 64 years old according to government estimation and also implicitly assumed in Professor Komiya's argument, can change, or can be changed, substantially. Examining the mandatory retirement age of a typical large Japanese corporation, we may say that retirement age was once deemed to be 55 years old some 30 years ago. It was around 60 years old 10–15 years ago, but now is approximately 64–65 years old. This means that the years worked by the average Japanese has increased by nearly ten years in such a relatively short period of time as 20–30 years. Therefore, when interpreting the kind of simulations quoted by Professor Komiya (Figures 3.1–3.3 in his paper), it is necessary to be very careful about the underlying assumptions. Deriving policies based strictly on that result would be rather misleading. One of the important policy implications to be derived from these simulations is that public policies should adjust all the relevant institutional arrangements necessary for a longer period of working years so that those who become elderly but who are still willing to work can be suitably accommodated.

My second example of how the percentage of the working-age population could be increased is by accepting immigration from overseas, instead of securing future workers domestically. This seems to be an extreme, and to some people outrageous, policy option. It is certainly a difficult issue upon which to form a national consensus, but given the nature of the relevant time horizon, these kind of options should not be excluded when formulating policies. In some other countries, such as Australia, Canada and the United States, immigration policy is important for a nation's human resources. In Japan also, there was in fact a similar policy debate during the 'bubble' period in the late 1980s as to whether and to what extent we should allow an intake of foreigners.

The third example, or rather a still bigger question in itself, is the validity of the policy goal as stated. Given the extremely long time horizon and adopting a global, or even planetary (!), perspective, which should take into consideration the entire worldwide increase in population, it is difficult to say whether a nation's long-term public policy which aims at increasing its population can be desirable and/or justifiable. Reconciling local birth rate policy with this global population question is extremely difficult, but the argument must not simply be dismissed, or at least the question must be borne in mind, even if only economic aspects are to be dealt with. All in all, a policy recommendation of raising birth rates requires much broader discussion if it is to be considered at all persuasive.

Another aspect which I am not very comfortable with is the author's conflicting perception of the openness of the Japanese economy to his policy prescription. On the one hand, he does point out, in fact he emphasizes, that Japan must be understood to be an open economy with international economic relations with other economies of the world (p. 80). If so, the existing amount of savings held by the Japanese, including those of the elderly, should be understood as claims not only on future goods and services produced domestically but also on those goods and services produced overseas. In this case, declining population does not lead immediately to a categorical need for higher birth rates, since foreign goods can be claimed in exchange for the saving. In this case, the policy implication would be to improve the market environment for international financial transactions so that exchange risks and other risks associated with foreign investments can be properly managed and hedged.

Policy Menu for Declining Population

Professor Komiya proposes four concrete measures to raise the birth rate. They are all apparently conducive to his stated objective, but the line advanced by his arguments seems somewhat patchy. The first three, namely, reduction in working hours, reinstatement after having children, and tax reduction for housing, are the policy objectives to be pursued not simply for achieving a higher birth rate but for other equally important purposes such as: enjoying life; allowing individuals, especially females, to be able effectively to contribute to society; and enjoying a higher standard of living.

On the other hand, the fourth measure, bonuses to parents for raising children, is a more direct measure to achieve this goal. Given what should be the basic principle of determining policy assignment – that is, when achieving policy objectives the more direct and most effective instruments should be chosen – this measure should, and can, be at the core of his proposal. Thus, the author's argument, though not exactly flawed, can be refined in this respect.

Sources of Inefficiency and Expansion of the Public Sector

Professor Komiya sharply and provocatively analyses the sources behind both the increasing inefficiency and the expansion of the public sector. His four-layer theory presented as an attempt to understand the Japanese public sector is a novel idea, at least when described in such a systematic way, and is extremely interesting. It is clearly linked to the system which employs and promotes government officials in Japan. By combining these analyses with an additional international factor, namely the continual US pressure on Japan to expand public investment, he draws the conclusion that there has been an expansion in both the size of the government sector and the government debt, as well as a growing inefficiency in Japanese public investment.

Thus, the author recommends two policies: one is the reform of the practices determining employment for government officials, and the other is to reduce government debt or shrink the budget deficit over the medium term. I have found these arguments quite convincing, and I should like to echo my support for these policies.

In the same vein, I should like to stress that public policies of the Keynesian type, pump-priming, aggregate demand policies, are not as appropriate as they used to be. Recent research (see Figure 3.4) shows that the end result of government investment seems to be far less effective recently in stimulating private demand than it was in previous years. Up until the late 1980s, government investment could stimulate private demand vigorously over a relatively short period, followed by some adverse side-effects due to the upward pressure on interest rates after an increase of aggregate demand (namely, the interest rate effect on private investment and the Mundell–Fleming effect on the net over-seas demand due to an appreciation of the yen). But in the 1990s, when business outlook generally has remained gloomy, the stimulating effect has become much smaller. And interestingly, subsequent adverse effects have also become very limited, due significantly to a persistently easy and accommodative monetary policy.

This means that traditional aggregate demand policy is not only less effective but, if utilized, would require a greater burden of debt in order

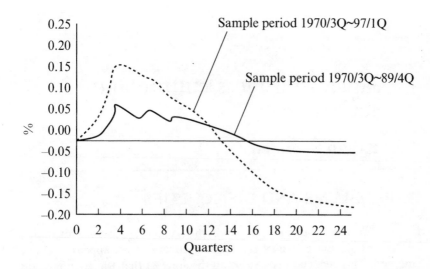

Notes: Shows the percentage point increase of private demands, when government investment increases 1 per cent initially (at period 0). Impulse response function of the vector-autoregression model incorporating six variables: private demands, external (foreign) demand, government investment, long-term interest rate, price level, and the yen exchange rate.

Source: Economic Planning Agency, *White Paper on the Japanese Economy*, July 1998

Figure 3.4   The effect of government investment on private demands: a comparison of two periods

to achieve a given level of effective aggregate demand. Therefore, various structural policies should be given priority. These include reforming the government sector as mentioned in the Komiya paper, as well as reforms in the financial sector and to the corporate governance system. These policies require more imagination and are more difficult to implement than traditional Keynesian policies. I look forward to hearing a further elaboration of his ideas for reforming the employment practices that characterize government bureaucracy.

4. Japan's business culture and society

Kyoko Sheridan

1. PROBLEMS AND DIFFICULTIES

It has been almost eight years since the Japanese economy dwindled into recession. Little sign of economic recovery as yet appears to have emerged. This recession is said to be the longest that the economy has ever experienced throughout its long history, putting at risk its hard-earned reputation as having the capacity to be dynamic, innovative and quick in responding to adversities. Many people, both inside as well as outside the country, regard such an unusually lengthy recession as a warning sign indicating that the economy has now come to an inevitable turning point. At this time the workability of the economic system itself and the relevance of its corporate management approaches need to be thoroughly evaluated. Without waiting for the result of the evaluation, the majority of the population sees the need for large-scale reform and for the restructuring of the economic system as well as of society in general. What, then, will the new economic society look like?

As early as the beginning of the 1990s a national search for that picture began. This implies that the search itself was not initiated by the subsequent economic slowdown, though it may well have been accelerated by these unfortunate events. Yet as we come to the end of 1998, there still has not emerged any specific picture, not even the vaguest outline, of a new economic society that would be supported enthusiastically by the population in general. Unless such a picture is drawn, the economy is not likely to find a clear way out of this recession.

In the past Japan seemed to clearly possess a special talent for:

- sketching the outlines of the future by collecting and collating information;
- accurately predicting future directions for the economy and society;

- composing 'vision plans' for building a better economy;
- motivating the population to achieve planned national objectives.

Does this leadership failure indicate the difficulty attached to interpreting the future of Japan under its current circumstances? Should the aim of this national search be to restore an economic society which previously was as prosperous as it was also too ambitious and progressive? Alternatively, does it mean that the Japanese people have lost interest in planning and guidance now that they have built an industrial state capable of providing, within bounds, a comfortable enough income and a stable, low-risk life?

It is true that the Japanese economy has grown large and affluent. This new-found status obliges Japan to assume a stronger leadership role in the world economy, as well as in the international political arena, than it had previously. Japan must now also make a significant contribution to promoting the development of the world's economy and to increasing the well-being of the world's population. Outside observers feel that a recession-stalled Japan unable to recover is just not acceptable. They demand that Japan resume her economic growth, open up her domestic market to international trade, invest actively in building production facilities, and transfer technologies offshore to help industrial development in other countries. While acknowledging the important role that the Japanese economy is able to play, given its size and accumulated capital and technologies, I strongly recommend in this paper that Japan should not be obliged by outsiders to fulfil expectations and demands which might lead her to make hasty decisions when selecting a future direction. Japan has come to an important turning point now that she has moved out of her industrial development stage. What Japan must do next is to:

- examine carefully and thoroughly the kind of problems which have emerged in the economy;
- challenge old precepts, ways and forms;
- reconsider which sectors in society should be changed;
- explore all the future possibilities and avenues which have opened up for the Japanese.

To discuss these future directions we must examine the decisions made in the past which led the Japanese to build their economic system, its corporate structures, the very forms and customs of business practices that are operating today. The problems we have now are inherited legacies of our previous making. To understand these legacies from the past I address my study in this paper *directly* to an examination of those customs and habits which promoted the construction of Japan's economic system and those business practices which helped her succeed.

This paper has two tasks. The first is to understand the shape and nature of those customs and habits that form Japan's 'business culture', with the aim of identifying the driving forces and the working principles which have guided the making of its economic system and its business practices. Understanding the particular form that business culture took will help us see the nature of the problems that now are emerging in Japan's economic society. The second task is to seek policy and research proposals which will help introduce an economic society that can be promoted as an alternative to Anglo-American models.

2. BUSINESS CULTURE

'Culture' is a concept often used to refer to a broad range of society's arts, habits and customs. In editing their joint work, *The Political Economy of Japan*, Kumon, a sociologist, and Rosovsky, an economic historian, gave their definition of culture as 'the design principles or fundamental patterns that act as organizers of more derivative social characteristics, such as a particular world outlook, set of policies, or forms of organization' (Kumon and Rosovsky 1992: 4–7).

I noted above that customs and habits guided the making of our preferred approaches to conducting business activity. I call it 'business culture' to indicate its influence in giving direction to people's decision-making at the level of corporate management and to their behaviour at the workplace in more general and fundamental ways.

Following the above definition given by Kumon and Rosovsky (1992), I intend to study business culture in order to see how design principles were formed in Japan to:

- influence the making of business systems and management practices;
- motivate a work ethic in the population;
- mould commonly held views on work;
- shape work behaviour.

Japanese business culture emerged during the initial stage of the country's industrialization. It was based on its people's understanding of the imminent importance of economic development. Subsequently this allowed enthusiasm to build for, and a commitment to the speedy promotion of, industrial development and the modernization of society.

Economists, economic historians and sociologists, among others, have all sought those factors that have played an important role in forming the business culture of pre-industrial Japan and the specific conditions and circumstances under which the country began its industrialization as a late-comer.[1]

Benefiting from those earlier research results, this paper discusses the development of labour management in Japan from a different standpoint. My purpose is to add further observations to Gerschenkron's hypothesis that economies coming late to development promote their industrialization at an accelerated speed. Developing economies benefit from ideas and technologies available to them from already developed economies. Their motivation to catch up is also enhanced by the recognition of the development gap between their own and the advanced economies. I aim to discuss how this catch-up process specifically influences the late-developing economies. In short, my concern is to understand the 'shaping' of their industrialization and not, as in Gerschenkron's work, its 'speed'. How has the use of foreign experience affected the specific nature of Japan's management systems and business organizations? This question leads us to see how particular experiences obliged the Japanese to formulate and develop their own specific economic and management systems and, by so doing, to build their own specific business culture.

To establish a modern industrial structure and begin its operation at a desired level of efficiency, people in business and government in early Meiji Japan travelled to the advanced industrial West and studied the behaviour and conduct of its business environment. The record of their 'learning' is well documented. Their progress and process has been charted carefully by economic and management historians.[2] It was an effort to transplant modern industrial technologies to an agrarian-based, traditional society as rapidly as possible. Particularly noteworthy are the many and varied experiments and experiences that were conducted by employers who aimed to educate and train their employees to be an efficient workforce, one which would be able to use the new imported tools and technologies. An equal and diverse number of experiments were made to design plants, offices, corporate organizations, work schedules, employer–employee communication channels and work relationships which could support the newly developed workforce and enable it to engage in production efficiently and effectively.

How were training programmes formulated and selected? How were workplace designs evaluated and accomplished?

A new set of rules and preferred approaches were identified out of such experiments and experiences which added to and supplemented old ones. People acquired an ever-increasing understanding of how to do business effectively and how to work efficiently in the newly emerging industrial environment that now characterized Japan.

The process of instituting new rules and approaches in Japan is always initially slow and gradual. It becomes even slower and even more gradual until eventually these rules secure the general acceptance and support of society as legitimate and worthy of being called a business culture. It is important to note that in this process efforts are made to evaluate whether the emerging business culture is in fact workable, relevant and desirable. So it was not until the end of the 1920s, after a full three decades of experiment and experience, that Japan's own approach was established. This formed the basis for any subsequent development of the employment system, management practices and business culture which came to constitute present-day Japanese management.[3] Slow it might have been in coming, but once established this approach became a grand principle, one which changed with the same deliberate slowness that marked its birth and development.

3. THE FORMATION OF JAPAN'S BUSINESS CULTURE

(a) Importance of Labour

It is no exaggeration to claim that labour has played a core role in generating economic growth and business development in Japan throughout her national industrialization efforts. In drawing up macro-economic plans, industrial policy, business strategy or social programmes, leaders in Japan have placed labour at the centre of their strategy map and based their plans on gaining the maximum possible contribution from workers. The working population responded to these employer initiatives by whole-heartedly deciding to behave in a manner which promoted their own well-being, their welfare at work and their self-development through working. As we shall see later, this approach differs distinctly from that followed by most countries in the West.[4] The making of a 'business culture' is largely defined by the employer's approach to labour management and the employee's attitudes towards work.

The importance of labour and the strategic use of labour is not limited to Japan and Japanese management alone. However, what is unique about Japan's case is that:

- the country lacks an adequate endowment of natural resources for industrial activities and land for cultivation and dwelling;
- she began her industrial development without waiting for an adequate accumulation of capital or sufficient technological advancement to support and supplement this shortage;
- the country decided to begin the industrialization of the economy as soon as it came into contact with the industrial states of the West and subsequently drew up national plans to achieve that task.

In the planning process, the Japanese decided that the task of industrialization should be promoted by relying heavily on the contribution of individual work efforts. How employers would organize the work efforts of their employees became the central strategic issue for the success of the industrialization of the country.

(b) The Transplantation of Business Ideas and Making Labour into a Resource

It was our observation that, with the aim of building a large and highly productive economic society, Japan made every effort to reach out to the advanced industrial West and to study the structure and conduct of these business environments. Such efforts were soon followed by the active transplantation of modern technologies and know-how from the advanced West.

New forms of management systems and business organizations developed. Newly imported elements were integrated into the traditional system of doing business. Out of such efforts a new form of business culture emerged. Let us follow the process of its formation.

First, we note the intensive commitment that the Japanese displayed in this transplantation. It was promoted in a highly organized way: they first made a selective 'shopping list' based on a careful investigation of the relative merits of importable ideas and technologies; subsequently they carefully studied their merits further to judge if their specific importation would help the growth of Japan's business and industry. In this process possible imports were designated as being at best acceptable technical tools for use within traditional Japanese social culture. The purpose of this procedure can be summed up by a motto *wakon-yosai* – 'Western technologies with Japanese spirit'. The spirit thus termed is used widely to portray the transplantation behaviour of the Japanese of the time. What I wish to add to this observation is an explanation of the practical reasons that led the Japanese to promote such behaviour.

I argue that this spirit only came to Japan in the actual process of transplanting foreign things. At the beginning of the process they saw their economy as full of backward (inferior) elements, inherited from the preceding feudal and village-based society, which would not be at all suitable for the purpose of developing a modern industrial basis for the country. They believed it necessary to replace those elements with new ideas and approaches. How quickly the country would succeed in promoting the proposed industrialization appeared then to depend on how quickly it could replace its traditional technologies, business systems and management practices with those foreign alternatives.

They first believed that these western approaches had universal value and were applicable to business activities in any country. Developing countries such as Japan had only to adopt them for industrial development to result. However, as soon as Japan began to transplant foreign ideas and technologies from the industrialized West it became obvious that the working of those western ideas and the adoption of their business approaches assumed a certain level of capital accumulation and the additional support of modern technological advancement. These were lacking in Japan in her early stage of industrial development. The adoption of foreign ideas and approaches turned out to be too expensive a luxury. Facing this problem, business leaders and government economic planners sought supplementary devices from within their own business culture. This important realization led them to establish a specific form of business culture which subsequently grew to become the fundamental rule and norm dominating the making of business systems and the formation of management practices. How they arrived at this idea and developed it, subsequently forming a business culture which served as a guiding principle in developing employment systems, may be understood by examining examples contained in the labour legislation debates at the turn of the century.

(c) Labour Legislation

At a time when government-led industrialization was transforming the feudal society into a modern state, labourers were moving from villages to fast-growing urban areas hoping to find better jobs and higher pay to improve their standard of living. Sadly, the reality was different. They were driven to work under extremely primitive conditions with long hours and meagre pay. There were soon frequent and large-scale disputes, both organized and disorderly, at mining sites and in textile mills. The government's first reaction was to introduce the Public Order and Police Law of 1900 in order to suppress disputes by force. But it soon became obvious that the problem was not only about social order but also, and more importantly, about worker productivity. In the early days of industrial development workers did not develop any adequate mechanical or other relevant skills. A high rate of turnover prevailed in almost all industries and workplaces, and employers found themselves unable to develop effective long-term investment strategies. A great number of new enterprises rose during the two *kigyo bokko* new enterprise booms of 1886–90 and 1895. Yet many failed to survive into a second or a third year.

The government felt obliged to undertake a public inquiry into the cause of such business failures. In 1883, investigators found appalling working and living conditions in textile factories and their workers' dormitories. Did the nation's export efforts really require such atrocious slavery and cheap labour conditions? It was time that Japan showed herself to be as civilized and modernized as the western nations with whom she traded. This demonstration was essential if Japan was to free herself from the humiliating Unequal Treaties imposed on her at the time of the Restoration.

The government sent missions to study existing labour legislation in western nations and decided to import the basic western approach of regulating labour markets. Among other things it would:

- make 12 years the minimum age for child labour;
- limit working hours to 12 per day;
- outlaw night labour for women and children under 16;
- establish guidelines for workers' accident compensation.

A great outcry came from business leaders, protesting that such a move was 'too early' given the infant stage of industrial development. It would reduce the cost competitiveness of many of the industries that were selling in the domestic as well as in the export market. By doing so, it would bankrupt the national economy in no time at all.

It was in the middle of this acrimonious dispute that Fukuzawa Yukichi proposed a workable alternative. He opposed the introduction of labour legislation at this stage of Japanese industrial development. He argued that:

- the legislation would reduce the working hours of labourers, limit their employment opportunities and reduce their earning capacities;

- it followed an inappropriate western approach which did not take into account specific customs and practices traditionally followed and appreciated as comfortable by people in Japan.

Fukuzawa wanted the legislation rewritten to build on the best potential of indigenous Japanese employer–employee relations and working conditions. The traditional *onjo* benevolent and affectionate relationship practised between landlords and tenant farmers should be the model for the new industrial relations system. This would provide pay and working conditions more appropriate to Japan's social culture as well as to her stage of industrialization. Similarly, those workers coming from villages would receive modern industrial training and education within the context of traditional customs and practice. Care and warm consideration on the part of employers was expected to make up the shortfall in monetary rewards (Sheridan 1993: 95–7).

Hirschmeier and Yui (1975: 191–4) observe that, except for a few progressive leaders of business, many employers in the period were of the opinion that employer–employee relationships ought to be guided by the time-honoured father–son principles. As for the workers themselves, T.C. Smith observes that from the 1890s to the 1920s they demanded 'improved treatment' and 'higher status' rather than higher pay. They felt that monetary motives and legally defined rights should not be permitted to spoil this personal relationship (1988: 119).

Whatever the perceptions of employers and the preferences of employees, there is no doubt that this is a makeshift approach for a backward economy. Specific cultural elements were selected to compensate for the shortage of capital and to contribute to economic growth as a substitute for capital. Some might praise Fukuzawa's plan as an 'innovative and pragmatic' device while others might condemn it as nothing but a 'cunning compromise', pushing people to work hard with the implied threat that otherwise they would be forced back to a pre-industrial mode of life. It is not our purpose here to evaluate Fukuzawa's proposal. We wish only to illustrate how Japan combined business logic with the potential of her own culture in developing a distinctive approach to industrial policy and management.

4. FROM MAKESHIFT DEVICES TO THE DEVELOPMENT OF THE MODERN JAPANESE MANAGEMENT SYSTEM

If employers in Japanese corporations had stopped at the stage where their management strategy drew exclusively upon labour to supplement capital, the industrial development that we see in today's Japan would not have been possible.

Employers invested in the training and education of their workers in order to develop an intelligent and efficient workforce in the economy. This initiative was more than adequately responded to by the employees themselves, whose intensive work morale made a valuable contribution to the industrialization efforts of the country. Research analysing corporate management has documented in detail how the Japanese became intelligent workers willing to organize themselves at the workplace and efficient operators of machines and other capital equipment. Workers demonstrated a remarkable level of interest in their work and a readiness to display initiative. These efforts added a contribution to the industrialization process which went far beyond anything a standard work manual would guide them to do (Inoki 1993).

The initial contribution of this early form of business culture lies in its role in directing people – leaders in business, managers, government policy writers, as well as workers themselves – to see labour as the most important and *strategic* resource for conducting business. At these early stages of labour legislation the importance of labour derived from its abundant availability compared with capital and natural resources. However, as we saw, employers soon saw the need to give labour adequate education and training to ensure their efficient productivity. This was promoted, as is seen in the examples of labour legislation, in combination with cultural elements and traditional work structures long practised in society. All of this led Japanese employers to recognize faster than most of their counterparts in industrial countries the importance of training and educating their employees and also cultivating their work motivation. Japanese management evolved based on this understanding, searching for better ways to develop human resources and use them to their maximum extent.

Dore (1973: 384) describes Japan's employment system as 'organisation oriented' and differentiates it from that of Britain which he describes as 'market oriented'.[5] What is this 'organisation oriented' system? We observe its characteristics dominating the decisions made by all three segments of the business economy. A preference for taking an organization-orientated approach rather than relying on the market was shown by employers when building corporations, arranging and managing the workplace, and structuring labour codes and employment practices. Government also followed this procedure in formulating its industrial policy. Workers, on their part, responded favourably to this approach so that it became a guiding principle in shaping their behaviour and attitudes to work. A focus on labour applied to all three fronts – in corporations, by government and with workers – reinforcing each other so that, in the end, they created a particular form of economic society in Japan.

Let us observe the development of this preferred organization-orientated approach on each of these three fronts. Japanese workers are more likely to commit themselves to a collective or corporate enterprise. Many see this as an important source of strength for Japanese corporations, allowing them to be competitive in the world market.[6]

Robert Lane (1991) sees the economic system in Anglo-American society as suffering a significant shortfall in welfare efficiency because its structure relies heavily on markets to generate and distribute people's work efforts (production of goods and services). He argues that, under this system, individuals are forced to seek economic welfare, happiness and satisfaction through market exchange; that is, people work and earn income with which they purchase goods and services for their own satisfaction. In a market system, Lane claims, that work is reduced to serving as a means to maximize income. This deprives the act of working of any intrinsic value and leads people to see work merely as a necessary burden and inconvenience. As a remedy, Lane recommends that the present Anglo-American economic system should be restructured so that people work for satisfaction as well. He proposes that a system be established in which people gain welfare and happiness directly at their workplace and seek their life's purpose in their individual work efforts rather than simply purchasing happiness as well as 'the meaning of life' in the market. In such an economy workers become not only happier and more content but also more efficient. He wishes people to see work itself as the core provider of welfare and happiness as a whole (Lane 1991: Parts V and VII). Is this ideal form of economic society mirrored in Japan's corporate society and enterprise community?

The life-time employment system and corporate welfare arrangements in many larger, established firms in Japan have been introduced to help their employees view work as having intrinsic value. This leads them to regard their work in a highly committed manner with both professional and personal interest as well as a marked degree of enthusiasm. It would appear that the system the Japanese adopted made them behave as if they were Lane's disciples, accepting his convictions and following his teaching.

Many hypotheses and observations have tried to explain how employers developed incentive structures which encouraged such an undefined but clearly observable commitment by employees to their own corporations and to the Japanese corporate community in general.[7] The way in which this was developed is outlined below. Employers offered their workers a place to nurture social relations, one which helped them to share a common goal that they could see as being larger than their individual aspirations. By working as a member of a team with common goals, many gained satisfaction that would have eluded their grasp if they had been encouraged to work for themselves alone. The system provided blue-collar workers with a wide range of education and training, meeting their desire to improve themselves through work. For white-collar office staff, the seniority promotion system led them to strive hard throughout their life-time in the hope of improving their economic living standard and social status at the workplace. With the specific sense of importance attached to economic and industrial development and growth in the country, corporate staff and workers gained social status as their corporation grew rapidly, became large, dominated national and international markets, accumulated assets and profits, and became internationally competitive and influential. In sum, we may say that it has been customary for the social status of employees to rise with the success of their corporation. This eventually results in an increasing level of commitment to the company.

Government also plays an important part in assisting the employers' management strategy so that corporations and industry operate most effectively by securing responsive support from their workers. By means of a public programme designed to maintain growth, promote efficiency in the running of the national economy and provide legitimacy to management techniques, employers succeed in deriving a maximum level of work effort from their employees.

Much existing research already explains the government–business cooperative relationship. We can observe, in fact, the effectiveness of cooperation throughout the pre- and post-war industrial development periods. It should be sufficient to note that the specific approach chosen by the Japanese government establishes a mechanism for providing welfare to individual people *within* the economy and does not establish any separate avenue or sources outside the economic system, as many welfare economies in the West have attempted to do. In essence, the government decided to increase the welfare and well-being of its people through economic growth and rejected those western approaches that introduce public provision, such as social security and other assistance measures for the unemployed, sick, aged and others with difficulties. The Japanese government feared that provisions of this kind would result in idle resources, become a drag on productive activities, and drain away economic growth and development opportunities (Sheridan 1998b: 21–3).

5. TRANSFORMATION TO A NEW CAPITAL-RICH SOCIETY FROM THE PRECEDING CAPITAL-SCARCE ECONOMY

Problems of Shortfall in Welfare and Living Quality

By the beginning of the 1960s the Japanese economy had accumulated enough capital to transform it into a capital-rich, labour-short economy (Minami 1986: 300).

The changeover caused business and government to adjust their labour management strategy and policy. Business acknowledged labour's changed bargaining position in this newly arrived at stage of economic growth. It decided to provide wage increases that would keep pace with labour productivity. This adjustment was intended to secure a continuing high level of work effort and to maintain employees' company loyalty. Government, on its part, aimed to improve equity among the population in general, as well as to reduce inequality specifically within the workforce. The object was to continue to maintain a national consensus which supported economic growth and further industrial development. Under this new labour shortage regime, business widely extended the benefits that skilled workers in big firms had been, thus far, exclusively enjoying (life-time employment and a corporate welfare system) to less-skilled workers and workers in smaller firms.

The time had finally come when labour could receive a fair share of the results of the country's industrial progress; but it was still all within the traditional business and government strategy which required making the best use of available labour to ensure continued economic growth. Neither business nor government attempted to go beyond this simple objective. No effort was made to take advantage of newly emerging opportunities that opened up with Japan's transformation into an affluent capital-rich economy. Instead, they saw the changeover only in terms of the potential problems emerging from labour shortages. Business and government particularly worried about the rising bargaining power of workers. They failed to appreciate the importance of the changeover and missed the opportunity of taking the economy in a new direction which would bring about an improvement of living standards for individual people and also improve Japan's social development.

Instead of introducing any new policies or innovative approaches, business and government together retreated in the direction of the familiar as soon as the economy was forced to grapple with the oil shocks of 1973 and 1978. In order to reduce production costs under the condition of rising energy prices and the consequent spread of hyperinflation across industry, management decided once again to try to solve its problems by imposing more intensive and longer hours of work. Workers not only complied with this management strategy but also agreed, once again, to withhold demands for wage increases. Government meanwhile invested heavily in infrastructure. Its activities were intended to support industrial objectives alone and not directly to improve the facilities and services available for 'quality of life' objectives. The aim was to assist business in its effort to overcome the difficulties posed by the oil shocks and to resume their previous growth and expansion process. Business, labour and government together opted to return to the old industrial and business approaches that were formed under labour surplus conditions. All of them ignored the economic transformation which was bringing a new level of affluence to Japan.[8] Figure 4.1 demonstrates this observation for the post-Second World

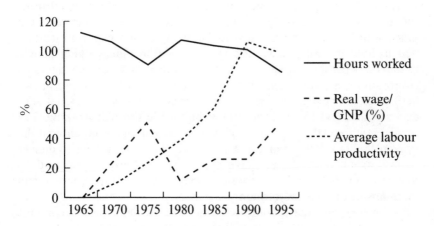

Figure 4.1   Relative changes in Japanese labour characteristics

War period. It is important to note that the rate of improvement in both wage payments and the reduction of working hours lagged even further behind in the 1970s and 1980s than at any other time.

Today, some observers of Japan's management system say that it has become 'excessively efficient'. Workers developed to be only human resources are forced to work intensively and efficiently to boost economic growth and to bring prosperity to their companies. But employees feel they are excluded from gaining a fair share of the benefit of such success (Baba 1992: 70). They wonder if this is due to the ingeniously structured mechanism of corporate management or, alternatively, to the country's economic system, which contains many government regulative networks and public institutions that aim to protect a variety of vested interests, rather than protecting the wages and salaries of the working population.

Whatever explanation they may accept, workers feel they are forced to work harder to increase their income in the hopes of improving their living standard and quality of life. But the reality, alas, is that in the existing system harder work does not improve their real economic well-being. Workers feel they are trapped in the web of an ingeniously structured economic system combined with a corporate managerial arrangement. Government, at the same time, has so far been unable to take any effective action to rescue workers from this dilemma. The only choice is to continue working harder to promote more efficient production which supports those already 'excessively efficient' business activities. So the syndrome of individual poverty in the midst of national and corporate prosperity continues (Sheridan 1993: 222–3).

Our study of Japan's business culture leads us to identify two distinctive features that characterize the economic system and management practice in the country. The first is the attitudes and expectations that people hold towards work. It is my observation that working people in Japan, whether workers in factories, office staff or managers in corporations, generally expect to gain welfare, satisfaction and happiness at their workplace. Many also expect to foster individual self-development and to establish a meaningful life through working. The second feature is the approach followed by Japan's government and the principles that it holds. Governments build economic systems to deliver desired social effects. Japan's government rejects alternative suggestions that recommend forming separate western-style welfare systems and mechanisms outside the economy.

Taken together, these features create a particular type of economic society in which people's personal and social activities are closely integrated with their economic activities so that the purposes of the former are not distinguished clearly from the objectives of the latter. The current popular criticisms of Japanese society that have emerged argue that a life-time employment system allows very few individuals to develop a career of their own and interests outside the set passage of that system. This leads to the propagation of *kaisha-ningen*, company men, who seek life's purposes only in working for their company. In addition, the absence of a public policy mechanism which would allow for a social policy independent of industrial and economic policy leads economic and industrial objectives to dominate social policy.

6. FUTURE

What form of an economy will the Japanese build?

(a) Economic Society

Will it still be an economic society in which social development, enrichment of community life and individual welfare objectives are to be promoted by economic activity as before? I believe it depends very much on how far people continue to hold their previous views and traditional attitudes towards work. Do they seek their welfare and happiness at work? Do they attempt to gain their life's purpose and personal development through work? I have so far not observed any clear signs of a break in this trend.[9]

If the working population continues to hold the same attitudes, and if business and government find it convenient as well, nothing will change. Japan's economic system will still depend heavily on self-sacrifice and hard work.

What is new is the forms of welfare and happiness that people seek from work. The trend will not be only to demand more jobs or work security, nor simply higher pay with reduced working hours: not even more comfortable working conditions will be sufficient.[10] It is the *quality of work* that is increasingly decisive. When people express their desire to improve their 'quality of life' rather than their level of pay, when people express the wish to gain welfare and happiness at work, and to find life's purposes through work, they are seeking work that itself provides satisfaction and a feeling of worth. It will therefore be the task of future societies to decide what *types* of goods and services to produce rather than merely *how much* of them to produce. Our main concern will be to decide not only appearance and quality but to determine for what purpose and function those goods and services should be produced. We may gain guidance from William Morris, who proposed to make our life-style simple and plain but rich in quality. He wanted to help us appreciate the value of nature, to understand the natural world and life itself as a whole (Paulson 1989: ch. 6). Will people be happy and content when they understand that what they produce achieves that *quality*? In this regard, the Japanese are expected to derive a considerable benefit from their past heritage of fine arts and crafts.

(b) Views, Expectations, Approaches and Behaviours of People Towards Work

Alternatively, there is no guarantee that people will continue to work as they previously did with such a high degree of motivation and interest. People may alter their view of and expectation from work and consequently behave differently. More leisure time may be sought, more flexible work arrangements and career paths may be preferred. We may expect Japan's future generation to be alien to the worlds described by McClelland (1967), Kinmonth (1981) and Lane (1991), to be divorced from those important ingredients for maintaining a 'diligent' workforce in society. Will the achievement of this capital-rich stage itself obstruct the future of the Japanese economy? Will women's progress into the workplace bring a new work culture into Japanese society and alter the current business culture altogether?

As we have seen, the formation and development of Japan's current business culture was a slow and gradual process. Will it be an equally slow and gradual process to revise that business culture if evaluation and reform efforts are left to the very people who are working under this business culture? Speedy reform may come only if society can create a *new breed of people*. Women and the new generation who were born and brought up in a capital-rich, labour-short economy may become this new breed of people.

(c) Tasks for Now: Capital and Saving

We have discussed the direction that activity in the proposed new economic society would take. Ideally, social purpose should receive priority before economic growth. The new economic society must be productive. We are not recommending that industrial activities should languish unpromoted. In fact, industrial production must be undertaken actively but only *within controlled conditions*. A wise and efficient way to conduct the new economic society would be to depend on the efforts of employers to structure corporations in a way which provides adequate working facilities. Corporations need to respond to the work expectations of employees. New investment alone cannot be expected to achieve this. We fear capital funds will go instead to the most profitable industrial activities. This would draw resources away from programmes for social development, welfare and 'quality of life', many of which may not bring the immediate prospect of large profits. Special public programmes accompanied by regulations may be necessary to secure ample flows of cheap capital into this social and welfare category of investment. In addition, public intervention may also be necessary if a newly structured Japan which provides more social services and welfare leads people to save less. Will it come in the form of tax reform, or the building of a new pension and annuity saving system?

Future generations living in a reformulated Japanese economic and business society should enthusiastically face these new challenges. Two possible approaches exist, both of which should call forth public debate.

(d) Learning from Their Past

There is no doubt that Japan has built a rich industrial state where people enjoy an adequate standard of living in a condition of equity and stability. Problems and dissatisfactions expressed today have emerged from the way this achievement up to now has been accomplished. To find a new passage to a better future it is essential to identify these problems and dissatisfactions and to understand their nature and causes. We must study the history of our economic and business development, the way in which it was promoted and with what results. Simple total rejection and general criticism is not useful. What needs to be done is to disentangle the economic networks and to unfold the business fabric. In order to decide what parts need to be revised, reformed, discarded or further developed, we have to perceive clearly the nature of the mechanism that drives it.

(e) Learning from Outside Once Again

Many economies and societies have accumulated useful lessons from past successes and failures. Following once again our Meiji leaders, let us try to reach out to that accumulated wisdom world-wide. This time, the Japanese should concentrate their efforts on examining as broad a variety of experiences and experiments promoted in other countries as possible. We need to go beyond simply investigating large European countries and America, which have been the traditional targets for such studies. Varied experiments in many economic societies have developed strategies for economic and social administrative development that are as many and varied as their histories and cultures. To study them in contrast to and in comparison with those of Japan would illuminate viable directions in which the Japanese may improve by developing their own traditional approaches and devices. Above all, we must remember that the quality of life enjoyed by each individual depends on following the principle that *the economy should serve people and not vice versa.*

There is nothing new in stressing the importance of this principle. Yet I believe it is necessary to reiterate its value before concluding this paper. We have argued that business culture has developed in Japan on the basis of business leaders' special efforts to formulate effective ways to use labour. Its original form was, technically speaking, a 'makeshift' approach that enabled employers to exploit labour by taking advantage of its relatively abundant supply and consequent weak bargaining position. As we saw, business leaders and managers in Japan did not stop short at this stage of developing their management techniques. They swiftly saw the importance of training and educating their employees, developing appropriate labour relations and fostering efficient labour management techniques. Despite this, it is my concern and my observation that people in Japan have never discarded their initial inclination to depend upon a 'makeshift' mentality which relies on this post-war approach whenever problems and difficulties arise in the economy. We saw this in the 1970s when the economy was challenged by two different oil crises. Is this tendency still dominant even in the 1990s, when Japan is suffering through an extended recession?

Only when Japan's management techniques and business strategies break free from this traditional tendency can they be studied and developed as a possible alternative to the Anglo-American model of corporate management and social progress. To achieve this reformulation of business culture, however slow and gradual in coming, it is necessary to see how the economy and how business actually serve labour.

NOTES

1. See for example, Miyamoto *et al.* (1996), ch. 2.
2. See, for example, Yasuoka *et al.* (1995).
3. Ibid., vol. 2.
4. We are told that religious, moral and other spiritual guidance was used for some time in motivating work activities in western countries such as England, America

and Germany. This trend appears to have disappeared along with economic industrialization. See Hirowatari (1993: 3–5) and Misumi (1993: 212–15).
5. See also Hirschmeier and Yui (1975). They make a similar observation.
6. An international study was conducted in eight countries (America, Britain, Belgium, Germany, Holland, Israel, Japan and Yugoslavia) in 1982 and again in 1992. A large number of people were asked how they view 'the meaning of working life'. Misumi, who undertook the Japanese study, reports that the proportion of people who viewed work as the most important activity in life (as compared with leisure, community, religion and family) is by far the largest in Japan. He also reported that such a positive view towards work appears to be acquired by people – particularly male workers in corporations – during their first actual working years. Misumi (1993: 220–7).
7. See Miyamoto *et al.* (1996) and Yasuoka *et al.* (1995).
8. We have observed that, throughout the long history of economic growth and industrial development in Japan, labour has received a slower increase in wages than productivity improvements would justify. A reduction of working hours has also been slow in coming compared with the growth rate of the national economy. See the argument put by Shinohara which is quoted in Minami (1986: 307–8) and Saito (1996).
9. See also Hirowatari (1993: 4–5).
10. Do Japanese people demand reduced working hours and more free time, as observed elsewhere in the West? See, for example, Sheridan (1998b).

REFERENCES

Baba, K. (1992), 'Gendaisekai to NihonKaishashugi', in Tokoyo Daigaku Shakaikaigaku Kenkyujo, *Gendai Nihonshakai*, Tokyo: University of Tokyo Press, vol. 1, ch. 1.

Dore, R. (1973), *British Factory – Japanese Factory: The Origins of National Diversity in Industrial Relations*, Oxford: George Allen & Unwin.

Hirowatari, S. (1992), 'Ima Naniga Mondaika?', in Tokyo Daigaku Shakaikagaku Kenkyujo (1992), *Gendai Nihonshakai*, Tokyo: University of Tokyo Press, vol. 6.

Hirschmeier, Y. and Yui, T. (1975), *The Development of Japanese Business 1600–1973*, London: George Allen & Unwin.

Inoki, T. (1993), 'Keizai to Anmoku Chi, Chishiki to Gino ni kansuru Ichi Kosatsu' (Economics and its implicit understandings, knowledge and technology) in K. Itoh (ed.), Nihon no Kigyo System, Jinteki Shigen, Tokyo: Yuhikaky, vol. 4, ch. 4.

Kinmonth, E.L. (1981), *The Self-made Man in Meiji Japanese Thought: From Samurai to Salary Man*, Berkeley, CA: University of California Press.

Kumon, S. and Rosovsky, H. (eds) (1992), *The Political Economy of Japan: Cultural and Social Dynamics*, Stanford, CA: Stanford University Press, vol. 3.

Lane, R. (1991), *The Market Experience*, Cambridge: Cambridge University Press.

McClelland, D. (1967), *The Achieving Society*, New York: The Free Press.

Masamura, K. (1997), *Nihonkeizai Suitai wa Sakeraruno-ka*, Tokyo: Chikuma Shobo.

Minami, R. (1986), *The Economic Development of Japan: A Quantitative Study*, London: Macmillan.

Misumi, F. (1993), 'Hatarakukoto no Imi – kikusai hikaku' [Importance of work], in H. Itami (ed.), *Nihon no Kigyo System* [Business Systems in Japan], Tokyo: Yuhikaku.

Miyamoto, M. and Takeshi Abe (eds) (1996), *Nihon Keieishi*, 2nd edn, Tokyo: Yuhikaku.

Paulson, C. (1989), *William Morris*, New York: Quantum Books.

Saito, O. (1996), 'Rodo', in K. Odaka, and O. Saito (eds), *Nihonkeizai no 200-nen*, Tokyo: Nihonhyoron sha, ch. 18.

Sheridan, K. (1993), *Governing the Japanese Economy*, Cambridge: Polity Press.

Sheridan, K. (1998a), 'Japan's economic system', in K. Sheridan (ed.) *Emerging Economic Systems in Asia*, St Leonards, NSW, Australia: Allen & Unwin.

Sheridan, K. (1998b), 'Seikatsu-ni sokushita Keizaiseisaku-zukuri', paper presented at Nihon Kokyo Seisaku Gakkai, Tokyo, 14 June.

Shinohara, M. (1986), *Nihonkeizai Kogi*, 2nd edn, Tokyo: Toyokeizai Shinposha.

Smith, T.C. (1988), *Native Sources of Japanese Industrialisation 1750–1920*, Berkeley, CA: University of California Press.

Yasuoka, S. and Masatoshi Amano (eds) (1995), *Nihon Keieishi*, Tokyo: Iwanami-shoten.

COMMENT ON SHERIDAN

Peter Drysdale

How Japan's business culture will change over the coming years is difficult to predict, given all the forces at work in Japan that will have their effect on institutional change and given the forces of change in the international economy and polity to which Japan is now so deeply exposed.

As I read the paper, Dr Sheridan suggests powerfully that change will be limited (the positive prediction) and that there is every reason why it should be (the normative judgement) because of the virtuous interactions between business culture and social goals.

There are therefore at least two ways in which we might comment upon this paper: one is to challenge the prediction, and the other is to challenge the normative judgement. I shall eschew both these approaches: I am too ignorant to attempt the former, and too much the pluralist to worry about the latter.

What may be helpful is to ask a few questions about the logic of the paper and to offer some comment on the factors that might be of relevance to the response of Japanese business and polity to Japan's current circumstance, for it is to Japan's current circumstance that the paper is ostensibly addressed.

In her concluding section, Sheridan asks the question: 'What form of an economy will the Japanese build?' (p. 131). She points to a range of influences that might bear upon this important social choice: established social virtues; economic and social goals; the experience of the past; the experience of outsiders. One is tempted to warn against forgetting the dinosaur syndrome. Where is circumstance in all this, and the intelligent response to circumstance? What are the circumstances in which such choices will have to be made, what are the forces inside Japan and outside Japan that demand change and adaptation in policy approach, strategic behaviour and institutional norms – and what is their urgency?

It is the sense of these challenges facing Japan and what might be an intelligent response to them that is missing from the argument of the paper – almost totally missing.

Japan is presently an economy, a society, in quite deep trouble. There is a growing sense of crisis, uncertainty – even fear – about this in Japan. Even if this sense of crisis were entirely lacking – and, for many reasons, but most importantly, because of the protectiveness of Japanese social systems, it has taken six years of relative stagnation to develop – Japan's problems are not less real because now they are no longer Japan's problems alone. They are also the region's problems, they are Australia's problems and the world's problems. Such is the stature and position of Japan and the influence of what it does upon society and upon the international economy.

What is wrong with the Japanese economy that demands policy response and institutional reform? It is not just six years of economic stagnation and lost potential; a banking system in deep crisis; financial reform that has run into the sand; and policy paralysis involving key government agencies. These all demand institutional change and, in my experience, the core of Japan's internationally competitive business community understands and advocates fundamental change, including the change of cherished labour market institutions.

Japan is also at the centre of a regional and global systemic problem which requires much more than Japan merely 'muddling through'. On top of all this, Japan is facing a long-term demographic transition, a declining population with a labour force whose numbers, given current institutional norms and social values, has peaked or will peak over the next year or two, and an economy riddled with pervasive doubts about its capacity for growth in productivity. Japan is a country which will have 25 million fewer people in the year 2050 than it has today. It would have been interesting to have some comment upon the effects of these changes, how this circumstance influences institutional transformation in Japan.

Let me conclude by noting that any analysis of these issues is incomplete without the inclusion of politics and the political processes in Japan. Japan might be characterized as a world-class industrial economy with a communal agrarian-based political system. The combination appears fatal to the management of current economic problems and the demands of longer-term social change. Whatever the case, we certainly need to know a great deal more about political structures and responses in Japan if we are to understand how Japan might make these important social choices – paradoxically, for the time being, without decisive influence from big business, because politics in Japan, despite the recent Upper House election, continues to be dominated by the interests of non-metropolitan Japan and the construction lobby.

REPLY TO DRYSDALE

Kyoko Sheridan

This paper explores business culture, how it is constructed in general, and how it works in the Japanese economy. I wrote the paper to provide an understanding of the general fundamental framework and the associated labour principles on which the Japanese economy has developed. The problems and difficulties that loom large in the economy have accumulated specifically within this framework and under these principles.

Since the presentation of this paper in August 1998, more people in Japan have expressed their strong discontent about the way their political and economic systems are structured and operate. Where has it gone wrong? What changes should be introduced? These are questions that are asked on a national level and involve all segments of the population: government, business and households.

We must not forget that the subject matter that we are wrestling with is *fundamental*. It is beyond any examination of economic performance or of business conduct. It requires more than an evaluation of institutional experience or of administrative or political process. It is about people's judgement of the acceptability of economic society and the value of its activity on their lives. It is about nation-building. Though we might like to speculate as to what sort of socioeconomic and political institutions will emerge and transform Japan's economic society in a new direction and construct a few plausible future scenarios, a more essential task must be undertaken first. This task is specifically for academic researchers: it is to examine exactly what problems the Japanese have today; why and how they have developed; what selection of policy tools is available; and if the tools are not adequate, what further devices should be developed?

Three different forces appear to be at work. They are political, economic and social, each following its own logic, but together generating a compound influence over the making of the new Japan. Politically the necessary reform efforts could be understood as completing the postwar effort to democratize Japanese society. This change came as a reaction to and reflection of the preceding authoritarian approaches in the Meiji days and developed up until and then throughout the Second World War.[1] Reform movements in the economic and social sphere which I discuss in the paper are fundamentally drawn from this political effort, which in general has led the Japanese away from those authoritarian, centralized and conformist ways of the past.

Economic analysis follows two logical streams. First is the macro-economic aspect which addresses the workability of the political economy. A large-scale reduction of government activities was introduced in Japan throughout the 1990s. It was promoted under the influence of a similar move initiated earlier in the US and Britain in the 1980s to meet their need to balance public accounts. Japan's reason was different: her economy continued to grow rapidly while the introduction of a welfare economy was delayed until as late as the mid-1970s. This allowed Japan to escape public deficit problems. The result was a delay in the need to evaluate the political economic system.

The second stream directly examines the efficiency and dynamism of industrial and business activities in seeking a way to reactivate business and investment, thereby resuming the growth of the national economy and ending the recession. To achieve this, the traditional approach of 'vision policy' was first attempted. When the robust booming economy collapsed in 1991 MITI began to compile its business proposals which called for individual entrepreneurial efforts to replace traditional managerial methods such as life-time employment and *keiretsu* business grouping network systems. MITI questions whether these standard approaches are any longer effective in an internationally competitive context.

People in Japan have now become more aware and are anxious to involve themselves in the 'what next' question. In raising this question, many have begun to think and behave as independent individuals highly conscious of the opportunities that now seem open to them in their choice of a personal life and in existing work patterns. Equally, there are, on the other hand, many who fear the increase in competitive pressures in the job market, at work and in daily living if and when the withdrawal of government regulatory measures and public programmes occurs as planned. This is aggravated by management reforms that are expected to reduce job security and corporate welfare provisions. People fear it will end the virtue of Japan's traditional approach which has aimed to provide 'stability' and 'equity' in economic life and the maintenance of 'civilized human relations' in the workplaces, though perhaps at the cost of economic efficiency. It is not clear at this stage which one of these two groups: the new breed of free competitive individual achievers on one hand, or the old traditional group-orientated members on the other hand, will dominate the re-evaluation process. As long as there remain those who value 'stability' 'equity' and 'civility' as being most important for a society, the future of economic society in Japan can be expected to follow a mixed economy form in which high 'competition' and 'efficiency' will be sought within, and not before, those three traditional values.

What actual forms of institutions, organizations and economic networks should be promoted to fulfil the people's desire for efficiency, democracy and quality of life is the research task that needs to be explored. It is good to see the question of the government's role examined in a free-thinking context, liberated from old public authoritarian ways. This role is sought not so much in the context of economic growth, expansion and efficiency but in the context of building a new economic society. An opening appears to emerge when people raise the 'what next' question. The Japanese have acknowledged that in changing their society they must demand fundamental economic reforms which will be implemented not only on the basis of their efficiency, but also for their potential to serve more adequately the well-being of people in society. It is not simply the economic system and industry structure, nor the employment system and management practices alone, but the very purpose of economic activities that is being questioned in its role of maintaining the well-being and happiness of people. A *new* economic society must be built that aims at providing happiness to people by making full use of the capital, technology and management know-how which has accumulated to a reasonable extent within Japan.

Note

1. Yasuhiro Nakasone, 'Sengo 50-nen, Nihon no Toji Kino Ron' [On the working of political governance of Japan in the post-war 50 years], in Seisaku Kenkyu-in (ed.), *Oral History as Policy Studies*, Tokyo: Chuo Koron Sha, 1998.

PART II

Current Problems

5. Why has the Japanese economy been stumbling for so long?

Masaru Yoshitomi

1. THREE DISTINCTIVE PHASES AND MAIN FEATURES

The Japanese economy has been stumbling since 1992. After growing by 3 per cent in 1991, the economy slid into recession in 1992 and stayed there for the next three years. In fact, during the last seven-year period the economy only registered a 0.5 per cent annual growth rate. However, it is wrong to dismissively picture Japan's economic perform-ance simply as one of prolonged stagnation. Rather, there have been three distinctive phases since 1992, and the proper characterization of each phase is important if we are to gain a better understanding of the reasons why the Japanese economy has been stumbling for so long.

The first phase comprises the period from 1992 to 1994, when the economy suffered a serious recession during three consecutive years. Two features stand out: first, this recession was caused essentially by a downward capital stock adjustment on the part of the private sector in response to excess business investment during the preceding boom in the second half of the 1980s. This excess investment was clearly demonstrated by the fact that incremental private business fixed capital formation was almost equivalent to that of private consumption during the boom period. Thus, business fixed investment declined more than 20 per cent on a cumulative basis during this first phase. Second, asset prices plunged sharply, which began seriously to impair bank capital. During the boom in the 1980s, the banks concentrated on extending bank loans to the real estate sector, lending heavily to construction firms and to non-bank lenders (*jusen*). A sharp decline in the price of commercial property reduced the market value of assets in the banks' balance sheets through mounting non-performing loans, while a sharp decline in stock prices reduced the value of the Tier II portion of the banks' capital.

The second phase describes the subsequent recovery period of 1995 and 1996, when the economy grew by 3 per cent per year in those two consecutive years. Three features stand out. First, business investment increased by 8 per cent per annum, reflecting both the completion of the aforementioned downward capital stock adjustment and new investment opportunities, particularly in information and telecommunication industries. Second, the exchange rate of the yen sharply appreciated, reaching 79 yen per US dollar in April 1995. In response to this appreciation, net exports declined, thereby reducing the economy's growth rate by nearly 1 per cent of GDP per year in 1995 and 1996. Third, responding to the sharp appreciation of the yen, the Bank of Japan reduced the official discount rate to 0.5 per cent in September 1995. The extreme overvaluation of the yen was rectified by 1996 when the rate depreciated to an average of 109 yen per US dollar. An exchange rate which ranges between 100 and 110 yen per US dollar reflects the equilibrium rate at which Japanese manufacturing industries can be, on average, internationally competitive. However, the Bank of Japan (BOJ) has maintained a historically low discount rate since then, because of the continued increases in non-performing bank assets. Despite the aforementioned recovery of the real economy, commercial property prices continued to decline. The policy of 'growing out' of a bad asset problem did not work. The *jusen* (specialized housing finance companies) débâcle broke in 1996. This threatened to bankrupt a large number of agricultural financial cooperatives which had extensively granted loans to the *jusen* towards the end of the real-estate boom. The government used 680 billion yen of public money to bail out insolvent agricultural financial cooperatives for political reasons.

The third phase covers FY 1997 and FY 1998, during which two features stand out. One is the start, beginning in April 1997, of a fiscal consolidation programme. Total tax increases amounted to 9 trillion yen, or 1.8 per cent of GDP (5 trillion yen from a consumption tax rate increase from 3 to 5 per cent, 2 trillion yen due to the termination of the temporary income tax reduction of 1994, and 2 trillion yen due to an increase in social security contributions for health care). In addition, public works expenditure was cut by 0.6 per cent of GDP. This fiscal consolidation reflected not only a simple response to a large deterioration in the budget balance of the general government (central, local and social security fund) from a surplus of 2.9 per cent of GDP to a deficit of 4.3 per cent of GDP between 1991 and 1996. The growing deficit was the result of discretionary stimulus policies (accounting for about half of the budget deterioration) as well as cyclical declines in revenues. The consolidation also reflected the budgetary implications of a rapidly ageing population. Besides these fiscal measures, the other major feature was 'financial deflation'. This started to hit the real economy from November 1997 when three large financial institutions, including one large deposit-taking commercial bank (Hokkaido Taku-shoku Bank, Hokutaku for short), went bankrupt. Deflation itself can be defined as a recession in the real economy combined with an absolute fall in the price level as represented by the GDP deflator. By financial deflation, I mean that its origin is financial in the sense that public confidence in the banking system becomes shaken. Lack of confidence curtails the marginal propensity to consume and discourages business investment sentiments. In addition, bank credit declines, undermining economic activities, particularly those of small and medium-scale enterprises. During January–March 1998, real GDP declined by 0.7 per cent from the previous quarter. The GDP deflator may have declined by 0.5 per cent from a year earlier, if we exclude the impact of the aforementioned increased consumption tax on the GDP deflator.

This financial deflation, which originated in the Japanese domestic banking problem, was aggravated by the Asian twin financial crisis (currency and banking). This effect came via an approximate 20 per cent decline in Japan's exports to Asia in the first quarter of 1998, when compared with the same period a year earlier. By the July–September quarter of 1997, the recessionary impact of the aforementioned fiscal consolidation was largely offset by an expansion in net exports, supported by the further depreciation of the yen from 109 yen per US dollar in 1996 to 121 in 1997 (as annual averages). More recently, the sharp reduction of exports to Asia since autumn 1997 has caused Japan's total net exports to decline sharply, aggravating its domestic financial deflation.

2. FINANCIAL DEFLATION AND POLICY CHOICES

The Japanese authorities have tried to confront the difficult policy problems which are unique to the current financial deflation. In financial markets, the following two 'abnormal' phenomena have appeared, particularly since November 1997. First, whereas the money supply (M2 + CD) has been growing by 3.5 per cent per annum in the most recent months of 1998, bank loans have been declining by 2 per cent during the same period. Second, whereas the riskless government bond rate has been steadily declining, reflecting a deepening recession in the real economy, private bond rates have been rising, reflecting an increase in credit risk premiums. The spread of interest rates between government and private bonds has been widening.

These two phenomena suggest that a traditional 'monetarist' policy, symbolized by helicopter money, will not work effectively. Indeed, aggressive open market operations by the Bank of Japan (BOJ) can increase banks' reserves, but banks do not necessarily have to extend more bank credit. Instead, they can purchase more national bonds in order to avoid perceived higher credit risks and to satisfy requirements for higher capital ratios relative to risk assets. As a result, the increased money supply leads only to lower interest rates on government bonds. In sharp contrast, however, bank credit continues to decline and private bond rates continue to rise so long as credit risks can not be reduced by such conventional easy monetary policy. In fact, the BOJ has been pumping increased amounts of high-powered money at a rate exceeding 10 per cent on a year-to-year basis. Since all bank deposits are protected by the government, there has been no serious incidents of classic 'bank runs', but bank deposits have shifted from problem banks to healthy banks via 'bank walks'. Hence total deposits within all commercial banks have increased by some 2 per cent. The associated key policy task is to figure out how to prevent bank credit and the related loans/deposit ratio from declining in order to cope with a credit-crunch induced recession.

It goes without saying that deflation as defined above deprives the monetary authorities of the power to lower interest rates in real terms, whereas the real value of debt liabilities and interest payments increases. The lower the general price level, the higher the debt liabilities and interest payments become in real terms, causing a recession to deepen. This in turn further lowers the price level, thus resulting in a deflationary 'spiral'.

On the fiscal policy front, too, the effectiveness of a conventional fiscal stimulus is substantially reduced under financial deflation. Because confidence in the banking system is shaken and there are greater uncertainties associated with the near-future economy, both consumer and business sentiments weaken, resulting in a lower marginal propensity to consume and to invest. Furthermore, Keynesian fiscal stimulus can only succeed as a pump-priming policy if the self-recovery forces of the private sector start to work and sustain an economic expansion after such a kick-start policy is undertaken. However, these anticipated self-recovery forces cannot gain sufficient strength to sustain an expansion because private consumption and business investment remain weak. Consumers' confidence remains shaken and bank credit does not increase to finance potential business activities. This is due to the existence of higher credit risks as well as the capital-cum-credit crunch. In general, given these conditions, fiscal multipliers must be noticeably smaller than usual.

3. IS THE 'TOO BIG TO FAIL' POLICY TO BE ADOPTED?

What is the root problem which has undermined the effectiveness of conventional monetarist and Keynesian stimuli by shaking the confidence in the banking system and generating a credit crunch and higher credit risk premiums? The huge amount of non-performing assets and potentially seriously impaired capital of the large banks is the underlying problem. Japan must somehow resolve this problem without threatening confidence in the banking system and without aggravating the credit crunch and increasing the size of the risk premiums. In November 1997, the government realized that it would be unable to close large financial institutions, including a large commercial bank (Hokutaku) in Hokkaido, without generating financial deflation. What should be done now?

While the aforementioned 'bank walks' gradually erode the deposit base of a problem bank, stock runs can take place against the problem bank based on the market's assessment of its solvency. Such stock runs immediately and adversely affect the bank's daily operation by creating greater difficulties in obtaining short-term funds in the inter-bank money market. This is exactly what happened to Hokutaku in November 1997 and to another large bank (Long-Term Credit Bank of Japan) in June 1998.

How can Japan foster the minimum level of confidence in the banking system required to forestall the possibility of financial deflation arising from the failure of large depository banks? In November 1997, the Japanese Ministry of Finance (MOF) did not adopt a 'too big to fail' policy. Instead, the MOF simply let Hokutaku go bankrupt without arranging for the purchase and assumption of the failed bank's good assets. Before and after the failure of Hokutaku, the BOJ had to provide the bank with a large amount of special loans (nearly two trillion yen) to cope with its liquidity shortage caused by deposit withdrawal. The BOJ's object was to avoid possible systemic risk to the financial sector. In addition, good clients of the failed bank suddenly faced enormous difficulties in obtaining working capital or settlement money. The resulting series of liquidity crises have forced a large number of clients, particularly small and medium-scale enterprises, to go bankrupt

although they remained potentially viable. The chains of bank credit
and inter-firm credit have broken down. Confidence in the stability
of the banking system has also been shaken and the aforementioned
'abnormal' financial situation has emerged. Bank credit has been cur-
tailed in the midst of money supply growth. Interest rate spreads have
widened between the rising ones of private bonds and the declining
ones of national government bonds. Thus, financial deflation has
developed since November 1997.

In the hopes of counteracting its policy mistake when trying to resolve
the banking problem, the government undertook the following two new
policy measures. One was the provision, in February 1998, of public
funds totalling 30 trillion yen (6 per cent of GDP), aimed both at
guaranteeing deposits of failed or failing banks and at recapitalizing the
capital-impaired weak banks. The other was the Bridge Bank scheme
designed by the government in early July 1998. This aimed mainly at
sustaining bank lending to sound and good-faith clients of failed banks
through bridge banks. Both these measures sought to avoid any further
deepening of the current level of financial deflation.

Two important policy tasks still remain. The Financial Supervisory
Agency (FSA), established 22 June 1998, by separating the Banking
Bureau from the MOF should set up a clear procedure for closing failed
banks. Failing or failed banks, identified by the Agency and based on
its own inspection of each individual bank's balance sheets, should start
liquidation by transferring non-performing assets to the already existing
Resolution and Collection Bank (RCB). All deposits of such banks
should be protected by using the aforementioned public funds. At
the same time, if no private banks immediately agree to take over the
purchase and assume the transactions of the failed banks, the Bridge
Bank scheme can be utilized to maintain credit to sound clients of the
failed banks. This should continue until such clients find new banks
whose operations are conducted under the supervision of the official
financial administrators appointed by the Commissioner of the FSA. If
these clients cannot find new banks in the due course of time, their
loans should be transferred to public bridge banks only if such loans
are proved viable. Within two years (with a maximum extension to five
years); both failed banks and public bridge banks should be totally
liquidated.

The other major task is to cope with capital-impaired but solvent
banks. The planned merger between Sumitomo Trust Bank and the
aforementioned Long-Term Credit Bank (now cancelled) could provide
a prototype for resolving the problems posed by these weak banks.
Even when such a merger takes place, it will still be indispensable for

weak banks completely to write off all losses due to non-performing assets. Impaired capital bases must be strengthened by the full utilization of designated public funds. What has actually prevented public money from being fully used to inject capital into weak banks is a lack of performance requirements or any appropriate mechanisms to enforce them. Enforced recapitalization is needed because top management of large banks do not want to assume managerial responsibility for either the large-scale downsizing or the organizational restructuring of the banks, including the forced resignation of CEOs or other top managers. The assumption of such responsibility should be a condition for the massive recapitalization of a seriously impaired capital base. Large banks plagued by weak corporate governance require a government-regulated capital infusion not only to support the stability of the financial system, but also to force top management to shoulder responsibility.

Although the Bridge Bank scheme is designed to make the liquidation of failed banks compatible with the maintenance of financial stability, particularly by continuing bank lending to their sound clients in good faith, the most difficult policy issue still remains. The policy authorities must somehow conduct the orderly resolution of these large banks' bad assets. A recent Federal Deposit Insurance Corporation (FDIC) study analyses the case of Continental Illinois Bank. Not only did the Federal Reserve Bank provide a substantial amount of liquidity, but the FDIC and a number of private banks provided the capital required to avoid a run on the nearly insolvent Continental Illinois Bank in 1984. All credits and deposits, including inter-bank deposits, were protected. This rescue package was labelled a 'too big to fail' (TBTF) policy. However, a recent FDIC study (1997) concludes that TBTF is an inaccurate term because Continental 'failed'. Top management was removed and shareholders lost their capital. Taking this result into consideration, 'too big to liquidate' (TBTL) would have been a more accurate label. This is because the sudden and uncontrolled failure of large banks will certainly generate spillover effects leading to a widespread breakdown of the bank and inter-firm credit network and will impair public confidence in the financial system. If a large bank is suddenly declared failing or completely insolvent by the FSA in Japan and its liquidation follows, this action would aggravate the current financial deflation. To actually implement the Bridge Bank scheme in the manner consistent with TBTL rather than TBTF requires the FSA to make very difficult policy choices.

Clearing up the root problem of the current financial deflation by dealing with the banking system's non-performing assets allows conventional Keynesian or monetarist stimulation policies to regain their effectiveness.

Entering 1998, the yen depreciated to around 140 per US dollar. The fundamental cause of this depreciation is the persistent financial deflation in Japan. So long as large banks continue to be heavily burdened by non-performing assets, the threat of financial deflation remains. The BOJ has no policy choice but to expand monetary aggregates further and also to lower interest rates. The existing weakness of the yen has been aggravated by sporadic speculative market sentiments. Therefore, the resolution of the huge amount of bad assets held by large Japanese banks will directly assist the recovery of those Asian economies now in crisis. By changing the expectations of the foreign exchange markets, resolving Japan's financial problems also will stop the depreciation of the yen and help stabilize the Hong Kong dollar and Chinese *renminbi*.

4.   FISCAL POLICY ISSUES

(a)   Issues About 'Too Little Too Late' Stimuli and 'Too Early' Consolidation

I have so far emphasized that the delayed and careless resolution of bad bank debts is the underlying reason why the Japanese economy has been stumbling for so long, namely this failure has caused the creation and continuation of financial deflation. However, fiscal policies have also come in for their share of criticisim. Fiscal stimuli were allegedly too little and too late during 1992–6 and the timing of the introduction of fiscal consolidation in FY 1997 was allegedly too early.

Since the structural budget deficit increased by 5 per cent of GDP between 1991 and 1996 (OECD, *Economic Outlook*, June 1998), an annual fiscal stimulus of about 1 per cent of GDP should not be considered as 'too little'. More importantly, many critics claim that the fiscal dose must have been too little because the economy fell into a prolonged recession and subsequently did not stage a strong recovery. Can the actual outcome of the macroeconomic performance be strong proof of the insufficiency of the fiscal stimuli?

As already mentioned, the downward adjustment of private capital stock was inevitable during 1992–4 due to an excess accumulation of business capital in the preceding boom period. The large adverse impact of such an inevitable downward adjustment was just cushioned by fiscal stimuli, registering a 0.5 per cent annual growth of real GDP during the same period. Otherwise, the economy would have fallen in a downward spiral due to an initially sharp decline in business investment, which in turn would have led to declining incomes, falling consumption and again to a further decline in business investment. Instead, private consumption increased by 2 per cent per annum throughout the period 1992–7.

Were fiscal stimuli introduced too late? The peak of the previous boom was dated March 1991 by the Economic Planning Agency and the first comprehensive policy package was introduced in August 1992, followed by four successive packages. However, such policy packages simply describe the scale of government expenditures and of public policy loans, but not actual government revenues or balances. A better way of measuring fiscal stimuli is to estimate changes in the cyclically adjusted structural balances caused by discretionary fiscal policies. From 1991 to 1992, the structural balance of the general government changed from a surplus of 1.9 per cent to a smaller surplus of 0.9 per cent of GDP, that is, a net fiscal stimulus of 1 per cent of GDP. This fiscal stimulus was unable to stop the Japanese economy entering a recession in 1992, but it prevented the downward spiral which might have arisen from sharply declining business investment. Because of the inevitably large downward capital stock adjustment, the earlier introduction of a Keynesian stimulus would not have prevented the recession.

Was the 1997 fiscal consolidation introduced too early? This issue is profoundly associated with the task of attaining fiscal policy consistency between a short-run Keynesian stimulus which creates larger deficits and medium-term consolidation for fiscal balance. This task certainly involves a timing issue. Fiscal consolidation should not undermine a sustained economic recovery. It should only be introduced when the recovery is strong enough to absorb the shock created by a fiscal contraction.

Where did the Japanese economy actually stand in terms of the business cycle in early 1997? There are essentially four phases in a complete business cycle:

1. the recovery phase from a trough to a middle point;
2. the prosperity phase from a middle point to a peak;
3. the contraction phase from a peak to a middle point; and finally
4. the recession phase from a middle point back to a trough.

While troughs and peaks are officially dated only by the Economic Planning Agency, the business cycle phase of the Japanese economy can be estimated by the BOJ's quarterly business survey (*Tankan*). This includes a difference index (DI) subtracting the number of companies judging business conditions to be good from those judging them to be bad. Where the DI is near zero (the number of optimistic and pessimistic companies is nearly equal), the macroeconomy is at a turning point. The economy is either moving from recovery into prosperity, or it is leaving a contractionary phase and sliding into recession.

The relevant DI suggests that the Japanese economy stood at a turning point in the second half of FY 1996. This is plausible, because the economy had been recovering at a rate of 3 per cent per annum for two consecutive years (1995 and 1996), mainly led by private invest-ment. This conjecture is further supported by the composite profit/sales ratio of all companies which returned to a level representing the average ratio for the past two decades. Therefore, the 1997 fiscal consoli-dation was not introduced in the midst of a recession, unlike President Hoover's contractionary fiscal policy in 1932. Of course, whether the scale of the 1997 fiscal consolidation was appropriate or not is another matter. In this regard, the following two issues can be raised.

One is the overall macroeconomic impact of fiscal consolidation, including its effect on net exports. In the extended Mundell–Fleming model under a floating exchange rate regime, fiscal contraction induces net export expansion by lowering the interest rate and hence weakening the exchange rate. How much the dampening effect of fiscal contraction will be offset by the induced expansion of net exports is an empirical question. In the July–September quarter of 1997, the expansion of Japan's net exports contributed 1.4 per cent to the growth of real GDP compared to a year earlier, while total domestic demand only reduced real GDP by 0.4 per cent, resulting in a 1 per cent growth in real GDP. This suggests the size of the offsetting effect of net export expansion, given that the fiscal consolidation equalled more than 2 per cent of GDP, as mentioned earlier. The long-term interest rate (ten-year national bonds) declined from 3.1 per cent to 2.4 per cent between 1996 and 1997, and the exchange rate depreciated from 109 yen to 121 yen per US dollar during the same period (all at annual averages).

Only in the October–December quarter of 1997 and the January–March quarter of 1998 did the aforementioned financial deflation cause total domestic demand to decline by 2.0 per cent and 4.7 per cent, respectively, on a year-to-year basis, the magnitude of which was far bigger than net export expansion. The actual fiscal contraction instituted by the Japanese government was not sufficiently large to account fully for such sizeable drops in domestic demand.

The other issue is whether the current banking crisis would have been avoided if fiscal consolidation had not been introduced in FY

1997. As mentioned earlier, the growing-out policy did not work while the recovery phase strengthened in 1995 and 1996. During this time the banking problem grew even worse. This suggests that, even without the fiscal contraction, the banking problem would not have disappeared but would have continued to worsen.

(b) Medium- and Long-term Fiscal Policies

Once financial deflation changed economic recovery into yet another recessionary phase, the Hashimoto cabinet launched a new policy package of 16 trillion yen, including an individual income tax reduction of 4 trillion yen and increased public work expenditure totalling 8 trillion yen. The new Obuchi cabinet intends to push through yet another package, including a freeze of the Fiscal Consolidation Act of 1997. This Act is aimed at reducing central and local government budget deficits to 3 per cent of GDP by the year 2003 from a level that reached nearly 7 per cent in 1996. It also seeks to eliminate new issues of so-called deficit bonds by the central government (which accounted for 1.5 per cent of GDP in the FY 1997 initial budget). However, as we emphasized earlier, medium-term fiscal consolidation should remain an important policy goal. In this regard, a key issue is whether medium-term fiscal consolidation is consistent with the underlying saving–investment balance in the economy. For example, suppose the optimal capital–income ratio is 4.0; further assume that the underlying growth rate for the Japanese economy can be estimated as running at an annual rate of 2.0 per cent for the period between 1991 and 2005. Domestic investment then requires saving to account for about 8 per cent of net national income. Total saving by the private sector is assumed to be 13 per cent, which has been the level actually achieved in the 1990s. The resulting excess of domestic saving over required investment is 5 per cent of net national income, divided between the general government deficit and the current account surplus. The target set by the Japanese government is to reduce the deficit of the combined central and local government to 3 per cent of GDP (hence, about 3.5 per cent of NNP) by the year 2003. This implies that the general government deficit will be 1.5 per cent of GDP (hence, about 1.8 per cent of NNP). In this case, the implied current account surplus will be 3.2 per cent of NNP or 2.7 per cent of GDP (net investment income accounted for about 1.2 per cent of GDP in 1997). Therefore, such medium-term fiscal consolidation strategy in Japan does not appear extremely off the mark, as implied by the sectoral distribution of the domestic saving–investment balance.

REFERENCE

FDIC (1997), 'History of the Eighties – Lessons for the Future: An Examination of the Banking crises of the 1980s and early 1990s', prepared by the FDIC's Division of Research and Statistics: Washington, DC.

6. Empirical determinants of banking crises: Japan's experience in international perspective

Michael Hutchison, Kathleen McDill and Rita Madrassy[1]

1. INTRODUCTION

The paralysis characterizing Japan's financial system in the late 1990s is not comparable to any other episode during the past 45 years. Stress in the Japanese financial system, especially failure to resolve the non-performing loan and bank problems, held back the economy and caused stagnation in a large part of the real-estate market for most of the decade. The problem reached a peak in 1998 with a flurry of actions designed to deal with insolvent financial institutions. These measures included a large commitment of public funds to protect depositors and recapitalize 'solvent' financial institutions (passed by the Diet in March), the creation of a new 'bridge bank' to take over the assets of failed banks (announced in July), and a political compromise allowing the commitment of public funds to the Long-Term Credit Bank of Japan (announced in September).

Although Japan's banking crisis is not unique among the industrial countries – several have faced banking crises over the past two decades – nowhere were the effects on the economy and the intensity of the problem so prolonged as in Japan. What made Japan special? Why was Japan still saddled with banking problems when other industrial economies, facing similar or even worse situations, resolved them much faster? Was Japan's delay in resolving its banking crisis and restoring confidence in its banking system related to almost a decade of enduring a weak economy and rising unemployment?

The general features of the banking crisis in Japan are by now well recognized (see, for example, Cargill *et al.* 1997, 1998; Hutchison 1997; OECD 1998), and in many respects resemble banking crises experienced by other industrial countries: booming economies and sharply rising asset prices, followed by recession, severe asset price declines and banking problems. The international character of the asset price boom, and subsequent collapse, suggests common explanatory factors. The existing literature investigating banking crises, however, consists for the most part of qualitative case studies and international comparisons.[2] Few quantitative studies or formal testing of hypotheses of the determinants and consequences of bank crises have been undertaken, and none have focused on Japan.

We investigate the Japanese banking crisis using a more quantitative approach, comparing features of Japan's banking crisis with the experiences of other industrial economies, and highlighting the special circumstances of the Japanese case. We review some of the basic statistical contours of bank crises in industrial countries, again highlighting Japan, and also design empirical tests of several propositions on the determinants of banking problems.

Our major finding is that Japan's banking crisis follows a pattern found in many other countries, and formal tests do not distinguish Japan as a special case. Our model predicts that Japan was particularly 'vulnerable' to a banking crisis in the early 1990s. The model indicates that there was a greater than 30 per cent probability of a banking crisis in Japan in 1992, given the configuration of asset prices, credit conditions and other economic factors prevailing at the time. We argue that the main factor distinguishing Japan from other industrial countries is the slow and poorly designed policy response of the Japanese government to resolve the country's financial crisis.

In the next section we review the basic features of Japan's banking crisis. In the third section we undertake a statistical analysis of the economic and institutional characteristics distinguishing those countries that have experienced banking crises from those that have not. We report the results from an 'event study' analysis considering the characteristics of economies in the lead-up to and aftermath of the banking crises. The fourth section undertakes a more formal probit analysis of the causes of bank crises in the industrialized countries and considers the predictions of the model for Japan. The final section considers Japan's regulatory response to the crisis and concludes the paper. In the appendix we review the literature on banking crises and compare the general characteristics of Japan's banking crisis with those of other industrial countries.

2. THE ORIGINS OF JAPAN'S FINANCIAL CRISIS[3]

Asset deflation in the early 1990s was the single most important factor affecting the profitability of Japanese financial institutions. This factor subsequently led to the present crisis engulfing a large part of the financial system. Deterioration in the quality of loans to the real-estate sector was the primary problem, but this was compounded by the drop in the value of banks' large equity holdings and growing loan problems associated with a prolonged period of slow growth and recession through most of the 1990s.

Japan's recession itself can in large part be traced to this decline in asset prices. Consumption fell as households saw the real value of their equity and real-estate holdings decline precipitously. The fall in consumption induced a fall in fixed investment, which was weakened further, in turn, by the overhang of excess capacity accumulated during the asset inflation phase and the credit crunch induced by the decline in bank 'hidden' capital.[4]

A number of features of the Japanese financial system in the mid-1980s made asset inflation more probable in the context of a newly liberated financial structure and accommodating monetary policy. These features of the Japanese financial structure include:

- financial deregulation and liberalization in the late 1970s and early 1980s, which had increased the portfolio flexibility of banks and other financial institutions, especially small depositories. Japanese financial institutions aggressively pursued lending to speculative real-estate ventures during the late 1980s and did so with very little oversight by the supervisory authorities;
- the shift to a slower growth path after the first oil-price shock in 1973 reduced the corporate sector's reliance on bank credit and services. As a result, banks sought out new markets – such as real-estate lending – outside traditional corporate finance and were willing to assume new and often higher risks of which they had little previous experience;
- the main bank system of industrial organization and corporate governance, which began to unravel in response to financial liberalization. No widely available financial-disclosure framework to evaluate and monitor risk was on hand to replace the main bank system;
- the considerable authority possessed by Japanese banks to purchase directly and hold equities, tying their 'hidden reserves' directly to the fortunes of the stock market;

- the regulatory monitoring system, which lagged behind market developments; 'administrative guidance' could not keep pace with the fast-changing financial environment;
- complete deposit guarantees which encouraged risk-taking at the very time that the Bank of Japan provided increased liquidity and financial liberalization which improved asset-diversification powers.

Asset Price Inflation

The process of financial liberalization in Japan in the 1980s failed to change the existing system of government deposit guarantees that had been designed for a more regulated and administratively controlled financial environment. As a result, government deposit guarantees provided incentives to assume risk, while at the same time regulatory and market innovations permitted depositories to manage and assume more risk.

However, financial liberalization and a lack of adequate supervision was only one of several factors contributing to asset inflation in Japan. The initial jump in stock and land prices during 1985–6 was most probably related to changes in fundamentals: aggregate productivity gains in Japan were very strong at the time, and demand for real estate – particularly in the Tokyo area – increased significantly. Further, expansionary monetary policy pushed interest rates to very low levels and contributed to a run-up in bond, stock and real-estate values. Against this background, structural changes were taking place: financial deregulation, changes in the flows of funds and increased risk-taking activity by banks also played a role at the beginning of the asset price inflation.

At some point, probably in late 1986 or early in 1987, the asset inflation process appears to have become a speculative bubble with little restraint either from financial institutions or regulatory authorities. Expectations of asset price increases fed upon themselves and price/dividend and price/rent ratios increasingly deviated from fundamental values until the crash in the early 1990s. Speculators during this asset inflation typically thought that even though the 'levels' of stock and land prices were abnormally high and would eventually fall, further investment was warranted as long as other investors thought prices would continue to rise. Many felt that they would be among the first to sell their asset holdings, realizing large capital gains, when the market started to fall. This kind of behaviour has been variously characterized as stochastic bubbles, herd instincts, momentum trading and bandwagon behaviour.

The Bursting of the Bubble.

Asset prices declined rapidly in the 1990–1 period. The Nikkei 225 stock price index reached its 38 915 peak on the last business day of 1989, and then tumbled. By 1 October 1990, the Nikkei stood barely above 20 000 – a decline of almost 50 per cent in nine months. It fell below 15 000 by summer 1992 and, despite considerable fluctuations, was still below that level in September 1998 (recording lows of around 13 500). Land prices began to fall in late 1991, and by 1995 prices were frequently only half of their peak values. At that time, the typical price for land was similar to that prevailing ten years earlier and it continued to decline in 1996 and 1997. Real-estate prices declined for seven consecutive years (to June 1998).

A combination of policy actions and the self-correcting mechanism of the speculative process (deflating the bubble) was responsible for the subsequent asset price decline. By mid-1989, the monetary authorities became fully aware of, and concerned about, asset price inflation and started to raise interest rates. The Ministry of Finance also introduced several measures to slow land price increases. The Iraqi invasion of Kuwait on 2 August 1990 further weakened the world economic outlook and the prospects for oil-dependent Japan in particular. Furthermore, once the decline in asset prices began, banks had an incentive to reduce lending for real-estate and other purposes. When the Basle risk-based capital ratio was negotiated in 1988 as an international minimum standard for banks with international businesses, Japanese banks were allowed to count 45 per cent of their equity holdings as part of their Tier II capital. As the value of these equities was devoted to meeting capital asset requirements, the cost of capital increased, reducing the incentive of banks to make loans and contributing to the drop in credit expansion.

Despite these factors, the most important reason for the collapse in asset prices was the self-correcting mechanism inherent in stochastic speculative processes. Expectations of further price declines generated selling, which in turn led to actual price declines. During the spring of 1990, for example, the Nikkei futures tended to lead the decline in cash markets. In fact, this was responsible for the view that futures transactions were making the stock market too volatile, and led to a tightening of margin requirements in the Nikkei futures market in Osaka in 1991.[5]

Onset of the Banking Crisis

The sharp decline of asset values and the slowdown in the economy in the early 1990s was quickly reflected in the balance sheets of financial institutions. Declines in real-estate values were particularly problematic for institutions with large loan exposure in that sector (for example, the *jusen* real-estate finance companies), as well as their parent institutions (city and regional banks). The sharp and prolonged downturn in the economy, the fall in equity values (financial institutions hold a sizeable share of their assets in equities), and the continued decline in real-estate asset values eventually led to serious financial distress.

Numerous small (including all but one of the *jusen*) and several large financial institutions had collapsed by mid-1998, including three of Japan's top 21 banks, one of the Big Four securities companies, and a mid-sized life assurance company. Non-performing loans were estimated at upwards of 12 per cent of GDP in early 1998 when the most far-reaching and concentrated government actions to resolve the banking problem were finally implemented.[6]

3.   INDICATORS OF BANKING CRISES FOR INDUSTRIAL COUNTRIES: WHERE DOES JAPAN FIT IN?

In the 1980s and 1990s a number of industrialized and developing countries experienced severe bank crises similar to that of Japan. A short review of the empirical literature on international comparisons of bank crises and general characterizations that emerge from the data are given in the appendix. Japan's experience seems to fit with the general characterization of the causes of banking crises in at least two ways: macroeconomic instability (boom and bust cycles in asset prices and real output) and weakness in financial structure (financial liberalization, deposit guarantees and weak supervision and regulation).

As discussed in the previous section, an expansionary monetary and credit policy was clearly evident in Japan in the latter 1980s and contributed to the boom and bust cycle of asset prices. Equally important, financial liberalization was undertaken against the background of a 'weak financial structure' – an increasingly competitive financial environment, shifts in the flows of funds, inadequate supervisory oversight, incentives to take on increased risk, deficiencies in accounting and financial disclosure frameworks, and the failure of governmental action to identify and manage the problem. Cargill *et al.* (1997, 1998) and Hutchison (1997) discuss these aspects of Japan's financial crisis in detail.

In this section we identify the key institutional and economic features of countries experiencing severe bank crises which distinguish them from other industrial countries. We compare these summary statistics with Japan, attempting to identify general and idiosyncratic features associated with the Japanese case. In our search for these key variables, we are guided by the findings of other studies (discussed in the appendix).

Identifying Bank Crises

We have identified and dated episodes of banking sector distress following the criteria of Demirgüç-Kunt and Detragiache (1998), updated using data from the Bank for International Settlements (1997). They identify banking crises as a situation where one of the following conditions holds: the ratio of non-performing assets to total assets is greater than 2 per cent of GDP; the cost of the rescue operation is at least 2 per cent of GDP; banking sector problems result in a large-scale nationalization of banks; and extensive bank runs take place or emergency measures such as deposit freezes, prolonged bank holidays or generalized deposit guarantees are enacted by the government in response to the crisis.

As the appendix discusses in some detail, the dating of banking crises is somewhat arbitrary. However, we follow the Demirgüç-Kunt and Detragiache definition to avoid any possibility of 'data mining', that is, identifying the date of the banking crisis after observing developments in macroeconomic and other variables thought to be determinants of the crises.[7] Japan's banking crisis, for example, is dated by the Demirgüç-Kunt and Detragiache criteria as starting in 1992. This is the first year of substantial government attention to the problem. However, the first significant plans for restructuring a large part of the financial sector did not come until 1993. Many observers wouldn't characterize the Japanese banking problem as a full-blown 'crisis' until 1995. On the other hand, using realistic estimates of non-performing loans as an indicator might date the beginning of Japan's banking distress as early as 1991.

We investigated 20 industrial countries over the 1980–97 period using annual data. The countries investigated are all OECD members: Australia, Austria, Belgium, Canada, Switzerland, Germany, Denmark, Finland, France, Great Britain, Greece, Ireland, Italy, Japan, the Netherlands, New Zealand, Norway, Portugal, Sweden and the United States. Using the four bank crisis indicators, seven countries are identified as having had bank crises since 1980: Finland (1991–4), Italy (1990–4), Japan (1992–7), Norway (1987–93), Portugal (1986–9) Sweden (1990–3) and the United States (1984–91).

Economic Characteristics

The variables considered are real GDP growth (gdp), the change in the spot exchange rate against the US dollar (domestic currency price of the US dollar; exrate), the rate of inflation (inf) and the real interest rate (rint). To capture the degree of foreign exchange exposure, we considered the ratio of a broad money aggregate to international reserves (m2ratio). To investigate whether excessive money and credit growth as well as asset price bubbles are associated with banking crises, we considered the rate of credit growth (credit) and the rate of change in stock prices (stock). The data are taken from IMF International Financial Statistics and various other sources.

Table 6.1 shows the differences in these economic characteristics between the group of countries experiencing banking crises and the group that avoided severe banking distress. The average values of these indicator variables are calculated over the full sample period for those countries which have not experienced a banking crisis. Then average values of these variables are calculated over the period leading up to the banking crisis in our focus group of countries (bank crisis). The objective is to identify different movements in these variables that distinguish the crisis and non-crisis countries during periods of relative tranquillity, that is, before banking problems become critical.

The first column of statistics shows the mean values for countries not experiencing a banking crisis and the second column shows the mean values for bank crisis countries. The third column shows the mean difference (t-statistic) tests, and the fourth column presents the corresponding value for Japan over the period prior to the banking crisis. The standard deviations are shown in parentheses below the mean values.

The mean difference tests indicate that the average rate of inflation, the increase in stock prices and the M2/reserve ratio are significantly higher in countries struck by severe banking problems. Average real GDP growth and average budget deficits also appear marginally higher (statistically significant at the 11 and 12 per cent level, respectively) in the crisis countries. By contrast, the average level of real interest rates (short-term) are lower in industrial countries experiencing banking crises – at least in the period prior to the crisis – than in the industrial countries not experiencing a banking crisis.

No statistically significant difference between the two groups of coun-

Table 6.1 Economic characteristics of industrial countries experiencing banking crises

	Countries not experiencing bank crisis	Countries experiencing bank crisis[a]	Difference in mean values (Pr>|t|)	Japan
Real GDP	2.27	2.72	0.11	3.97
growth	(2.23)	(1.79)		(0.99)
Exchange rate	2.04	2.92	0.68	−5.41
Depreciation	(13.00)	(15.08)		(13.64)
Inflation	5.57	8.66*	0.00	2.12
	(5.39)	(6.18)		(1.22)
Real interest	3.33	1.91*	0.00	2.55
rate	(3.65)	(3.12)		(0.89)
M2/reserve	13.39	28.97*	0.00	44.26
ratio	(9.83)	(26.47)		(7.52)
Credit growth	5.91	5.10	0.41	6.46
	(11.11)	(5.12)		(2.60)
Stock price	11.62	23.16*	0.01	13.90
change	(19.30)	(29.50)		(18.60)
Budget surplus	−3.96	−5.12	0.12	−4.25
	(4.14)	(5.21)		(2.60)

Notes:
[a]   Values prior to banking crisis.
*   Statistical significance.

tries is found in the pattern of credit growth or exchange rate change. By contrast with conventional wisdom, credit growth in those industrial countries experiencing banking crises was somewhat lower, on average, than in the non-crisis industrial countries.

Where does Japan fit in this general pattern differentiating economic developments in the crisis countries from the non-crisis countries? No simple pattern emerges. Similar to other bank-crisis countries, Japan's average real GDP growth and rise in stock prices was faster than the group of industrial countries not experiencing severe financial problems. The M2/reserve ratio was also substantially greater.

The similarities end at this point, however, as prior to the start of the crisis Japan experienced less exchange rate depreciation (indeed, strong appreciation), lower inflation and somewhat higher real interest rates than even the non-crisis countries. The Japanese average budget deficit during this period was between the sample means of the crisis and non-crisis countries. Credit growth was faster in Japan than the non-crisis group (and much faster than the crisis countries), conforming to conventional wisdom but not consistent with economic developments in the other industrial countries experiencing banking crises.

Economic Developments Before and After Banking Crises

Table 6.2 shows the economic characteristics of industrial countries experiencing banking crises at different periods: prior to the banking crisis, the first year of the onset of the crisis, during the banking crisis, and after the crisis. The number in parentheses below the mean value is the standard deviation of the variable and the number in square brackets is the probability that the mean value indicated is the same as the previous value. For example, real GDP growth following crisis episodes averaged 3.53 per cent per annum (with a standard deviation of 1.46), a significant jump (less than a 1 per cent probability that the values are the same) from the 1.47 per cent average (with a 2.20 standard deviation) recorded during the crisis episodes.

The 'asymmetric' information explanation for bank crises, expressed for example by Kaminsky and Reinhart (1996), would suggest that a booming economy and sanguine views of the future (for example, strong stock markets and rapid credit growth) tend to be followed by a slowdown in economic activity and a fall in stock values and credit growth.

The basic time-series statistics support the 'asymmetric view'. The four variables which indicate a distinct shift over crisis episodes are real GDP growth, exchange rate depreciation, credit growth and stock price increases. Real GDP growth drops during the crisis episode and rises significantly following the crisis. Credit decreases during the crisis and jumps markedly following the crisis.

Perhaps the most striking feature is the development of stock markets: booming prior to the crisis (a 23 per cent annual rise), sharply declining in the first year of the crisis (an average 6 per cent drop), and rising around 10–11 per cent per annum on average during the remaining years of the bank crisis episode as well as following the crisis episode. The 11 per cent per annum stock price rise is the same as the average for the non-crisis countries over the full 1980–97 sample period. Although not statistically significant, inflation and real interest rates also tend to decline after the onset of banking crises.

Japan experienced a similar pattern over time as other countries experiencing bank crises: a booming economy (rapid real GDP and

Table 6.2 Economic development prior to, during and after bank crises

| | Seven crisis countries | | | | Japan | | |
	Prior to crisis	First year of crisis	During crisis	After crisis	1980–91	1992	1993–7
Real GDP	2.72	1.32	1.47	3.53*	3.97	1.02	1.45
growth	(1.79)	(4.19)	2.20)	(1.46)			
Pr>|t|		[0.42]	[0.93]	[0.00]			
Exchange	2.92	–4.68*	3.56*	–1.69*	–5.41	–0.36	0.82
rate	(15.08)	(9.83)	(10.73)	(8.21)			
depreciation		[0.10]	[0.08]	[0.06]			
Inflation	8.66	9.71	4.09	4.13	2.12	1.73	0.06
	(6.18)	(12.8)	(3.37)	(3.94)			
		[0.84]	[0.29]	[0.97]			
Real interest	1.91	0.80	3.73	4.09	2.55	1.52	1.07
rate	(3.12)	(10.26)	(2.75)	(3.93)			
		[0.78]	[0.48]	[0.74]			
M2/reserve	28.97	34.50	28.64	24.41	44.26	56.72	32.27
ratio	(26.47)	(40.54)	(28.42)	(29.24)			
		[0.76]	[0.75]	[0.65]			
Credit	5.10	2.77	–1.078	2.97*	6.46	1.17	0.83
growth	(5.13)	(10.86)	(5.34)	(4.61)			
		[0.59]	[0.39]	[0.01]			
Stock price	23.16	–6.21*	11.21*	10.15	13.90	–25.95	0.99
change	(29.50)	(18.57)	(22.95)	(14.32)			
		[0.01]	[0.01]	[0.85]			
Budget	–5.12	–4.59	–5.62	–4.75	–4.25	0.31	–1.54
surplus	(5.21)	(5.21)	(4.52)	(3.04)			
		[0.81]	[0.65]	[0.49]			

Note: Parentheses indicate the standard deviation of the variable. Square brackets indicate the probability that the mean is different from the mean of the category to its left. * indicates statistical significance.

credit growth along with rising inflation) and strong asset markets (rapid stock price increase) prior to the bank crisis, followed by a sharp slow-down and falling asset prices. All these indicators suggest the recessionary conditions and asset price deflation that typically characterize banking crises. Japan clearly fits this pattern.

Focusing again on asset price developments, Figure 6.1 shows stock

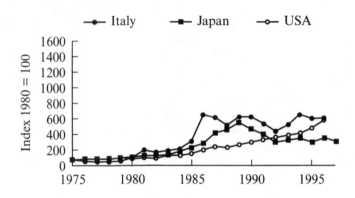

Figure 6.1   Stock value index

price indices for industrial countries experiencing banking crisis in the 1980s and 1990s (excluding Portugal). The countries experiencing the largest stock market booms prior to the onset of their banking crises were two countries in Scandinavia. In particular, Sweden and Finland experienced stock market increases of more than 700 per cent, followed by sharp declines, in the decade prior to the onset of their banking crises (1990 and 1991, respectively).

Similar, though less dramatic, patterns are seen in Italy (1990), Japan

(1992) and Norway (1987). Between 1980 and the peak prior to the onset of their banking crisis, stock indices in these countries climbed, respectively, approximately 500 per cent, 400 per cent and 250 per cent. Japan's boom and bust in asset prices around the time of the banking crisis is not unusual compared with other industrial countries facing similar difficulties. By contrast, stock prices in the United States rose only about 30 per cent between 1980 and 1984 and did not decline at the time of the savings and loan crisis.

4. PREDICTING BANKING CRISES

This section presents a model linking economic developments and institutional structures to banking crises. We investigate whether economic and institutional characteristics of countries are associated with the onset of banking crises and use the model to see if Japan's banking problems fit a pattern seen in other industrial countries. Our objectives are both to investigate the general characteristics associated with banking crises and to determine whether Japan's experience (or the circumstances surrounding the banking crisis) is idiosyncratic. Using panel data encompassing 20 industrial countries over the 1980–97 period, we use a multivariate probit analysis to estimate how a particular variable changes the probability of the occurrence of a banking crisis holding constant the other explanatory factors.

This is the relevant question for policy analysis and it cannot be addressed using simple univariate descriptive analysis. Three previous empirical studies of which we are aware have formally addressed this issue. Kaminsky and Reinhart (1996) use a probit model, associating banking crises with two explanatory factors: the incidence of financial liberalization (measured by a dummy variable taking a value of unity if 'financial markets are deregulated' and zero otherwise) and the previous occurrence of a balance of payments crisis. Only the financial liberalization dummy variable is statistically significantly and positively associated with banking crises.

Demirgüç-Kunt and Detragiache (1998) also use probit analysis in their investigation of the determinants of banking crises. However, they consider a larger number of potential explanatory factors (using annual data) than Kaminsky and Reinhart (1996). They find that low real GDP growth is contemporaneously associated with banking crises. They do not find that rapid real GDP growth is a leading indicator of banking crises, however. They also find that (a) high real interest rates, (b) high inflation, (c) external vulnerability (measured by a high ratio of broad money to international reserves), (d) low values of a 'law and order' index (a proxy for a weaker regulatory and supervisory structure), and (e) the existence of an explicit deposit insurance scheme (increasing moral hazard) are significantly associated with banking crises. By contrast, they find little evidence that terms of trade deterioration, rapid credit growth or the exchange rate also are systematically associated with banking crises.

Eichengreen and Rose (1998) also employ probit models to estimate the probability of a banking crisis, but focus on developing countries. They find that external factors, especially increases in world interest rates, are an important determinant of banking crises in developing countries. Overvalued real exchange rates and slowing output growth also play a role. However, differing exchange rate regimes and domestic credit booms do not add predictive power to the model.

Following these studies and the descriptive studies of the previous section, we estimate the probability of a banking crisis by means of a multivariate probit model which uses maximum likelihood estimation. In each period the country is either experiencing a crisis or it is not. Our dependent variable takes on a value of zero if there is not a crisis and a value of unity if there is a crisis. The probability that a crisis will occur (at a particular time in a particular country) is modelled as a function of a vector of explanatory variables $X(i,t)$, where i denotes country i and t denotes the time period. Our panel data set has 237 observations.

We employ two categories of explanatory variables in the analysis: institutional variables (that do not vary over time but show significant differences across countries) and macroeconomic variables (which vary substantially over time and across countries). The institutional variables we consider are the average number of strikes per year and a measure of central bank independence.[8] A relatively high frequency of strikes indicates a substantial degree of labour unrest and could indicate greater economic volatility. Greater risk of economic turmoil, in turn, may contribute to a country's vulnerability to a banking crisis. A more independent central bank, on the other hand, might indicate greater supervisory control, less political intervention and less vulnerability to a banking crisis. The macroeconomic variables employed are standard: stock price (percentage change), exchange rate depreciation, real GDP growth, inflation and credit growth. Annual data are employed.

Basic Results

Table 6.3 reports the results from the estimated probit equations with contemporaneous values of the explanatory values. The estimated coefficients (standard errors) are shown in the third column of the table. The fourth column shows the relevant statistic of significance (z), and the fifth column shows the probability that the point coefficient estimate is not significantly different from zero. The results indicate that two of the variables are marginally significant and one variable is highly significant. The 'pseudo' R^2 is 0.236, suggesting a moderate degree of explanatory power for the model.

Table 6.3 Probit estimates: contemporaneous, excluding all years after first crisis year

Bank crisis	Coefficient	Std error	z	$P > |z|$
Strike	–0.207	0.745	–0.277	0.781
Central bank independence	–2.570	1.650	–1.558	0.119
Stock price change	–0.029	0.014	–2.052	0.040
Exchange rate depreciation	–0.029	0.019	–1.560	0.119
GDP growth	–0.070	0.086	–0.824	0.410
Inflation	0.002	0.055	0.032	0.974
Credit growth	0.003	0.016	0.016	0.987
Constant	–0.882	0.696	–1.268	0.205

Notes:
Number of observations = 225
Pseudo R^2 = 0.236

The coefficient estimates indicate that a high degree of central bank independence decreases the probability of a banking crisis. Moreover, a fall in stock prices and currency depreciation is associated with an increased likelihood of a banking crisis. By contrast with the conclusions of many individual case studies and descriptive international comparison studies, we find that real GDP and credit growth does not significantly add explanatory power to the model. That is, these variables do not help predict the occurrence of a banking crisis after controlling for the movement in stock prices, exchange rates and institutional factors.

Current problems

In Table 6.4 we report the estimates from our probit model where alternative measures of economic activity (real GDP as a deviation from potential GDP) and credit growth (nominal credit growth less nominal GDP growth) are used as explanatory variables. Both of these variables are plausible alternative measures of, respectively, the state of the business cycle and the extent of excessive credit growth. However, the results are uniformly weaker in Table 6.4 compared to Table 6.3. The state of the business cycle and of credit growth is not systematically correlated with banking crises after controlling for other factors.

Table 6.4 Probit estimates: contemporaneous, including alternative definitions of variables of GDP and credit growth, excluding all years after first crisis year

Bank crisis	Coefficient	Std error	z	$P>|z|$
Strike	−0.193	0.746	−0.259	0.796
Central bank independence	−2.421	1.647	−1.470	0.141
Stock price change	−0.030	0.014	−2.128	0.033
Exchange rate depreciation	−0.022	0.019	−1.179	0.238
GDP deviation	0.069	0.087	0.796	0.426
Inflation	0.001	0.058	0.015	0.988
Credit growth above GDP growth	0.002	0.015	0.132	0.985
Constant	−1.103	0.679	−1.625	0.104

Notes:
Number of observations = 225
Pseudo R^2 = 0.236

Predictions for Japan

The model estimates reported in Table 6.3 cover all the industrial countries and may or may not do well in predicting the likelihood of a banking crisis in a specific country at a particular moment in time; that is, the model could have relatively high predictive accuracy in general but do rather poorly in predicting the actual occurrence of any particular banking crisis. Our question is whether the general statistical characteristics of bank crises identified by the model help to explain the timing and likelihood of the bank crisis which occurred in Japan.

To this end, Figure 6.2 reports the predicted probability of a banking crisis occurring in Japan during the 1980–97 period. The line labelled 'predicted in-sample' uses the coefficient estimates from Table 6.3 to predict the probability of a banking crisis in Japan for each year. That probability is below 10 per cent until 1990, at which time the probability jumps to over 15 per cent. The probability climbs further to almost 20 per cent in 1991 and peaks at about 30 per cent in 1992. The estimated probability then drops sharply to below 10 per cent in 1993. These results indicate that the model does quite well in predicting the occurrence of the Japanese banking crisis. Since the institutional variables are quite stable, the results are driven by the collapse in stock prices in 1990–2 and the shift from strong currency appreciation to exchange rate depreciation.

It is noteworthy that the model's predictive accuracy is not driven by the fact that Japan is included in the data sample from which the model coefficients are estimated, and then used to predict the probability of a banking crisis (an 'in-sample prediction'). The line labelled 'predicted out-of-sample' in Figure 6.2 shows the predicted values for Japan when Japanese data are excluded from the estimation equation. The coefficients from the model excluding Japan are then matched up with actual macroeconomic developments in Japan to predict the probability of a banking crisis. Although somewhat lower in magnitude, the general pattern of a sharply rising probability of a banking crisis is again clearly evident.

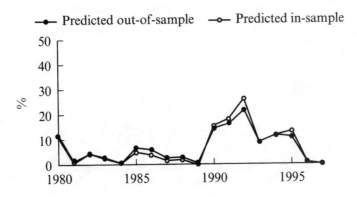

Figure 6.2   Predicted probability of a banking crisis in Japan

The model also predicts the onset of banking crises for the other industrial countries quite well. Figure 6.3 reports the predicted values for the other industrial countries. The country acronyms placed next to a particular point on each line of the figure indicate the year of the onset of a banking crisis. The probability of a banking crisis occurring in Finland was over 25 per cent in 1991 when it occurred (peaking the year prior). The probability of a banking crisis also climbed significantly prior to the event in Sweden (peaking at the time of the crisis), Italy (peaking a year after the onset of the crisis) and Norway (peaking a year after the onset of the crisis). Only the predicted values for the United States did not climb prior to the onset of a banking crisis.

The results reported in Table 6.3 and Figures 6.2 and 6.3 are for macroeconomic variables that are contemporaneously associated with banking crises and, hence, caution should be exercised in interpreting these as causal relationships. It is possible that the onset of a banking crisis may, for example, in turn trigger a fall in stock prices or currency depreciation. In Japan's case, however, we know that the fall in the stock market (which peaked on 31 December 1989) preceded the banking crisis by a full two years, indicating a causal link running from a collapsing stock market to the onset of a banking crisis.

What value has an exercise of this nature for policy analysis? Clearly, we have not estimated a forecasting model and are not able to use current macroeconomic conditions to predict the onset of future banking problems. However, the warning signs of a sharp asset price

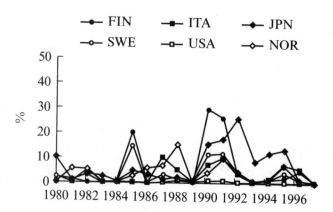

Figure 6.3   Predicted crises

boom or currency depreciation should put bank supervisory authorities on notice. Moreover, to some extent these variables are under the control of the policy authorities and, through this channel, banking stability may play a role in macroeconomic policy deliberations.

Several studies reviewed in the appendix suggest that some variables may be useful leading (as opposed to contemporaneous) indicators of bank crises. The descriptive statistics reported in Table 6.2 also suggest a discernible pattern to macroeconomic developments prior to the onset of a banking crisis. A closer look at the evidence, however, indicates that no empirical study has had much success in systematically forecasting banking crises (or currency crises) in the context of a rigorous multivariate model. That is, macroeconomic variables in a formal forecasting sense have not been reliable leading indicators of banking crises.

None the less, we also estimated a simple forecasting model: a probit equation where all the macroeconomic explanatory variables shown in Table 6.3 were lagged one year. Not surprisingly, the same institutional variable (which does not change over the sample) is statistically significant. However, none of the lagged macroeconomic variables appears systematically to lead the onset of banking crises. By contrast with conventional wisdom, we do not find that rapid GDP and credit growth, or a run-up in stock prices, systematically helps to predict banking crises in the industrial countries. We also estimated the model with two-year lags of the explanatory variables and obtained the same basic results.[9]

5. CONCLUDING OBSERVATIONS

The previous sections indicate that, in most dimensions, the Japanese banking crisis is similar to those experienced in other industrial countries. The analysis of macroeconomic developments before and after bank crises indicates that Japan followed a pattern similar to many countries facing bank crises, and our model successfully predicts the increased likelihood of a banking crisis in Japan in the early 1990s.

The factors leading up to the Japanese banking crisis were not unique: financial liberalization, expansionary credit growth, rapid real GDP growth and an asset price bubble. The immediate aftermath also followed a pattern seen in other industrial economies experiencing severe bank crises: recession and deflation, falling asset prices, and a credit 'crunch'.

At this point, however, the similarities end. Japan's banking crisis has had greater adverse effects than in other countries. The duration of the banking crises in other industrial countries in some cases was as long as Japan's (Italy's continued for eight years; Norway's for seven years; the USA's for seven years). And in several cases the magnitude of the problem, measured at the peak in terms of non-performing loans as a percentage of GDP, was substantially greater than in Japan (Italy, Finland, Norway and Sweden). But in no case was the general malaise over the economy felt more deeply than in Japan: that is, the intensity of the crisis was felt longer and more sharply in Japan than in other industrial countries. This is illustrated by the failure of asset prices to recover and by the weak GDP growth/near-recession that prevailed in Japan over much of the 1990s.

If the determinants and timing of the bank crisis in Japan seemed to conform to experiences elsewhere, why then was the Japanese problem so severe and the sense of a crisis situation so prolonged? The slow policy response and numerous half-measures to resolve the banking crisis appear to be the main factors setting the Japanese experience apart from bank crises experienced in other industrial countries.

A voluminous literature has studied the Japanese policy response to the banking crisis (see Cargill *et al.* 1997; Hutchison 1997). The proximate causes of the problem are clear: (a) the failure of the regulatory authorities to recognize early the full magnitude and implications of the banking crisis; (b) the delayed response of the regulatory authorities, especially the failure to deal decisively with bankrupt institutions; and (c) the difficulty the political system had in confronting the problem in Japan and committing public funds to a major financial restructuring, delaying until very late in the process. Commitment of sizeable public funds in 1998 to shore up deposit insurance, restructure financial institutions and establish a new 'bridge bank' were only forthcoming after many years of political wrangling while the banking problem worsened. It is necessary to draw on deeper political economy arguments as to why these initiatives were so late in coming, and why Japan was apparently not able to draw on the lessons from other industrial countries (for example, the United States, Finland, Norway, Sweden and others) facing similar problems.

APPENDIX

Empirical Literature Using International Comparisons of Banking Crises

Recent reports by the International Monetary Fund (1998) and the Organization for Economic Cooperation and Development (1998) have highlighted the topic of financial crises. The IMF and OECD reports and a number of other studies (for example, Caprio and Klingebiel 1996; Kaminsky and Reinhart 1996; Kaminsky *et al.* 1997; Demirgüç-Kunt and Detragiache 1998; and Eichengreen and Rose 1998) have attempted to identify characteristics common to countries experiencing bank crises and to investigate whether there are signs or indicators suggesting particular vulnerability to a major financial problem.

Identifying Bank Crises

A bank crisis may be defined in a variety of ways, but generally refers to a situation in which 'actual or potential bank runs or failures induce banks to suspend the internal convertibility of their liabilities or compel the government to intervene to prevent this by extending assistance on a large scale' (IMF 1998: 74–5).

Banking crises are usually difficult to identify empirically, however, because of data limitations. The potential for a bank run is not directly observable and, once either a bank run or large-scale government intervention has occurred, the situation will probably have been preceded by a protracted deterioration in the quality of assets held by banks. There is a risk of dating the crises too late in that financial problems usually begin well before government intervention. But there is also a risk that the crisis date is set too early in that the peak of the crisis is often reached much later than the initial government intervention.

Identifying bank crises by the deterioration of bank asset quality is also difficult since direct market indicators of asset value are usually lacking. This is an important limitation because most banking problems in recent years are not associated with bank runs (the liability side of the balance sheet) but with a deterioration in asset quality and with a subsequent government intervention. Government intervention usually follows a sustained build-up of non-performing loans in banks' portfolios, large fluctuations in asset prices (real-estate and stocks) and a rise in business failures. Moreover, it is often laxity in government analysis of banking fragility, and the slow follow-up action once a problem is recognized, that allows the situation to deteriorate to the point of a major bank crisis involving large-scale government intervention.

Given these conceptual and data limitations, most studies have employed a combination of events to identify and date the occurrence of a bank crisis. Institutional events usually include forced closure, merger or government intervention in the operations of financial institutions, runs on banks or the extension of large-scale government assistance. Other indicators frequently include measures of non-performing assets, problem loans and so on. Case studies are frequently relied upon in dating the onset of a banking crisis. This is because institutional setups and financial structures vary so greatly across countries.

General Characteristics of Bank Crises

Despite the difficulties of identifying and measuring the magnitude of banking crises, several common features of countries experiencing such crises emerge from the literature. The IMF (1998) study, drawing on previous work, identified 54 banking crises in both industrial and developing countries between 1975 and 1997. Most of these crises were concentrated in the second half of the sample period, and the incidence was greater among the developing countries (42 crises) than the industrial countries (12 crises). The fiscal and quasi-fiscal costs of restructuring financial institutions to resolve the banking crisis were often large, reaching over 40 per cent of GDP in some cases (Argentina and Chile in the early 1980s). The real output costs were also substantial as financial institutions and markets failed to function effectively.

The IMF report identifies several general categories of problems which are frequently associated with financial crises (both banking and currency crises): unsustainable macroeconomic policies; weaknesses in financial structure; global financial conditions; exchange rate misalignments; and political instability.

Macroeconomic instability, particularly expansionary monetary and fiscal policies spurring lending booms and asset price bubbles, has been a factor in many bank crises, including most experienced by the industrial countries in the post-war period. External conditions, such as large shifts in the terms of trade and world interest rates, have played a significant role in financial crises in emerging-market economies. By affecting the profitability of domestic firms, sudden external changes can adversely impact banks' balance sheets.

Weakness in financial structures refers to a variety of circumstances ranging from the maturity structure and currency composition of international portfolio investment flows to the allocation and pricing of domestic credit through banking institutions. These weaknesses often arise in times of rapid financial liberalization and greater market competition, when banks are taking on new and unfamiliar risks on both the asset and the liability sides of balance sheets.

Weak supervisory and regulatory policies under these circumstances have also increased moral hazard by providing an incentive for financial institutions with low capital ratios to increase their risk positions in newly competitive environments, and allowing them to avoid full responsibility for mistakes in monitoring and evaluating risk. Further, deficiencies in accounting, disclosure and legal frameworks contribute to the problem because they allow financial institutions (or financial regulators) to disguise the extent of their difficulties. Governments have frequently failed to identify problem institutions quickly or to take prompt corrective action when a problem arises, resulting in a larger and more difficult crisis situation.

A general interpretation of these stylized features, put forward by the IMF (1998) report, is that a prolonged period of macroeconomic overheating – high inflation, large current account deficits, rapid credit growth, increased short-term capital inflows – together with recently liberalized financial systems, make the financial system vulnerable. Adverse economic developments, such as a rise in world interest rates or a fall in the terms of trade, capital inflows or asset prices, then strike an already vulnerable financial system. If the weakened financial situation is also faced with serious deficiencies in its institutional and regulatory environment, there is an increased likelihood that a banking crisis will develop. Deficiencies in the institutional and regulatory environment, in turn, are often associated with recent liberalization of the financial system undertaken without prior strengthening of the regulatory and accounting framework and bank supervision.

Specific Indicators of Vulnerability

Beyond these general qualitative features of banking crises, a few specific indicators that appear to precede them emerge from the literature. Few of these warning signs consistently predict crises, however, and often give false signals (that is, they predict a crisis during a tranquil period). The wide range of experiences surrounding banking crises, in terms of institutional and economic environments, belies any simple characterization.

The IMF (1998) report, using simple plots of the data, finds a number of characteristics which are broadly consistent with other studies. A rising ratio of broad money to narrow money (interpreted as an indication of financial liberalization) and a rapid growth of domestic credit (reflecting expansionary macroeconomic policies) often precede banking crises. Deposit growth and high real interest rates also tend to peak around the time of a banking crisis. The report finds that stock markets often decline and real activity tends to weaken about a year prior to a banking crisis. Stock market declines in these instances are accompanied by a drop-off in real-estate prices. By the time crises are underway, the report finds that output growth is significantly lower than its average during tranquil periods and stock prices are significantly lower.

Caprio and Klingebiel (1996) find that some set of macroeconomic factors was at least a contributing factor in all the bank crises in their sample (29 cases). Adverse terms of trade movements of at least 10 per cent preceded the bank crisis in most countries, as did a rapid and sometimes explosive loan growth. They also find that a fundamental weakness in financial structure played a prominent role in most banking crises. 'Weakness in financial structure' is defined in this context as a structure which: (a) provides incentives for banks to assume excessive risk; (b) allows lax accounting standards and ambiguous regulations about reporting problem loans; (c) maintains a system of weak government supervision of banking institutions (often politically motivated); and (d) allows political or other non-economic (for example, fraud) factors to influence lending decisions.

In their descriptive empirical work, Kaminsky and Reinhart (1996) argue that the asymmetric theory of banking crises – crises are most likely when bad news immediately follows a period of sustained high loan demand and sanguine expectations – is supported by the data. In particular, they present summary statistics which suggest that output growth and the stock market peak about a year before the beginning of a banking crisis. The stock market (and real-estate market) falls about a year prior to the banking crisis and continues a long and protracted decline. By the time the crisis begins, output growth slows significantly and a recession ensues. Real exchange rate appreciation and lending booms also tend to precede the onset of banking crises. A rising money multiplier and high real interest rates are also associated with banking crises, perhaps reflecting financial liberalization.

Operational Characteristics

The studies surveyed suggest that several macroeconomic and institutional variables may be correlated with banking crisis, with varying time lags.

One year or more prior to bank crisis

- Rapid domestic credit growth (IMF);
- rise in the ratio of broad to narrow money (IMF);
- real exchange rate appreciation (Kaminsky and Reinhart);

- stock market peak (Kaminsky and Reinhart);
- business cycle peak (Kaminsky and Reinhart);
- high real interest rates (Kaminsky and Reinhart);
- rising money multiplier (Kaminsky and Reinhart);
- financial structure weakness (Caprio and Klingebiel).

One year or less before the bank crisis

- Stock market and real estate market decline (IMF; Kaminsky and Reinhart);
- fall in economic activity relative to trend (IMF);
- rapid growth in bank lending (Caprio and Klingebiel);
- adverse movement in terms of trade (Caprio and Klingebiel).

Contemporaneous with the bank crisis

- Peak in deposit growth (IMF);
- peak in high real interest rates (IMF);
- output significantly below trend growth (IMF);
- stock market significantly below peak (IMF).

Our choice of macroeconomic variables employed in the statistical analysis of the third and fourth sections above was guided by the results from these studies.

NOTES

1. Hutchison is also Research Associate at the Center for Pacific Basin Monetary and Economic Studies (Federal Reserve Bank of San Francisco) and the Economic Policy Research Unit (University of Copenhagen). The authors thank the UC Pacific Rim Research Program, the International Centre for the Study of East Asian Development, and the UCSC Committee on Research and Division of Social Sciences for financial support. We are grateful to Rita Madarassy for her help in the data collection and preliminary analysis phase of this project.
2. See International Monetary Fund (1998) for a review of the literature.
3. This section draws on Cargill *et al.* (1997, 1998).
4. Japanese banks are permitted to hold equities in non-financial corporations. Bank equity holdings form an important part of the 'customer relationship system' or main bank system. Regulation permits 45 per cent of the latent capital gains (market value minus value at which equity was originally booked) to be counted toward Tier II bank capital. The fact that the majority of equities were obtained in the past and are carried on the balance sheet at historical cost means that the bank's balance sheet understates capital during a bubble phase because equities appreciate in value. This 'hidden' capital erodes, however, with the decline in stock prices.
5. The increases in the margin requirements on Nikkei futures trading in the Osaka

Securities Exchanges are commonly thought to have contributed to a decline in trading volumes in Osaka and an increase in trading volumes in Singapore, where the same product is traded.
6. Patrick (1998) provides an excellent discussion of the extent of the banking crisis in Japan and its effects on particular financial institutions.
7. The only exception is the United States. We date the Savings and Loan crisis in the United States from 1984, using the dating scheme of Caprio and Klingebiel (1996), rather than the Demirgüç-Kunt and Detragiache (1998) date of 1982. We find little support in the literature for a date as early as 1982. It is noteworthy, however, that our judgement in using the 1984 date weakens our empirical results in section 4.
8. The strikes variable is from Barro and Sala-i-Martin (1995) and the central bank independence variable is from Cukierman (1992).
9. These results are not reported to save space but are available from the authors upon request.

REFERENCES

Bank for International Settlements (1997), *Annual Report 1997*, Basle: BIS.
Barro, Robert J. and Xavier Sala-i-Martin (1995), *Economic Growth*, New York: McGraw-Hill.
Caprio, Gerald and Daniela Klingebiel (1996), 'Bank insolvencies: cross-country experiences', Washington, DC: World Bank, mimeo.
Cargill, Thomas F., Michael M. Hutchison and Takatoshi Ito (1997), *Political Economy of Japanese Monetary Policy*, Cambridge, MA: MIT Press.
Cargill, Thomas F., Michael M. Hutchison and Takatoshi Ito (1998), 'Preventing future bank crises in Japan', paper presented at a conference on 'Preventing Banking Crises: Analysis and Lessons from Recent Global Bank Failures,' sponsored by the Federal Reserve Bank of Chicago and the World Bank, Washington, DC: World Bank.
Cukierman, Alex (1992), *Central Bank Strategy, Credibility and Independence: Theory and Evidence*, Cambridge, MA: MIT Press.
Demirgüç-Kunt, Asli and Enrica Detragiache (1998), 'The determinants of banking crises in developing and developed countries', *IMF Staff Papers*, 45 (1): 81–109.
Eichengreen, Barry and Andrew Rose (1998), 'Staying afloat when the wind shifts: external factors and emerging-market banking crises', NBER Working Paper 6370, New York: National Bureau of Economic Research.
Hutchison, Michael M. (1997), 'Financial crises and bank supervision: new directions for Japan?', Federal Reserve Bank of San Francisco *Economic Letter* 97–37, 13 December.
International Monetary Fund (1998), 'Financial crises: characteristics and indicators of vulnerability', in *World Economic Outlook*, Washington, DC: IMF, ch. 4.
Kaminsky, Graciela and Carmen Reinhart (1996), 'The twin crises: the causes of banking and balance-of-payments crises', mimeo (February), Washington, DC: International Monetary Fund.
Kaminsky, Graciela, Saul Lizondo and Carmen Reinhart (1997), 'Leading indicators of currency crises', Working Paper WP/97/79, Washington, DC: International Monetary Fund.

Organization for Economic Cooperation and Development (1998), *Economic Outlook* (June), Paris: OECD.

Patrick, Hugh (1998), 'The Causes of Japan's Financial Crisis', Center on Japanese Economy and Business, Columbia University, Working Paper 146.

COMMENT ON HUTCHISON, McDILL AND MADRASSY

Eileen Mauskopf

A major goal of this paper is to quantify the probability of the onset of a banking crisis by looking at various economic and institutional characteristics of a country. It asks are there particular macroeconomic policies or macroeconomic developments, or institutional and regulatory factors, which have been common to banking crises in industrialized countries and which either precipitate a bank crisis or occur simultaneously with the onset of the crisis? If so, which are the most important factors? And can these factors predict retrospectively the onset of the Japanese banking crisis or, alternatively, is the Japanese crisis different in fundamental ways from bank crises that have occurred in other industrialized countries?

This is really an ambitious goal and an important task because if we are ever going to have a testable and usable theory of what triggers a banking crisis, we need to develop some quantitative models of the principal determinants of these crises. However, it is a difficult task and, to some extent, it requires that we oversimplify the events leading up to banking crises. If we think back over recent banking crises – even restricting the pool of crises to those of the industrialized countries alone – we know that despite factors common to many (such as financial deregulation, the consequent changes in the composition of bank portfolios; and the failure of prudential supervision to keep pace with the changes in the cyclicality and riskiness of the banks' asset holdings), there are also differences among the countries both in the precipitating factors and in the relative importance of the common factors.

For instance, in the US as in many other countries, the boom and bust sequence of the savings and loan institutions (and the banks to a lesser degree) was greatly influenced by the boom and bust cycle of commercial (and residential) real-estate markets. In many countries, financial deregulation provided the opportunity for banks to increase their exposure to the commercial real-estate industry. The greater availability of credit to this industry no doubt led to rapidly rising real-estate prices. But in the US, there was another important factor that contributed first to the rise and then to the demise of the real-estate bubble and the consequent fortunes of financial institutions. In the early 1980s Congress enacted very generous tax depreciation allowances for real estate; buildings were built which, even if they were never occupied, were still a worthwhile investment for some because the 'tax losses' on these buildings (which generally were well in excess of the true losses) could be used to shield other unrelated income from taxation. So we had an enormous building boom, and doctors and lawyers (and other such entities!) were buying factories and hotels, and financial institutions were happily lending (sometimes more than 100 per cent of the cost) and even taking equity positions in real-estate development. In 1986, however, the tax scam was sufficiently well known that Congress felt obliged to clamp down by passing the so-called 'passive-loss' provisions, which basically said that you could not offset the income tax you owe on your wage with the loss (whether a real loss or a loss on paper only) you had from some real-estate holding if that holding was incidental to the way you earned your living. The passive-loss provisions accelerated the subsequent collapse of the commercial real-estate market, a collapse that was probably inevitable given the enormous amount of overbuilding by then. (Interestingly enough, though, bank lending for real-estate ventures did not peak until a few years after the passive-loss rules became law, further contributing to the stock of empty office buildings.) Although other countries appear to have liberalized tax depreciation allowances around the same time as the US or shortly thereafter, the subsequent reversal of the real-estate tax law in the US appears not to have occurred elsewhere (or at least not widely) and therefore is not going to contribute to the explanation of why the real-estate bubble burst, and with it the fortunes of financial institutions. But exactly what precipitates a banking crisis may depend on just such idiosyncratic factors. Ignoring these factors or bundling them up in broad terms – like financial deregulation or a collapse in asset prices – could obscure the important details in the evolution of the crisis. This, of course, is an inevitable compromise in economic models of all sorts and ultimately how well a model predicts tells us whether the omitted details and idiosyncratic factors are more important than the common quantifiable factors.

Notwithstanding the inherent difficulty of the task, the authors are to be complimented for trying to sort through the myriad details that characterize these crises in order to isolate the common factors and to quantify the effect these common factors have on the probability of the onset of a banking crisis. In this regard, the paper is an important contribution to a new and relatively sparse literature. It is also reassuring in that the paper confirms the results of other recent studies – that indeed there are factors which appear to be common to the onset of a banking crisis – specifically a fall in stock prices and a currency depreciation. At the same time, the authors note that factors cited by others as commonly occurring just prior to or around the onset of a banking crisis – such as rapid growth of real GDP and credit – are not statistically significant in their own analysis of the industrialized countries' banking crises.

Although I applaud the authors' efforts, I am left with a less than satisfied feeling that the probit regressions are going to help me predict future banking crises. Part of my unease is due to what I have already mentioned: that trying to fit very complicated temporal relationships between institutional structures, macroeconomic policies and circumstances into probability models of banking failures may lose a lot of the richness and diversity of the crises. How well *this* particular model does is hard to say. First, in a regression that relates the probability of a crisis to the state of the economy one year prior to the onset of the crisis, not a single macroeconomic indicator is statistically significant. *So the model is not useful in real time as a predictor of future crises.* The authors are most successful in estimating a *contemporaneous* relationship between the macroeconomy and the onset of a banking crisis, although, as they note, this begs the question of causation. However, even here, it is hard to gauge the ability of the model to forecast crises properly. The reported measure of the goodness of fit, a 'pseudo R^2' says nothing about the model's ability to predict the onset of a banking crisis. The moderately high R^2 (0.38) may only mean that the model is pretty good at predicting the absence of the onset of a bank crisis. That is, given that only 7 out of 225 or 237 observations are associated with the onset of a banking crisis, a relatively high R^2 can be achieved if the model generally predicts a low probability of a banking crisis and *never correctly predicts the onset of a crisis*. The reported measure of the goodness of fit is not an informative measure. The authors acknowledge this, but they need to go further and provide alternative information: at the very least, they should show, for each of the seven banking crises, the model's predicted probabilities over time for the onset of the crisis. These probabilities were given for Japan and they should be provided for other countries also. Only with this information can we tell how useful this model is.

There are some methodological issues that are a bit troubling. First, the authors rightly acknowledge the difficulty in dating the onset of a banking crisis. Yet the nature of this probit analysis requires that they pick a starting date. To do so, they use a set of criteria proposed by others that are arguably somewhat arbitrary: for instance, a crisis would be deemed to exist if the ratio of non-performing assets to total assets is greater than 2 per cent of GDP. Suppose this criterion were modified so that the critical ratio is 1.5 or 2.5 per cent. Does that alter either the number of countries identified as having a crisis or the year currently identified as the onset of the crisis? If it alters either of these, by how much do the regression results change? That is, how robust are the results – both the statistical significance of, and the estimated contribution of, the common determinants to the probability of crisis? Confidence in the model would increase if the estimation results were robust to small changes in the criteria used to identify a banking crisis.

Second, because the main interest in this paper is how well the model predicts the onset of the banking crisis in Japan, it would be preferable if the model had been estimated on data that *excluded* Japan and then used the results to predict the probabilities of a banking crisis for Japan. In general, if we look at time series models, how well the model does should be determined by its out-of-sample predictions. Similarly, for cross-sectional data, *the object of interest should not be included in the data used to estimate the model*. Sometimes these conventions are not very important – for instance, if you are interested in the forecasts of some variable for, say, 1997 and 1998 and your estimation period extends from 1950 to 1998, chances are good that the estimated relationship will not be particularly sensitive to the inclusion or exclusion of the 1997 and 1998 observations in the estimation period. But, in this paper, there are only seven observations of an onset of a banking crisis and therefore any one of the seven can in theory heavily influence the estimated relationship. So it would be preferable to see both how different the estimation results would be if Japan were excluded from the estimation base and how well the resulting model would do in predicting the onset of the Japanese banking crisis. I am concerned that the results could be quite different and that the model's forecast that there was a 50 per cent probability that a banking crisis would occur in Japan in 1992 (the year it is identified as having begun) may be unduly influenced by the inclusion of Japan in the sample period. That is because, as the authors note, virtually all of that 50 per cent probability is due to the very sharp decline in Japanese equity prices in 1992 (by about 24 per cent, from the end of December 1991 to the end of December 1992). The estimated model (when Japan is included) indicates that contemporaneous declines in equity prices are the most statistically significant of the economic variables in determining the onset of a crisis. Would contemporaneous declines in stock price be so strongly associated with the onset of a banking crisis if the Japanese experience in 1992 were to be excluded from the estimation period? And, if not, would the model have any predictive ability in identifying the Japanese banking crisis or would we instead conclude that the Japanese experience is highly idiosyncratic?

Some of the explanatory variables in the probit analysis – both those that are statistically significant and those that are not – seem somewhat strange or ill-defined. Are riots really associated with the probability of banking crises in *industrialized* countries? Are these riots related to bank runs or all sorts of things? Undoubtedly, the US is the most violent of the industrialized countries, but the only recent riot I can think of was the Los Angeles riot when Rodney King was abused by the police force. It is hard to make a connection between that and the probability of a banking crisis here. More importantly, many of the economic variables need to be adjusted or scaled to be more meaningful. For instance, the authors find that neither the rate of real GDP growth nor the rate of credit growth appears to be significant in determining the onset of a banking crisis. But GDP growth by itself, when comparing countries, is pretty meaningless. It is better to think of actual GDP growth relative to potential GDP growth; only then can one come up with an unambiguous measure of excessive growth. Similarly, shouldn't credit growth be measured relative to nominal GDP growth to make sense of its magnitude? A rapidly growing country can support rapid credit growth without necessarily risking financial fragility and breakdown. Is it nominal or real exchange rate depreciation or both that seems to be an important determinant of banking crises? Finally, the authors need to beef up their set of explanatory variables. Somewhat surprisingly, real-estate price changes were not included among the explanatory variables despite the importance of real-estate as collateral in industrialized countries. As it stands now, the probit analysis says that countries with labour unrest, less independent central banks and crashing stock markets (and, to a lesser extent, exchange rate depreciations) have a higher probability of banking crises. That is just not very informative. For policy-makers, the theory needs to be richer, more precise and more specific in the timing and sequence of events. Otherwise, this and similar models may predict crises that never occur and fail to predict those that do.

Let me turn briefly to an issue that was raised but somewhat short-changed in the paper: why is the Japanese banking crisis still going on? From the viewpoint of an American investor interested in Japanese equities, it has been surprising that Japanese companies have for some ten years now been earning rates of return – measured as dividends plus capital gains, divided by the capitalization values – that are sharply lower than those earned by US corporations. No doubt, a big part of the difference reflects the fact that the US economy has been booming during much of this time while the Japanese economy has been stagnating. But taking a longer perspective, say starting in 1980 and going through 1997, the rate of return on US equity has averaged around

16 per cent, compared to about 7 per cent on Japanese equity. The discrepancies between the US and the Japanese rates of return remain even after correcting for the effect of extensive cross-holdings of corporate equity in Japan and even after adjusting for the lower rate of inflation in Japan.

One question would have to be: to what extent do differences between the two countries in corporate governance account for the differences in shareholder returns? Corporate governance is really remarkably different in the US and Japan. Research, including that of my colleagues at the Federal Reserve Board – particularly Michael Gibson, has shown that equity ownership in Japan is dominated by insider stakeholders: lenders, customers and suppliers who have financial or product market relationships with the firm. Managers of the firm are more beholden to these insider stakeholders than to the outsider shareholders, and as a result profit maximization – which would benefit outsider shareholders – is not the exclusive, nor most important, consideration of the managers. *The data show that insider stakeholders are especially dominant in the financial sector.*

Relative to the US, Japanese managers are also insulated from shareholder pressure for profit maximization by the smaller representation of institutional shareholders among total outside shareholders. In the US, pressure from institutional investors is much more likely to get management's attention because they are the ones who can vote *en masse*. Japanese institutional shareholders are both small in number and have no history of pressuring firms to maximize shareholder returns. Japanese managers are also insulated from pressure by the firm's board of directors because Japanese boards are dominated by company insiders.

Again, relative to the US, there is a very limited market for corporate control in Japan, as measured by the value of mergers scaled by GDP. Takeovers appear to be incompatible with the Japanese system of long-term relationships with suppliers and customers, and, in addition, would be difficult to effect because of the pervasive system of cross-shareholding.

These differences in corporate governance would seem to account for some of the divergence between equity returns in the US and Japan. But more important to the issue at hand is the role of the Japanese corporate governance traditions in the stagnation and seemingly catatonic state of the Japanese economy and the Japanese banking system.

REPLY TO MAUSKOPF

Michael Hutchison

Some basic problems remain (for example, not that many crises in industrial countries, not a forecasting model, and so on). However, we could address some of your other points. In particular, (a) we estimated the model 'out of sample' (excluding Japan) and presented the Japan predictions; (b) we tried your suggested measures of credit and real GDP; (c) we reported predictions for all the countries experiencing banking crises; (d) we dropped the riots variable (I couldn't come up with a good story, as you note, for the industrial countries and the timing of the LA riots doesn't fit – neither the recent ones nor the Watts riot!). We have made a number of other editorial and smaller statistical changes.

7. Crisis? What crisis? The policy response to Japan's banking crisis

Jenny Corbett

INTRODUCTION

In the process of the economic slowdown and, ultimately, recession which has occurred in the Japanese economy since 1991, a great deal of attention has been focused on the banking crisis. Even international commentary has created the impression that the crisis is not only unusual but that it is particularly severe and has been handled in a noticeably inept fashion. In all these judgements the implicit comparators are not stated. Yet a recent IMF book on banking crises (Lindgren *et al.* 1996) has pointed out that in the 1980s and 1990s over 130 countries, nearly three-quarters of the members of the IMF, have experienced some degree of financial difficulty. Of those, 36 countries were classified as experiencing bank 'crises'. Importantly, these were not all developing and emerging markets. Several of them were industrialized countries with well-developed bank supervision regimes and standard regulatory structures. It is all the more remarkable, therefore, that there are so few attempts to make international comparisons when considering the Japanese banking problem and to search for lessons from other experiences. As happens so frequently in studies of Japan, the US Savings and Loans crisis of the early 1980s has usually been assumed to be the only valid comparable example.

The general analysis of banking crises has been expanding rapidly and there are now a number of studies of the causes of a crisis. There are fewer, but still a significant number of studies, on defining and measuring the severity of crises and still fewer on analysing the responses to crises. This paper cannot consider all these issues and concentrates only on the latter.

The title of the paper is not intended to imply that there is no banking crisis in Japan. Its purpose is to highlight the perception that Japanese policy-makers have been denying that a crisis exists and taking no policy action in response to what they have claimed is a non-existent problem. The paper seeks to put in perspective the Japanese response by examining what has been done and when. It also asks the question whether the popular perception that Japanese policy-makers have reacted inappropriately is correct. To answer that question the paper proposes a method for 'benchmarking' policy against both theoretical and empirical criteria.

The first section of the paper describes the difficulties in identifying crises. The point is to show that Japanese policy-makers are not alone in wanting to delay action until the severity of a crisis is clear. Policy inaction may be costly but policy responses also have costs. Despite this point, many observers would argue that by 1994 or 1995 the deterioration in the banking sector was so clear that policy-makers could have responded on the basis that the direction of change was clear. This point is borne out by the empirical work of Hutchison, McDill and Madrassy (Chapter 6 in this volume).

The two subsequent sections survey the empirical and theoretical literature which assesses the success of different rescue packages. From the survey the paper extracts five policy areas which make up the sum of the rescue packages in banking crises. The first three policy areas apply to the handling of failed, or insolvent, banks and consist of rules for:

- bankruptcy procedures;
- asset management of failed institutions;
- depositor protection.

The last two areas relate to the handling of still-solvent banks with a significant amount of bad loans. These are:

- recapitalization;
- cleaning balance sheets.

Within these policy areas there are a number of contrasts between theoretical propositions and observed policy operations. The most notable of these are:

- On closure ('bankruptcy') of banks there is a contrast between theory and practical policy advice. Theoretical models can lead to the counter-intuitive suggestion that *ex ante soft* policy may have better incentive effects on banks' desire to continue rolling over bad loans while the clear-cut policy advice provided by international organizations is that tough closure policies are desirable.

- Whatever agency takes over the management of the assets of failed banks must have incentives to undertake workouts of bad loans rather than roll them over. There is no clear evidence on the superiority of particular institutions. Empirical studies draw completely contrary conclusions on whether central banks can be successful.
- Depositor protection may in theory be a contributing factor to moral hazard in bank lending but in practice no crisis country has inflicted significant losses on depositors. Other stakeholders in banks (management, shareholders and creditors) should, in principle, bear some of the burden but again practices have varied significantly.
- Unconditional recapitalization is never optimal but there is little agreement on the type of conditionality which should apply. Theory suggests that verifiable actions should form the main conditions but practical policy advice has been limited to comments on the forms of refinancing (long versus short, debt versus equity).
- Optimal policy for cleaning balance sheets depends, in theory, on how much information asymmetry exists between banks and regulators, how much incentive there is for banks to roll over loans (hide the quality of their balance sheets) and how many borrowers-in-default are non-viable. Leaving debt on banks' balance sheets ('self-reliance') can be optimal under some circumstances. While earlier policy advice (particularly to economies in transition) tended to favour debt cancellation, IMF advice favours transfer combined with a tough workout policy.

The final sections of the paper describe the key characteristics of Japan's policy responses so far, and compares them with benchmarks derived from the empirical and theoretical literature. The paper concludes that by empirical 'best practice' standards, such as they are, Japan may perhaps be regarded as moving in the right direction and scoring a medium grade against the benchmarks. There remain doubts about the crucial aspects of (a) the design of *ex ante* bank closure policies; (b) policies to clean banks' balance sheets; (c) incentive-compatible recapitalization policies; and (d) policies which will induce the optimal degree of bad debt workouts.

1. WHAT DO WE KNOW ABOUT BANKING CRISES: WHEN IS A CRISIS NOT A CRISIS?

It may seem obvious that policy authorities will know when a banking crisis is occurring, but in fact one of the most compelling explanations for the observed 'forbearance' of policy authorities (that is, a period in which nothing is done about growing banking difficulties) is that it is quite difficult to establish when balance sheet problems in some banks threaten to become a systemic banking crisis. Yet all policy advice (see below, pp. 196–8) assumes that rescue policies are inappropriate except in cases of threatened systemic crises. At the same time policy authorities are urged to act *before* a crisis actually becomes systemic. Identifying the development of a crisis is obviously crucial.

At a general level it is clear that there is in fact little agreement on when banking problems become a crisis. A survey of the definitions of a crisis offered in the main empirical studies highlights the difficulty. Sundararajan and Balino (1991: 3) offer five definitions, drawing upon literature published between 1904 and 1986. Only one of the five refers to banks becoming insolvent and to banks collapsing. The definition which they settle on for their own study is when:

> a significant group of financial institutions have liabilities exceeding the market value of their assets, leading to runs and other portfolio shifts, collapse of some financial firms, and government intervention. Thus the term crisis refers to a situation in which [various causes lead to] generalized solvency problems in a financial system, and lead to liquidation, mergers, or restructuring.

Clearly, this is a definition which can only be applied with hindsight and, indeed, after the crisis is full-blown. It is not a definition which policy authorities would want to rely on to determine when to intervene. By the time all these features have been observed, intervention would be too late.

Caprio and Klingebiel (1996: 84) acknowledge that 'since banks are opaque, defining what constitutes a crisis or systemic event is inherently subjective'. They note:

> There are three general types of bank insolvency: those limited to a single or a small number of banks . . .; overt banking system runs; and a more silent form of financial distress. Overt runs happen suddenly and end quickly. Financial distress of the banking system, when a significant portion of the system is insolvent but remains open, is perhaps the most pernicious . . . Financial distress can persist for years.

Their definition is narrowed 'to the case in which the net worth of the banking system has been almost or entirely eliminated ... it should be easy to agree that if the banking system is insolvent ... then the problem is systemic'. On the basis of this definition, which in concrete terms means assuming that unprovisioned non-performing loans measuring 5–10 per cent of total loans would usually be enough to eliminate bank capital, they included Japan amongst the 69 countries judged to have systemic bank problems.

Lindgren *et al.* (1996: 9) state that:

> A sound banking system may be defined as one in which most banks are solvent ... Solvency is reflected in the positive net worth of a bank ... in other words the distance between soundness and insolvency can be gauged in terms of capitalization ... It is difficult to precisely classify a banking system as 'sound' or 'unsound' because there is no benchmark measure of systemic insolvency ... Obviously, a high reported level of nonperforming loans would indicate fragility. However, there is always an element of judgement in projecting and valuing uncertain future returns ... In addition, owners and managers of unsound banks have incentives to ... show loans as performing in order not to lose their bank ... These weaknesses in information explain why banking problems emerge with little apparent warning.

They give a useful survey of what these difficulties mean for the problem of predicting bank solvency problems but conclude that, so far, studies have been largely case-study based and qualitative in nature. The lessons from the studies available at their time of writing were country-specific rather than general (though evidence has been supplemented more formally since by Demirgüç-Kunt and Detragiache 1997; and Hutchison *et al.* Chapter 6 in this volume). For their own operational definition they return to Sundararajan and Balino (1991: 1) and define crises as cases where there were runs or other substantial portfolio shifts, collapses of financial firms or massive government intervention. Extensive unsoundness short of a crisis is termed 'significant' but fails to constitute crisis. On this basis Japan in 1995–6 was considered to have 'significant' problems but not a crisis (in contrast to Caprio and Klingebiel 1996).

It is obvious that there is no agreed-upon definition of exactly when a system is in crisis, but worse, that even if there were, serious difficulties would arise in collecting reliable data in advance of the crisis becoming systemic. Compounding the difficulty for policy-makers, there is also no agreement on measures of how bad a crisis has become. It is not clear, for example, whether systemic crises can be more or less severe and whether all systemic crises, regardless of their severity, require intervention.

Corbett (1999) uses a number of benchmarks to measure severity, including profitability, provisioning, bad loans and lending to real-estate, to place Japan among a sample of eight crisis countries. That paper also used the severity of the decline in credit growth at the bottom of the crisis cycle as a measure and observes that a lack of internationally comparable data made measurement of severity extremely difficult. It is clear from that study that there is no generally accepted empirical indicator of the severity of a crisis. However, the paper ventures the conclusion that up until 1996 a limited set of indicators would place Japan only in the middle range of severity when compared with a group of industrialized countries which Lindgren *et al.* (1996) classified as experiencing crises.

2. POLICIES FOR RECOVERY: HOW DO WE ASSESS RESCUE PLANS?

Given the difficulties of crisis identification, it is perhaps understandable that any individual country will be slow to react. However, it is fairly remarkable that of the large number of countries experiencing crises relatively few have undertaken systemic bank restructuring programmes. Alexander *et al.* (1997), following up the study by Lindgren *et al.* (1996), claim that only 30 members of the IMF have undertaken such programmes (of the 133 member countries with banking problems) over the last 15 years. This is the more remarkable because of the frequency of bank rescues (c.f. Goodhart and Schoenmaker 1995). This section considers the question of how to assess the appropriateness of policy put into place once a banking problem has been identified.

There have been a number of studies of banking sector restructuring (Sundararajan and Balino 1991; Goodhart and Schoenmaker 1995; Caprio and Klingebiel 1996; Sheng 1996; Alexander *et al.* 1997) but only Alexander *et al.* attempt to draw clear policy lessons about the design of restructuring measures. These studies are descriptive and do not attempt to link empirical observation with the growing theoretical literature which tries to shed light on the effects of, and optimal design for, restructuring policies. Nevertheless, it is useful to describe briefly their findings about a broad range of experience with restructuring policies.

Sundararajan and Balino (1991: 1) look at seven countries experiencing crises in the 1980s (all countries which might be termed emerging markets). In drawing lessons about the design of rescue policies they conclude that the 'detailed institutional arrangements ... such as whether to set up a separate agency for asset recovery – will vary according to factors specific to the situation ... However, the chosen arrangement should preserve transparency and avoid shifting the losses to the central bank.' The implication is that there are few general lessons about policy design which can be gained from considering past experience. However, they do attempt to establish objectives for rescue policies which stress restoring bank viability and minimizing cost to the government. Other authors also cite these as key criteria.

Goodhart and Schoenmaker (1995) survey 104 bank failures in 24 developed countries from the 1980s to the early 1990s and find that about two-thirds were rescued one way or another (while only one-third were liquidated). Of the methods for dealing with failing banks 45 cases involved rescue packages or the use of special administrations to run failed banks; that is, a degree of direct government intervention. Their main concern was to determine, given the available evidence, which institution was most capable of carrying out rescues. The authors also evaluate potential conflicts between the aims of rescue operations and the monetary policy objectives of central banks. They conclude that the frequency of bank failures is not strongly related to whether or not there is a separation of central banking from banking supervision. Since central banks usually retain responsibility for stability of the monetary system and lender of last resort facilities they will want some involvement with the supervision role even if it is formally separated.

Caprio and Klingebiel (1996) provide data on 69 countries experiencing crises and give details of recovery policies for a subset of 26 countries. They also score all the countries' success in the restructuring exercises against four macroeconomic criteria (financial deepening, development of real credit, real deposit interest rates, recurrent problems) and find that few countries handle crises well. As with Goodhart and Schoenmaker (1995), however, they do not attempt to analyse whether some types of rescue measures were either more successful or less costly than others.

Dziobek and Pazarasioglu (1997) in Alexander *et al.*, provide a descriptive analysis of 24 countries' rescue packages with useful details concerning the types of policy used. They use the data to try to spell out 'best practice' policy towards bank restructuring. To do this they assess which policies seem to have permitted countries to make 'substantial' progress (in the areas of restoring banking system viability (six indicators), and which help to restore intermediation capacity and an appropriate level of banking services relative to the GDP (six indicators)) compared with the policies used by countries which made only 'moderate' or 'slow' progress. They conclude that there are 12 features which constitute best practice:

1. a comprehensive approach correcting not just immediate problems but accounting, legal and regulatory problems in banking;
2. prompt action: speed is of the essence. Countries using some form of prompt corrective action (PCA) do better;
3. operational restructuring of the banks themselves which directly address management deficiencies;
4. a designated lead agency which should coordinate and implement systemic bank restructuring and should have some degree of autonomy. The lead agency should be separate from the central bank (in contrast to the finding of Goodhart and Schoenmaker) but Deposit Insurance Corporations (DICs) have been successful;
5. continuous monitoring of the process;
6. central bank liquidity support may be needed but it should not provide long-term finance to banks;
7. firm exit policies: policy should avoid the 'too big to fail' syndrome;
8. government financial support of insolvent banks is unavoidable but bond transfers and other financial instruments are not always successful. The support needs to be incentive-compatible;
9. loss-sharing should be a principle, though in practice few countries impose losses on depositors. DICs funded by private banks are one mechanism to achieve this;
10. removing non-performing loans from banks' balance sheets and transferring them to a separate loan recovery agency is effective;
11. loan workouts, which can be done either by central organizations or loan collection agencies tied to individual banks. No strong case exists for a particular institutional setup;
12. positive economic growth also helps.

3. THE THEORY OF RESCUES AND CLEANING UP BAD LOANS

The main conclusion to be drawn from this survey of empirical studies is that there is no agreed framework for assessing the success or appropriateness of policy responses to banking crises. None of the studies has been designed to test hypotheses about policy design or effectiveness and each has been carried out with a different set of initial questions and a different set of criteria for policy success. This section of the paper, therefore, turns to three important theoretical works which address the best design of rescue policy. It should prove useful to add whatever theoretical insights we can draw to the purely empirical understanding provided by the literature above. Theoretical work has been rather sparse despite the recent frequency of bank crises and bailouts. Aghion *et al.* (1998) make the point that rescue policies have generally been *ad hoc* and have not had institutional or legal support. Policy-makers have not had theoretical analysis available to help in the design of policy.

The theoretical works surveyed here, against which a later section measures Japan's performance, cover two particularly important areas of bank rescue strategy. The first is the issue of when policy-makers should intervene in the running of failing banks and liquidate them (or remove managers) and when they should rescue them by recapitalization. The second area is the choice of strategies used to clean potentially solvent banks' balance sheets.

Two papers address the question of bank rescue (a 'passive' strategy which normally does not affect the management of the bank) versus intervention by supervisors to close or restructure a bank (an active, or tough policy). Mitchell (1998a: i) analyses the choices that banks make to roll over quite passively any loans in default versus a policy that pursues their claims; and the choices regulators make to 'punish' passive and insolvent banks versus the attempt to rescue them. In her paper she states:

> Banks may choose to roll over loans in order to hide their poor financial conditions or to gamble for resurrection. Regulators can reduce creditor passivity through their *ex ante* choice of monitoring capability and their *ex post* choice of policy for distressed banks. Yet, if too many banks are discovered to be passive or insolvent, a situation labelled 'too-many-to-fail' (TMTF) may arise, whereby it is less costly to rescue than to close large numbers of banks. Banks may implicitly collude through their choice of actions in order to trigger TMTF. A principal result of the analysis is that when the regulator reacts to the threat of banks triggering TMTF, it is by 'softening'. One form of softening involves lowering the *ex ante* monitoring capacity and 'punishing' a smaller number of banks *ex post*. More undetected passivity will thus exist in equilibrium than if TMTF could not be triggered.

Although the optimal policy in the face of this type of problem is not spelled out, it is clear that banks have incentives to roll over debt. The possibilities for banks are, however, even richer:

> When banks are faced with default on their balance sheets, they choose between being 'passive' or 'active'. A choice of passivity is a decision to passively reschedule loans ... A choice to be active is a decision to actively

recover the outstanding debt, either through out-of-court workout or through a formal bankruptcy proceeding.   (Ibid.: iii)

Banks may choose passivity either to avoid signalling their poor financial condition, to 'gamble for resurrection', or to attempt to trigger TMTF. Since bank behaviour will be the result of both the severity of monitoring by regulators and the expected *ex post* policy towards insolvency, insolvent banks will always choose passivity to avoid revealing their financial state. Solvent banks may also choose passivity as a gamble for resurrection or to trigger TMTF:

> Thus in economies where TMTF is a threat, it may be impossible to establish tough prudential regulations without risking a bailout of the entire banking system. The equilibrium choice of monitoring capability and *ex post* policy will depend on the proportion of distressed banks expected to be insolvent, the costs of recapitalising banks, and the likelihood that banks will implicitly collude to trigger TMTF.   (Ibid.: iv)

The likelihood that monitoring will be softened and that a smaller number of banks will be recapitalized rises with each of these.

Aghion *et al.* (1998) extend Mitchell's model to ask (a) when and whether to bail out a failing bank; and (b) if a bailout is desirable, how to bail out the bank. Their objective is to design a bailout scheme which preserves bank managers' incentives to liquidate defaulting borrowers while keeping the bailout bill as small as possible. In this version of the model the assumption of informational asymmetry between the regulators and the banks takes on greater significance. Regulators cannot observe exactly what proportion of bad loans banks carry because they do not know which borrowers are in default. Only banks have this information and can, as a result, cover up the true extent of their problems; they can misrepresent the true net worth of the bank. Since actual defaults can be observed, banks which want to misrepresent the net worth of the bank do this by extending further loans to problem borrowers:

> Once it is recognized that bank managers can delay insolvency by hiding the extent of their bank's loan losses and that they may refrain from liquidating bad loans in an attempt to hide loan losses it should be clear that strict bank closure rules requiring the closure of any insolvent bank may be counterproductive. Such rules may simply induce bank managers to hide the size of their loan losses for as long as they can.   (Aghion *et al.* 1998: 2)

The result of the analysis is initially somewhat puzzling but can be understood in the light of this quote. Their results show that:

a tough recapitalisation policy in which the bank manager is always dismissed results ... in the bank managers rolling over bad loans in order to conceal the extent of their loan losses and therefore in the softening of the firms' budget constraints. Vice-versa, a soft approach to recapitalisation (in which the manager of a failing bank is not dismissed) encourages her to take an overly tough approach to firm liquidations, while exaggerating her own recapitalisation requirements. (Ibid.: 3)

The interesting result here is that when the banking system as a whole is known by the government to be in crisis, a soft bailout policy is preferable to a tough one because the cost of not sufficiently liquidating the loans of defaulting borrowers is greater than the cost of excessive recapitalization which deflects managerial incentives into overstating the needs of more solvent banks. Since the policy trade-off only arises because the government cannot distinguish the true net worth of banks, a policy which encourages banks to reveal their true state is better than either the simple 'soft' or 'tough' policy. One method for achieving this which Aghion *et al.* (1998) suggest is to make recapitalization depend on the observable (by the regulators) action (by the banks) of carrying out liquidations. This is effectively a policy of recapitalizing by buying bad loans on a non-linear pricing formula. The first tranche of liquidations are paid a lower price than the next tranche. This discourages banks with only a small proportion of bad loans from applying for recapitalization and enables regulators to distinguish banks with a lot of bad debt from those with only a little.

Aghion *et al.* (1998) point out that the counterintuitive result that soft policy dominates tough differs from some other literature which recommends tough policy (on moral hazard grounds) precisely because the information asymmetry creates the incentive for banks to cover up their real problem. In a full information model this would not arise. They note that this asymmetry is more likely to be a problem in economies in transition, for which their model was developed, than in other cases. However, it is so commonly observed that banks do behave in this way, and so commonly asserted in the case of Japan that the true extent of bad loans cannot be known, that this does not seem an unduly strict assumption. Mitchell's original result adds another reason why tough policies may fail: the possibility that they will induce banks to be passive towards loans in order to trigger the TMTF problem.

The other area where theory has begun to clarify policy options relates to the methods for cleaning the balance sheets of potentially solvent banks. An early paper by Mitchell (1998b, originally 1995) produced the first analysis of trade-offs between different strategies to clean banks' balance sheets of bad debts. It uses a three-tier hierarchy, consisting of regulators, banks and firms, to analyse three types of policies that have been advocated: debt cancellation; debt transfer to 'hospital' or bad-debt banks; and 'self-reliance', which leaves debt on the books of banks. The analysis identifies direct effects of policies on bank behaviour and indirect effects on firm behaviour as a function of the banks' response. The analysis demonstrates that differing policies applied to financially distressed banks have differing real effects on firms' and banks' assets. The paper is thus able to spell out conditions under which each policy would be optimal.

The model considers the government's choice of policy, followed by the banks' choice of whether to roll over or 'work out' (whether through liquidation or restructuring of firms) the debts in default. If banks roll over debt, inefficient firms continue in business but, worse, the managers of non-viable firms have the opportunity to dissipate assets through mismanagement. The model is intended to describe the economies in transition in which managers of state-owned firms may engage in the theft of assets. In the context of other economies, however, the same result could be achieved by allowing managers to continue to appropriate assets or to diminish the value of firms in the usual principal–agent manner because of a lack of effective governance. The government's objective function should be to maximize the value of banks' and firms' assets. The direct costs of policy arise from issuing government debt to recapitalize banks, but since the improved banks' balance sheets enter the government's objective function these costs disappear. Ultimately, the costs of bad policy come from the cost of creating the wrong incentives for banks to roll over the debt of defaulters and to allow asset dissipation to occur. The result of the analysis is that:

1. debt cancellation is better than self-reliance if the default rate is high because banks will roll over rather than work out debt under a self-reliance approach. If asset dissipation by non-viable firms as a direct result of debt cancellation is not too high, then debt cancellation could be preferred to self-reliance even when banks do work out these bad debts;
2. debt transfer is better than self-reliance only if the default rate is high (so that banks will be inclined to roll over, not to work out, debt) since it is assumed that bad debt banks (asset management companies) will always be worse at workouts than will commercial banks (because the latter are assumed to have inside information about defaulters);
3. debt transfer will be better than debt cancellation if the bad debt

bank is fairly good at workouts and debt cancellation does not reduce asset dissipation by viable firms.

This allows a specification of the conditions under which each policy would be the optimal choice:

- debt cancellation would be optimal if all bad debtors were viable and there was no dissipation of assets by bad debtors (that is, the default was not very 'bad' and there was a greater risk of excess liquidation);
- debt transfers would be optimal if the bad debt bank was effective at workouts and it could prevent asset dissipation when it did the workouts;
- self-reliance would be optimal if commercial banks agreed to fewer rollovers than the bad debt bank and all bad debtors were non-viable (so there would be no risk of excessive liquidation).

4. JAPAN'S PERFORMANCE

This section considers how Japan's policy has developed over the course of the 1990s, while the next section tries to judge how the changes look in the light of the empirical and theoretical literature surveyed above.

Table A7.1 (pp. 214–22) shows the development of policy towards the growing banking crisis from 1991, when banks first showed signs of difficulty. After surveying the theoretical literature, five broad areas emerge as important when attempting to find some general patterns in these changing, *ad hoc* policies:

1. the legal basis for closing or restructuring banks: that is, dealing with the question of who should close failing banks and on what grounds;
2. the decisions about who should take over the assets and liabilities of institutions which fail, who should carry out loan workouts of bad debts and how to ensure that viable borrowers are protected;
3. the degree of protection to be offered to depositors in failing institutions: this question has implications both for 'moral hazard' issues and for the incentives for depositors, shareholders and other creditors to monitor banks;
4. the degree of recapitalization support for banks with bad loans but which are not expected to fail;
5. the method of cleaning balance sheets of non-failing banks.

The theoretical literature demonstrates that all these areas are inter-linked because of their effects on bank incentives and behaviour, but it is useful to have some mechanisms for considering broad categories of policy changes. The first three policy areas apply mainly to insolvent or failing institutions while the last two apply more to solvent banks which are continuing in business.

Policy falls fairly naturally into two periods: the 'pre-crisis' period of growing fragility, from 1991 to mid-1994, and a 'crisis' period from late 1994 onwards, although, as noted above (p. 194), there are difficulties in deciding when problems become a crisis.

Pre-crisis

Consider the policy developments in the five areas outlined above.

(a) Bankruptcy
Regarding the legal basis for closing financial institutions, the striking feature is that there was no mechanism for supervisory agencies to undertake reorganizations or to initiate bankruptcy proceedings. Any such action had to be initiated by the institution itself, its shareholders or its depositors. As a result there was also no clear basis for taking such action. Aghion *et al.* (1998) note that the lack of bankruptcy procedures for banks is not uncommon although they also comment that: 'it is generally up to the regulators to decide how to deal with an insolvent bank and regulators have by and large too much discretion and little guidance on how best to restructure or liquidate' (Aghion *et al.* 1998: 1). It followed from this situation in Japan that some guidelines set by supervisory agencies had no legal force. For example, compliance with BIS capital adequacy standards was a voluntary matter. Failure to comply carried no regulatory penalty, although banks operating in foreign markets were penalized by their inability to raise funds if *their* credit ratings were affected.

(b) Management of assets after failure
As a consequence of the first point, there was no clear position on who, or what institution, would take over the assets and liabilities of failing institutions. By implication, since the initiation of liquidation was a private matter, the takeover of a viable business and the workout of bad debt would be left to whatever private institution (normally another bank) became involved. In practice, since policy was geared to pre-venting financial collapses, arranged takeovers and mergers were the usual solution.

(c) Depositor protection

There was ostensibly a limited degree of depositor protection provided by the Deposit Insurance Corporation (only deposits up to 10 million yen per depositor were insured). The DIC was set up under the Deposit Insurance Law of 1971 and was a small fund with capital provided by the government, the Bank of Japan and private financial institutions in roughly equal amounts. The DIC came under the supervision of the Ministry of Finance and insurance premium contributions were required from all banks, credit associations and credit cooperatives. It was widely acknowledged that the DIC had insufficient funds to meet claims in the event of any significant failure, but since no banks had ever failed and no depositors had ever lost money the crisis never arose. It is likely that depositors assumed they would somehow be reimbursed in full. From 1991, however, following the collapse of Tokyo Shinkin credit association, the funds of the DIC were occasionally used to provide support for financial institutions which took over the operations of failing institutions (for example, Sanwa Bank took over Tokyo Shinkin in 1991, Iyo Bank took over Toho Sogo Bank in 1992, in 1993 Iwate Bank took over Kamaishi Shinkin and Osaka Koyo merged with troubled Osaka Fumin Shinyo Kumiai; all received funds from the DIC).

(d) Recapitalization

It followed from the lack of a clear policy about when to close failing institutions that there was no clear guideline on when banks would be recapitalized. In practice, this issue was closely bound up with the interpretation of the obligation of the DIC to protect depositors. As noted above, in all cases of merging failing institutions with healthy ones, the acquiring institutions received some financial assistance in the form of either capital injections, donations, forgiveness of claims or low interest loans.

(e) Cleaning balance sheets

The treatment of bad loans on the books of solvent banks was also *ad hoc* in this period. In 1992 the Cooperative Credit Purchasing Company (CCPC) was established to allow banks to move bad loans off their books at less than book value. Packer (1994) and others have noted that this was mostly designed to allow some tax deductibility for capital losses on loans rather than a real mechanism for removing those loans from these banks. The capital for the CCPC came from the banks themselves. In Mitchell's (1998a) terms, this was tantamount to a policy of 'self-reliance'.

Crisis Period

After the collapse of two credit associations (Tokyo Kyowa and Anzen) in December 1994 there were distinct changes in both the operation and legal basis of policy. From this period on, arguably, there was both growing evidence that the problems were fairly serious and widespread and a changed policy perception that a more systematic approach was needed. Changes in each of the five areas are examined below and, in the next section, related to the theoretical literature.

(a) Bankruptcy procedures

A number of credit cooperatives failed between December 1994 and August 1995 (after Tokyo Kyowa and Anzen came Cosmo, Kizu and then Hyogo Bank). In each of these cases the institutions themselves announced that they were suspending business so there was no immediate change in the role of supervisors. In December 1995 the report of the Financial System Stabilization Committee of the Financial System Research Council (advising the Ministry of Finance), set up in recognition of the growing seriousness of the problem and based on six months of meetings, proposed a number of significant changes. These ultimately were enshrined in six new pieces of legislation enacted in June 1996. Of these, the Law to Provide Special Procedures for Reorganizing Financial Institutions enabled supervisors of institutions to resort to existing legal procedures for corporate reorganization and bankruptcy, thus at least giving them a basis for an active role in liquidating failing institutions. In reorganizations the DIC was empowered to act on behalf of depositors, instead of leaving them to represent themselves as previously.

The Law to Implement Measures for Ensuring the Sound Management of Financial Institutions established the procedure known as Prompt Corrective Action (PCA). PCA establishes procedures by which supervisory agencies undertake corrective measures automatically under certain conditions. The system is similar to the PCA system introduced in the US as part of the Federal Deposit Insurance Corporation Improvement Act (FDICIA) of 1991. The initial proposal in Japan was fairly vague, specifying that action could be taken on the basis of some criterion such as capital adequacy, but the exact criteria were only spelled out later. As a result of the advice of a study group advising the Banking Bureau of the MOF, the criteria were set out (as shown in Table A7.2, pp. 222–3). Compared with the criteria provided in a Federal Reserve Board summary of US procedures, these capital adequacy tripwires (see Goldstein 1997) seem fairly concrete and leave relatively little discretion to supervisors. The logic of PCA is, as Goldstein (ibid.: 46) points out: 'to use regulatory sanctions to mimic the penalties that the private market would impose on banks (as their financial condition deteriorated) if they were not insured and ... to reduce greatly the discretion that regulators have in imposing both corrective actions and closure of a bank'. The principles may be sound as far as they go but, as Benston and Kaufman (1997) point out, in the US case there is still a degree of discretion for supervisors (which they felt was excessive) and capital ratios could have been set higher. This latter criticism might well be levelled at Japan, since business suspension only becomes mandatory when capital adequacy is negative and even then is subject to discretion. Furthermore, there has yet to be any serious test of the system in the US, which has had a buoyant economy and few banking problems since the system was implemented.

PCA was to have come into effect in April 1998 but, in the Emergency Measures to Stabilize the Financial System of December 1997, it was postponed for banks with no overseas operations. In the Comprehensive Plan for Financial Revitalization (July 1998) the new Financial Supervision Agency (FSA) was given the responsibility for carrying out inspections which would then be followed by PCA.

In the course of the political debate over the fate of the Long-Term Credit Bank (LTCB) during August to October 1998 these plans were modified. Under the Emergency Measure for Financial Stabilization, a new Financial Revitalization Committee will take over the role of the FSA (by January 2001) and absorb the MOF's financial system functions. It will decide the treatment of banks according to their capital standards but institutions will now fall into one of four categories rather than the three of PCA, and tougher conditions will apply than under PCA. Furthermore, banks which are not necessarily insolvent but which may 'have difficulty repaying despositors' may be temporarily nationalized. Thus between 1995 and 1998 the system had moved from supervisors having no power to close banks, through giving them recourse to the standard corporate bankruptcy law, to their having considerable powers to inspect banks and decide whether to liquidate, nationalize or put them into a bridge bank.

(b) Management of assets after failure

The assets of the two failed credit associations were transferred to the Tokyo Kyodo Bank, set up in December 1994 explicitly for this purpose. Capital for the new bank was provided from both private and public sources. It was not initially clear whether the new bank was to be a public or a private body. It later took over the assets of the Cosmo and

Kizu cooperatives but it could not be said that this yet represented a clear policy decision about the management of such assets. In the bank failures of 1995 and 1996 the same procedure of establishing new private banks to take over the assets of the failed banks was followed. A more consistent policy began to emerge out of the fiasco of the *jusen* resolution package in June 1996, when the Housing Loan Administration Corporation (HLAC) was established to take over the business of seven *jusen*. The HLAC is clearly a public body although with some private capital contribution. Shortly afterwards, the Tokyo Kyodo Bank was restructured as the Resolution and Collection Bank (RCB). Both the HLAC and the RCB have responsibility for collecting bad loans as well as managing performing assets, and they are now under the DIC. The RCB was further strengthened in the Emergency Measures to Stabilize the Financial System in December 1997 to cover banks as well as credit institutions.

The Bridge Bank plan of July 1998 would have allowed failed banks to be put under administration while good and bad loans were separated. The good loans would have gone to the bridge bank (to be called the Heisei Financial Revitalization Corporation and to come under the DIC). The bridge bank would have been wound up after a maximum of three years if it could not be transferred to private management. The difficulty of the plan was that it implied that the recapitalization of the failing bank would occur before the separation of good and bad loans and before sending it to the bridge bank. This was seen as too lenient on shareholders. There were also some doubts that it could be applied to large banks because of the potential cost and the need to ensure continuous services for their large, sound borrowers. By the end of October 1998 (see appendix) legislation for a more elaborate scheme had been passed which would permit failed banks to be either liquidated, temporarily nationalized or sent to the bridge bank. The RCB and the HLAC were to be merged into a Japanese version of the US Resolution Trust Corporation (RTC) which would handle bad loans and would be set up as a private corporation. Another new feature was that a bank could request temporary nationalization without declaring insolvency and its bad loans would be taken over by the RTC. This allowed for a form of 'debt transfer' whereby a bank which would ultimately continue to function as a private bank (although under different ownership) would have bad debts removed and be recapitalized. The purpose of introducing the nationalization route was to deal with large banks in such a way as to protect the good borrowers and to avoid a credit crunch.

(c) Depositor protection

While there have been occasional remarks from the Ministry of Finance about the need for depositors to become more aware of the quality of banks and to monitor them, in practice the tendency throughout the period has been towards strengthening and widening protection. In the Emergency Measures of December 1997 and in the Comprehensive Plan of July 1998 the commitment to full depositor protection was explicit. The DIC's functions and powers have been expanded well beyond merely an insurance agency and it now plays a central role in policies toward failed banks, as noted above.

(d) Recapitalization

There has been a shift away from a case-by-case approach, which had been applied only to banks taking over the major part of a failing institution and often involving a non-subordinated loan element, to a more general policy. The Emergency Measures of December 1997 reflected the concern that the bad loan problem had become universal and, in line with this perception, provided resources for the DIC to inject capital into non-failing banks. Although the legislation for this strengthening of the DIC (February 1998) contained criteria to be fulfilled by banks applying for capital injections, all major banks appeared to be eligible and a small amount of capital was injected into 21 of the banks. Subsequently, political battles were fought over this issue, starting in the middle of 1998. These clearly reflect the problem noted below that recapitalization was not sufficiently conditional. The legislation which resulted in the October 1998 agreement provided public funds for:

- banks with capital below 8 per cent (for banks operating inter-nationally or 4 per cent domestically) to sell bad loans to the RTC and receive capital via government purchases of preferred shares or subordinated debt;
- banks below 4 per cent (international, 2 per cent domestic) to be partially nationalized (the government taking a 50 per cent stake);
- banks below 2 per cent (international, 1 per cent domestic) to come under full state ownership for a temporary period;
- banks with capital above 8 per cent also to be recapitalized if they meet conditions similar to those set out in the earlier legis-lation which gave a committee of the DIC the responsibility for deciding when recapitalization would occur (clear cases occur when solvent banks take over failed institutions, but what other

circumstances, such as a threat of financial instability, might also apply are not clearly specified).

Initially, tough conditions on management responsibility, dividend payouts and restructuring were contemplated but these were progressively softened as it became clear that banks would be reluctant to apply for recapitalization if conditions were too tough. It is not clear at present whether the conditions are still so tough that they deter banks applying.

(e) Cleaning balance sheets

Until mid-1998 there had been no explicit policy to address this issue. The Bridge Bank plan applied to failing banks but did not provide a mechanism for potentially solvent banks to carry out liquidations, to engage in workouts, or to move bad debts off their balance sheets. In Mitchell's terms, the policy was still one of self-reliance. The Comprehensive Plan of July 1998 acknowledged this problem to some extent in the section on 'aggressive disposal of bad loans' which noted the need to create markets for loans and for collateral but did not address the question of bank incentives. Subsequent revisions to bills have made it possible for banks applying for recapitalization (including solvent banks with adequate capital ratios) to sell bad loans to the RCB (under the DIC), and presumably to the new RTC when established, so that a form of debt transfer, previously lacking, has been introduced.

5. ASSESSMENT: HOW DOES THE POLICY MEASURE UP?

A Theoretical Check List

(a) Bankruptcy policy

Both Mitchell (1998b) and Aghion *et al.* (1998) point out that a tough policy may be counterproductive both because it may encourage banks to roll over loans as a way of hiding the level of defaults and because it can trigger the TMTF problem. If the whole banking system faces problems and there is information asymmetry between banks and regulators then *ex ante* a soft policy dominates a tough one. Since both these features appear to exist in Japan there is a *prima facie* case in favour of a soft policy which should increase workouts (and might reduce asset dissipation by defaulters). In such a case prompt corrective action (PCA) type policies with no discretion for regulators would be undesirable, but even PCA with discretion may not work because it is not clearly an *ex ante* soft policy. The later revisions, with even tougher conditions than the original PCA, may exacerbate the problem. The uncertainty about how regulators will treat banks may still cause those banks to hide their true status. The response by banks so far to the new policies suggests that this is the case. Thus the Japanese policy of PCA with discretion, which may be characterized as *ex ante* tough, but *ex post* soft, does not seem desirable.

In addition, Mitchell (1998b) points out the problem that *ex ante* tough policies may be impossible to implement because of TMTF. Faced with the threat of a TMTF policy, authorities may be tempted to soften monitoring and rescue fewer 'failing' banks, leaving more marginal banks undetected. It appeared that Japanese policy was moving in the direction of a tougher policy by establishing PCA and setting up the FSA but all moves since December 1997 have been consistent with a fear of a TMTF situation. PCA was softened for those banks most likely to fail (smaller banks with no international business).

Aghion *et al.* (1998) also note that the simple application of corporate bankruptcy procedures (as in Japan after 1996) is inappropriate. Banks require different bankruptcy laws which take into account the special nature of the banking business. This was not addressed in Japan in the first phases of legal reform but is partially dealt with by the new procedures which include nationalization.

(b) Managing assets of failed banks

There is not much theory directly relating to this policy feature in the three papers reviewed here but it is clear from Mitchell (1998a) that the effectiveness of any institution taking over a bank's bad debts under a debt transfer policy is crucial in determining the optimality of a policy to clean balance sheets. If the same institution is to manage the workouts of the bad loans of both failed and still-solvent banks (in the event of a debt transfer policy) then its effectiveness in imposing workouts, rather than rolling over debt, is important. In Japan this institution is the new RTC. There is not yet sufficient evidence upon which to judge it.

(c) Depositor protection

What theory exists about the design of protection policy (which is not reviewed here) does not clearly relate to the success of restructuring policies (it has more to do with the causes of crises than the cures). In practice, most countries have protected depositors more or less fully but despite this there appears to be no objection to giving the depositor protection agency (the DIC) a lead role in restructuring, as has been done in Japan.

(d) Recapitalization

Aghion *et al.* (1998) show clearly that unconditional recapitalization policy is not optimal. The best policy is recapitalization based on observable actions such as workouts or liquidations. Policy can be used to elicit information on the true level of defaults faced by banks. Mitchell (1998a) simply notes that recapitalization creates credibility problems for governments but does not propose solutions.

Japanese policy seemed to have moved initially in precisely the wrong direction in this respect. Starting with case-by-case recapitalizations, policy since December 1997 has moved towards across-the-board recapitalizations which, though ostensibly based on observable characteristics, do not create incentives for banks to be tougher on rollovers. This policy appears very similar to Mitchell's TMTF scenario. Although the policy subsequently softened its *ex ante* monitoring (probably to reduce the number of banks needing bailouts), initially the authorities toughened monitoring (with the introduction of PCA) but were able neither to enforce the banks' liquidations of defaulters nor to prevent banks from continuing to roll over loans. The new conditions on recapitalization perpetuate the problem since they still do not provide incentives for banks to perform workouts. They do, however, provide the opportunity for banks to transfer bad debts to the RTC.

(e) Cleaning balance sheets

Japan's policy for non-failing banks had been similar to Mitchell's (1998a) policy of 'self-reliance' (leaving bad debts on banks' balance sheets) while proposing debt transfers for failed banks. The Bridge Bank proposal was in the same vein for failed banks. Mitchell shows that self-reliance is optimal if commercial banks are not soft on workouts (do not allow rollovers and do not permit borrowers to dissipate assets) and if many defaulters are non-viable so there is less risk of excessive liquidation. Certainly, the first condition does not characterize Japan while the second is unclear. Legislation now provides the possibility of debt transfer by still-solvent banks.

It appears that the theoretical best policy, given that commercial banks have proved soft on rollovers and that there is information asymmetry between banks and regulators about the true degree of default, would be either to transfer debt along with a tough policy by the bad-debt bank on debt workouts, or self-reliance combined with an *ex ante* soft policy on bank closures which make recapitalizations conditional on observed workout performance by banks. Japan's policy is some way from either.

An Empirical Check List

The Dziobek and Pazarasioglu (1997) study shows that Japan has used eight measures in its bank restructuring policy, compared with an average for industrial countries of between three and six. Of these measures, four (a loan workout unit; closure, mergers and splits of banks; provision of central bank liquidity; and the disciplining of banks' managers) are also part of the list of best practice policies, while two of the remaining three are considered bad practice (central bank loans and new equity) and one is neutral.

From the list of twelve measures representing best practice, Japan has partially implemented five (comprehensive restructuring of accounting, legal and regulatory systems; prompt action mechanisms; operational restructuring of banks; loss sharing with creditors but not depositors; and debt transfer to a loan recovery agency) and has definitely implemented a further three practices (designated lead agency; central bank liquidity support; and strict closure policies). It has failed to implement incentive-compatible recapitalization policies, has tended to make long-term capital available rather than short-term lending, has not implemented a loan workout policy or institution, and has not delivered positive economic growth while restructuring was under way. The record is at best mixed.

More importantly, perhaps, is that the list of best practice policies is in conflict with what theory suggests may be desirable. Thus PCA-type policies with strict closure rules are regarded by this IMF study as unambiguously desirable (and Japan scores on both counts although PCA was not promptly introduced) while we have seen that under some circumstances this may not be the case. The list also suggests that debt transfer policies are always desirable while theory again suggests that this depends on certain characteristics of the particular banking crisis.

CONCLUSION

By empirical 'best practice' standards, such as they are, Japan may perhaps be regarded as moving in the right direction and scoring a medium grade against the benchmarks. However, one must have some doubts about whether all the elements of average best practice make sense in the Japanese context. Taking into account recent theoretical developments, there remain doubts about the crucial aspects of the design of *ex ante* bank closure policies, of policies to clear banks' balance sheets, of incentive-compatible recapitalization policies, and of policies which will induce the optimal degree of bad debt workouts.

APPENDIX

Table A7.1   Key dates in policy development to resolve the banking crisis in Japan

FY 1991 (April 90–91)   Banks' pre-tax profits fall 27 per cent. Bad debt provision triples. MOF estimates 21 major banks have 7–8 trillion yen in non-performing loans (2 per cent of total loans).

June 1992   Diet passes law reforming financial system. The new law lowers barriers between banks and securities firms (end of Article 65).

August 1992   Price Keeping Operations (PKO) under way to support stock market prices and ease banks' problems. MOF announces 'The present guidelines for administrative management of banking sectors' to reassure markets.

October 1992   Estimate of city banks' non-performing loans reaches 12.3 trillion yen (as of March 1992).

1992   BIS capital standards (8 per cent capital/asset ratio) are imposed. These must be met by **April 1993**. Japanese banks are allowed to include 45 per cent of unrealized capital gains on securities portfolios as Tier II capital.

September 1992   Definition of provisions to qualify under the Provisions in Special Accounts for Loan Loss Write-offs are eased to encourage write-offs of non-performing loans by allowing tax-exempt charge-offs.

December 1992–January 1993   Cooperative Credit Purchasing Co. Ltd (CCPC) is established by the Bankers' Association to purchase bad debts of banks at fair value and allow tax relief on losses. Initially it is capitalized by private institutions. Sales of bad debts to the CCPC begin in March 1993.

1994   Individual banks are allowed (a) to set up 'bad banks' (special purpose companies (SPC) which are privately capitalized) to restructure bad debts, and (b) to set up property auction subsidiaries individually or jointly with other banks.

FY 1994   Banks announce first actual after-tax losses.

December 1994 Tokyo Kyowa and Anzen credit associations fail with bad loans totalling 82 per cent of loan portfolio. Disposal scheme involves a new bank, Tokyo Kyodo Bank, which is set up to hold their assets. The necessary capital is injected by private banks, the Tokyo local government, the Deposit Insurance Corporation and the Association of Credit Cooperatives (with the Bank of Japan's cooperation).

March 1995 Non-performing loans are estimated at 40 trillion yen (first figure for whole banking system).

July–August 1995 Cosmo Credit Coop (fifth largest) is subject to a deposit run (14 per cent of deposits withdrawn in one day) and business is suspended. Its business is taken over by Tokyo Kyodo Bank.

August 1995 Kizu Credit Coop business is suspended. Business is transferred to Tokyo Kyodo Bank. The DIC's special financial assistance is extended to cover all losses incurred in excess of the payoff cost limit (this requires some legal amendments).

August 1995 Hyogo Bank fails. The resolution scheme transfers business to the newly created Midori Bank which is capitalized by private institutions but with a subordinated loan from the Bank of Japan.

December 1995 Statement by the Minister of Finance ('Measures to improve banking inspection and supervision') based on the Report of the Financial System Stabilization Committee of the Financial System Research Council (FSRC) which includes a proposal for the resolution of the *jusen* problem and three proposals for other legislation to deal with bad loans.

March 1996 Taiheiyo Bank collapses. The irrecoverable assets are written off with assistance from four supporting banks. The whole business is transferred to Wakashio Bank, a new bank established as a subsidiary of the Sakura Bank.

June 1996 Six financial reform laws are enacted arising from the FSRC report: (a) Law Concerning Special Packages for Promoting the Disposal of Debts of Specified *Jusen*, (b) Law to Amend the Deposit Insurance Law; (c) Law to Amend the Agricultural and Fishery Cooperative Savings Insurance Law; (d) Law to Provide Special Procedures for Reorganizing Financial Institutions (to establish disposal procedures using judicial procedures such as corporate reorganization and bankruptcy); (e) Law to Implement Measures for Ensuring the Sound Management of Financial Institutions ('Prompt Corrective Action');

Table A7.1 continued

and (f) Law Concerning Special Packages for Suspending Prescription of Claims Owned by Specified *Jusen*.

Government package for liquidation of *jusen* assets involves a total of 6 trillion yen with 685 billion yen of public money.

July 1996 Housing Loan Administration Corporation (HLAC) set up as part of the *jusen* resolution to hold *jusen* assets and collect *jusen*-related claims. It is created as a subsidiary of the Deposit Insurance Corporation (that is, it is not privately held). Seven *jusen* are dissolved. Half of HLAC's capital of 200 billion yen is provided by the Financial Stabilization Contribution Fund which the Deposit Insurance Corporation establishes with contributions from private financial institutions (totalling 1007 billion yen) and the other half from the Bank of Japan with the funds being channelled through the Deposit Insurance Corporation. Funds to purchase *jusen* claims are financed by low interest rate loans from lender financial institutions including *jusen* founding financial institutions. Losses already recognized upon the transfer of claims to the HLAC are to be covered by a government contribution of 680 billion yen through the Emergency Financial Stabilization Fund, as well as the renunciation of loans and grants of lender financial institutions. Also, if the amounts collected prove to be less than the acquisition prices and cause further losses to the HLAC, then the operating profit of the Financial Stabilization Contribution Fund and government funds are to cover the loss equally (Nagashima 1997).

September 1996 Tokyo Kyodo Bank is restructured as the Resolution and Collection Bank (RCB) (based on the US Resolution Trust Corporation) to hold failed credit cooperatives' assets and to engage in resolution and collection of loans. As with the HLAC, it is a subsidiary of the Deposit Insurance Corporation.

October 1996 Election.

November 1996 Prime Minister Hashimoto announces financial Big Bang. The concepts of 'Free, Fair and Global' are used. 'Free' implies promoting new entries and wider fields of business (examples include revision of the FETCL). 'Fair' refers to improvements in disclosure. 'Global' means moving towards internationally standardized accounting and supervision practices.

November 1996 Hanwa bank failure is the first to be treated under the new laws of June 1996. A new bank assumes all the business of

Hanwa Bank, including the repayment of deposits. All assets are purchased by the DIC. The DIC places the administration and collection of assets with the RCB.

10 October 1997 Two regional banks merge: Fukutoku Bank with bad loans of 123 billion yen (8.08 per cent of loans) and the Bank of Naniwa with bad loans of 22.9 billion yen (6.88 per cent of loans).

4 November 1997 Sanyo Securities (seventh largest broker) collapses with debts of 373 billion yen.

17 November 1997 Hokkaido Takushoku Bank (tenth largest city bank) collapses. Some part of its business is transferred to the local North Pacific Bank. A buyer is sought for the other parts. The collapse heightens demands for development of a system which utilizes public money.

25 November 1997 Yamaichi Securities (fourth largest) collapses.

November 1997 Tokuyo City Bank (second-tier regional bank) fails. Business is transferred to the Sendai Bank.

December 1997 Long-Term Credit Bank (LTCB) is the first bank to reveal an estimate of its exposure to the stock market.

December 1997 Government proposes an economic stimulus package, part of which includes the 'Emergency Measures to Stabilize the Financial System'. It promises 30 trillion yen of public money (10 trillion yen in government bonds to the DIC and 20 trillion yen in guarantees). MOF also announces that it will postpone implementation of Prompt Corrective Action (due to start in April 1998) for banks with no overseas operations and will permit some accounting and tax-deductibility changes which would cosmetically improve banks' balance sheets. Main points of the programme are to increase financing for the DIC to 'protect deposits in full' and to expand its scope to cover not only cooperatives but other financial institutions. The DIC's ability to collect bad loans is to be increased. The RCB is upgraded 'as a bank that takes over the business of possible insolvent institutions'. The plan requires amendments to the DIC Law and new legislation to permit use of public funds (via the DIC and the RCB with inspection by a 'fair and neutral examining board') as a source of capital injection (preferred stocks and subordinated bonds). 'This operation will be examined and decided on by an examining board based on strict criteria, in order that it be distinctive from the aiding of individual financial institutions' (that

Table A7.1 continued

is, it is a systemic bank rescue plan for recapitalization, which does not involve restructuring or debt workout plans).

January 1998 MOF scandal. Prosecutors investigate bribery of MOF bank inspectors by banks. Senior MOF official commits suicide.

February 1998 Two pieces of legislation are passed by the Diet to strengthen the DIC (proposed under the 'Emergency Plan' of December 1996). More public money is made available to protect depositors of failed deposit-taking institutions and to provide capital injections to sound institutions. On 26 February detailed criteria for the capital injections are announced by the newly appointed committee within the DIC. It consists of four representatives from the authorities, including the Minister of Finance and the Governor of the Bank of Japan, and three private sector representatives. The criteria for determining whether a bank is eligible to receive a capital injection are:

1. the bank is taking over assets from a failed bank;
2. the bank's financial condition is not significantly weak in terms of profitability and capitalization. A bank qualifies as weak if it has reported net losses for the past three consecutive years or has not distributed a dividend for the three-year period;
3. there is a risk that, if no capital is injected, the bank might face a liquidity crisis leading to a chain of failures which would jeopardize the economy;
4. the capital injection is not provided to help the rehabilitation of a troubled bank but to enhance the soundness of the banking system and to ensure it is able to fulfil its role in the economy;
5. a high probability of the bank's failure after the capital injection is not to be expected;
6. it should not be extremely difficult to redeem the preferred shares.

Criteria 1 and 3 are sufficient conditions for eligibility; the rest are necessary conditions. All major banks are believed to have applied for capital injections.

March 1998 Scandal at the Bank of Japan. Officials are arrested for providing information to banks. In May the executive director in charge of the internal Bank of Japan investigation commits suicide.

FY 1998–9 Introduction of self-assessment method of disclosure of bad loans based on US Securities and Exchange Commission (SEC) definitions.

June 1998 The Financial Supervisory Agency is established to investigate and regulate the financial sector. In July the FSA announces an inspection of the top 19 banks.

July 1998 The second report of the Government–LDP 'Comprehensive Plan for Financial Revitalization' is published, including the Bridge Bank proposal. There are four key action areas of the plan:

- aggressive disposal of bad loans (including some measures to create a secondary market for bad loans and to facilitate disposal of collateral);
- prompt restructuring of financial institutions (no details provided);
- improvement of transparency and disclosure (restates measures already implemented for self-assessment based on 'standard' US SEC definitions of bad loans);
- strengthening of bank supervision and prudential standards (to provide more detail on the operation of the FSA).

The most controversial part, the 'bridge bank' concept, is presented as 'virtually equivalent to the bridge bank scheme in the US' (Comprehensive Plan for Financial Revitalization: Second Report) but actually differs in some crucial respects. The main difference is in the timing of the transfer of a bank into the publicly owned bridge bank status. In the Japanese scheme a failed bank will come under the administration of a receiver who will manage the assets for some period before the bank is divided first into loans to sound borrowers (which will be transferred to a public 'bridge bank' if they cannot be passed on to another financial institution). While these good assets are intended to go to the bridge bank, problem loans will be transferred to the Resolution and Collection Bank (RCB) for disposal. The 'bridge bank' will come under a DIC funded holding company, tentatively named Heisei Financial Revitalization Corporation, and will continue to provide loans to sound borrowers. The bridge bank will then be required to wind down operations within a two-year period in principle, but this can be extended for a further three years.

Mid-August 1998 The FSA declares that the LTCB is not insolvent on an unconsolidated basis. Government suggests that the LTCB will be allowed to use some part of the 13 trillion yen fund set up to help

Table A7.1 continued

still-solvent banks. The intention is to permit a merger with Sumitomo Bank by allowing the LTCB to write off some bad loans. The opposition parties object, claiming that the LTCB is insolvent and public money should not be used. Passage of the legislation relating to the Comprehensive Plan is held up in the Diet.

September 1998 Negotiations between the LDP and the Opposition continue through the month. On 19 September a compromise is 'agreed' upon. The key points are:

1. the new 'financial revitalization committee' (*kinyuu saisei iinkai*), under the direction of the cabinet minister responsible for financial matters, will take over financial supervision from the MOF (and absorb the FSA) and will decide when to declare that a bank has failed and which method to use for dealing with it (of the three set out below). Legislation to set up the committee is scheduled for enactment in the next ordinary session of the Diet, but no time is set for establishing the committee;
2. all *failed* banks may either be (a) liquidated; (b) put under administration, recapitalized and put into a bridge bank (the government's original plan); or (c) (new Opposition proposal) put under 'special state administration' (that is, temporarily nationalized, with the government compulsorily buying up ordinary shares) and later sold back to private interests. The nationalization request may come directly from a bank without the bank first declaring insolvency (so it may apply to *still-solvent* banks);
3. all bad debts of failed banks are to go to the new Resolution Trust Corporation (*seiri kaishu kikan*);
4. the RTC is to be established as a private limited company (*kabushiki kaisha*) to absorb the HLAC and the RCB;
5. the Financial System Stabilization Law (February 1998) is to be abolished, which means that the special fund of 13 trillion yen to recapitalize banks lapses;
6. no specific plan is proposed for the LTCB – the wording deliberately leaves options open.

The plan nearly fails when the LDP appears still to contemplate injecting public funds into the LTCB without nationalizing it, while the Opposition expects it to be nationalized (without necessarily being declared insolvent). Some factions in the LDP also do not accept the removal of powers from the MOF.

The proposals leave unclear the issue of recapitalization for still-solvent banks and provide no replacement for the abolished 13 trillion yen fund. By late September, agreement is reached on the temporary nationalization of LTCB and on removing financial powers from the MOF. The LDP then lays down conditions for using public funds to recapitalize still solvent banks (higher provisioning against doubtful loans, 'accountability' by managers). Public funds are to be available for:

- banks with capital below 8 per cent (for banks operating internationally or 4 per cent domestically): these banks would sell bad loans to the RTC and the government would buy preferred shares or subordinated debt;
- banks with capital below 4 per cent (international, 2 per cent domestic): these banks would be partially nationalized (government 50 per cent stake);
- banks with capital below 2 per cent (international, 1 per cent domestic): these banks would trigger full state ownership for a temporary period.

3 October 1998   Law for Emergency Measures to Revitalize Financial Functions ('Financial Revitalization Bill'). Eight bills pass the Diet. These:

- replace the three-option scheme for failed banks (and still-solvent banks, at their own request);
- establish the basis for the Financial Revitalization Committee (under the Prime Minister's Office) to be set up by January 2001 (its aim being to 'collaborate' with the MOF in handling financial crises);
- set up the RTC.

October 1998   In the closing days of the Diet session the LDP revises its proposals on recapitalization to clarify the conditions for injecting funds into banks above 8 per cent capital. These conditions are similar to those in the legislation of February 1998 (the now abolished Financial Stabilization Law) which were scheduled to be imposed by the DIC (that is, taking over a failed bank, and so on) although it also now allows the DIC to purchase bad loans from these still-solvent banks. Debate continues concerning the amount of money needed for recapita-

Table A7.1 continued

lization until finally a package is passed on 16 October (the Financial
Stabilization Bill) which sets up 17 trillion yen to deal with failed banks.
It allows 18 trillion yen to deal with undercapitalized banks. These will
apply directly to the DIC. (The FRC will decide whether preferred or
ordinary shares will be used.) Banks with capital over 8 per cent
(preferred shares or subordinated debt) will receive 25 trillion yen.
Banks may continue to use the cost method to calculate their capital
ratios (opposed by the Democratic Party). No new conditions are
imposed for extra provisioning. The final plan is supported by some,
but not all, the Opposition parties. The Democratic Party wants stiffer
conditions on public money injections to weak banks and opposes
injections for healthy banks. They also want higher provisioning against
Category 2 loans. If the Democratic Party forms a government before
the banking crisis is resolved, changes in legislation are possible.

23 October 1998   The LTCB applies for nationalization under the new
laws

Table A7.2 Prompt corrective action

Capital category	Capital adequacy ratio		Corrective action
	International	National	
1	Less than 8%	Less than 4%	Must submit business improvement plan and implement it.
2	Less than 4%	Less than 2%	Submission of capital restoration plan required. Growth of total assets restricted or reduction of total assets required. New lines of business prohibited or the reduction of the existing scope of business required. New branches and subsidiaries at home and abroad prohibited or a reduction in existing ones required. Dividend payments are restricted or

Capital category	Capital adequacy ratio		Corrective action
	International	National	
			prohibited. Bonuses to senior executives are restricted. Deposits with high interest rates are restricted or prohibited.
3	Less than 5%	Less than 0%	Business is suspended either partly or entirely. May be subject to category 2 corrective action only if the institution: (a) has a positive net worth inclusive of unrealized gains or assets; or (b) can be expected to return a positive net worth based on an overall view of the business improvements being made, profitability, the level of non-performing assets, etc. Institutions classified under categories 1 and 2 may be subject to business suspension if their net worth is negative (inclusive of unrealized gains on assets), or if it is expected to turn negative.

Source: Nagashima (1997: 206)

REFERENCES

Aghion, P., P. Bolton and S. Fries (1998), 'Optimal design of bank bailouts: the case of transition economies', EBRD Working Paper 32, London: EBRD.

Alexander, W.E., J.M. Davis, L. Edrill and C-J. Lindgren (1997), *Systemic Bank Restructuring and Macroeconomic Policy*, Washington, DC: International Monetary Fund.

Benston, G. and G. Kaufman (1997), 'FDICIA after five years: a review and evaluation', *Journal of Economic Perspectives* 11: 139–59.

Caprio, G. and D. Klingebiel (1996), 'Bank insolvency: bad luck, bad policy, or bad banking?', paper presented to the Annual World Bank Conference on Development Economics, Washington, DC: World Bank.

Corbett, J. (1999), 'Japan's banking crisis in international perspective', in M. Aoki and G. Saxonhouse (eds), *Finance, Governance and Competitiveness in Japan*, Oxford: Oxford University Press.

Demirgüç-Kunt, Asli and Enrica Detragiache (1997), 'The determinants of banking crises: evidence from industrial and developing countries', Washington, DC: World Bank, mimeo.

Dziobek, C. and C. Pazarasioglu (1997), 'Lessons and elements of best practice', in W. Alexander, J.M. Davis, L. Edrill and C-J. Lindgren (eds), *Systemic Bank Restructuring and Macroeconomic Policy*, Washington, DC: International Monetary Fund, 75–143.

Goldstein, M. (1997), *The Case for an International Banking Standard*, Washington, DC: Institute for International Economics.

Goodhart, C. and D. Schoenmaker (1995), 'Should the functions of monetary policy and banking supervision be separated?', *Oxford Economic Papers*, 47: 539–60.

Hutchison, M., K. McDill and R. Madrassy (1999), 'Predicting banking crises: Japan's financial crisis in international comparison', 157–83

Lindgren, C.-J., G. Garcia and M.I. Saal (1996), *Bank Soundness and Macroeconomic Policy*, Washington, DC: International Monetary Fund.

Mitchell, J. (1998a), *Strategic Creditor Passivity, Regulation and Bank Bailouts*, CEPR Discussion Paper 1780, London: Centre for Economic Policy Research.

Mitchell, J. (1998b), 'The problem of bad debts: clearing banks' balance sheets in economies in transition', Brussels: ECARE, Free University of Brussels, mimeo.

Nagashima, A. (1997), 'Role of the central bank during problems of bank soundness: Japan's experience', in C. Enoch and J.H. Green (eds), *Banking Soundness and Monetary Policy*, Washington, DC: International Monetary Fund, 191–227.

Packer, F. (1994), *The Disposal of Bad Loans in Japan: A Review of Recent Policy Initiatives*, Center on Japanese Economy and Business Working Paper 88, New York: Columbia University.

Sheng, A. (1996), *Bank Restructuring: Lessons from the 1980s*, Washington, DC: World Bank.

Sundararajan, V. and T. Balino (1991), 'Issues in recent banking crises', in V. Sundararajan and T. Balino (eds), *Banking Crisis: Cases and Issues*, Washington, DC: International Monetary Fund, 1–57.

COMMENT ON CORBETT

Takatoshi Ito

The paper covers a wide range of theoretical issues related to a banking crisis in general and then applies its theoretical conclusions to the Japanese experience. Many other papers and policy discussions on the Japanese banking problem are written without reference to theory. This paper is highly recommended as a means of understanding the issues at hand in some kind of formal framework. The paper is also very balanced, in the sense that each step of the policy measures is interpreted from a theoretical base. In some places I feel that Professor Corbett gives too much credit to Japanese monetary authorities, but her argument still makes sense. In other places, the paper appropriately questions the measures taken by the Japanese authorities. The paper should be recommended to all researchers and people who are dealing with the banking problem in Japan.

Let me express my views on the banking situation in Japan. I think that measures to deal with the bad debt problems have been developed over the past six years. They were in the right direction, but the progress was too little and too late. Japan is not unique in experiencing this type of banking problem. However, this does not mean that Japan's problem could have been controlled to arrive at a situation different from the present one.

Let me comment on the Corbett paper, step by step. The first section describes the difficulties in identifying banking crises, especially, *ex ante*, distinguishing it from a banking 'problem'. Corbett cites her own work (1999) elsewhere to conclude that 'up until 1996 a limited set of indicators classified Japan as experiencing difficulties only in the middle range of severity when compared with a group of industrialised countries which Lindgren *et al.* (1996) classified as experiencing crises'. The statement is a reasonable one, with only one reservation. I think that back in 1995, her indicators would have been pointing distinctly towards a severe problem, namely that without additional measures being taken Japan was likely to drift into a banking crisis. So the fact that the situation did not develop into a crisis until 1996 does not relieve the policy-makers of bearing full responsibility. To repeat, there were ample signs and indicators that were pointing to an upcoming crisis by 1995.

In the first section, Corbett argues that it is difficult for the authorities to know when a problem becomes a crisis. She states that '[A]t a general level it is clear that there is in fact little agreement on when banking problems become a crisis' (p. 194). Moreover, some of the definitions of a crisis are only applicable with the benefit of hindsight.

In the second section, Corbett surveys the literature. Dziobek and Pazarasioglu (1997) conclude that there are 12 features which constitute best practice. Let me borrow their points and grade the performance of the Japanese bank supervisors:

- **Comprehensive approach** *Grade:* Marginal pass, but too late. *Explanation:* Only taken in 1998, in the Total Plan proposed by the LDP. It should have been taken in 1995.
- **Prompt action** *Grade:* Fail. *Explanation:* It should have been done in 1995.
- **Operation restructing** *Grade:* Fail. *Explanation:* Banks were too late and too little in their restructuring.
- **Designated lead agency** *Grade:* Marginal pass. *Explanation:* It is clear that the Ministry of Finance has acted as the leading agency. Unlike the United States, where there are several competing agencies that supervise, the Japanese system is straightforward on this point. The performance of the lead agency is another question.
- **Continuous monitoring** *Grade:* Pass. *Explanation:* Unlike many critics, I think that the Ministry of Finance knew what was happening. Monitoring was fine.
- **Liquidity support** *Grade:* Excellent.
- **Exit policy**; avoid 'too big to fail' *Grade:* Fail. *Explanation:* The authorities are still thinking in terms of 'too big to fail'.
- **Incentive-compatible government support** *Grade:* Marginal pass. *Explanation:* Now that 30 trillion yen is promised, the support is sufficient for the time being. However, it took several events to convince the government and the public to allow for that amount. It is still questionable whether it will be 'incentive-compatible' (see conditions for government's subscription to banks' preferred shares).
- **Loss-sharing rule** *Grade:* Marginal pass. *Explanation:* I think that it would be dangerous to deny depositors a full guarantee. However, losses should be shared by shareholders and executives without question, and maybe by bond holders.
- **'Effectively removing non-performing loans from banks' balance sheets and transferring them to a separate loan recovery agency'** *Grade:* Marginal pass. *Explanation:* The CCPC (Cooperative Credit Purchasing Co. Ltd) was created first. However, this was just a device for shifting the assets off balance sheets with back

finances (from the bank of asset origin to the CCPC). The final losses were not determined until the assets were sold off. The Tokyo Kyodo Bank was created as the successor of the two credit unions that failed in December 1994. This bank later became the Resolution and Collection Bank (RCB). It does function as a recovery agency. But until the bank 'fails', assets cannot be moved to the Resolution and Collection Bank. The CCPC was reformed in July 1998 so that it can now buy assets from banks without backfinancing. However, it is not clear how CCPC losses, if materialized, will be covered after the final sales of the assets.

- **Loan workouts** *Grade:* Marginal pass. *Explanation:* It was only recently that the Bridge Bank formula was put forward which protected the good customers of a failed bank. Non-performing loans are to be shifted to the RCB (Resolution and Collection Bank) from a failed bank. The Bridge Bank will take over good and doubtful loans. It is not clear how the Bridge Bank will 'work out' those doubtful loans.
- **'Positive economic growth also helps'** *Grade:* Fail. *Explanation:* No substantial growth since 1992. A faint recovery in 1996 was killed off by the tax increase in April 1997.

At the end of the paper, Corbett assesses the progress as follows: 'Japan has used eight measures in its bank restructuring policy, compared with an average for industrial countries of between three and six. Of these measures, four are also part of the list of best practice policies, while two of the remaining three are considered to be bad practice and one is neutral. From the list of twelve measures representing best practice, Japan has partially implemented five and has definitely implemented a further three practices. It has failed to implement incentive-compatible recapitalization policies. The record is at best mixed' (p. 213).

In the third section, Corbett reviews the theory of rescues and cleaning up bad loans. She takes up Aghion's argument (Aghion *et al.* 1998): ' "a tough recapitalisation policy in which the bank manager is always dismissed results ... in the bank manager rolling over bad loans in order to conceal the extent of their loan losses and therefore in the softening of the firms' budget constraints. Vice-versa, a soft approach to recapitalisation (in which the manager of a failing bank is not dismissed) encourages her to take an overly tough approach to firm liquidations, while exaggerating her own recapitalisation requirements." The interesting result here is that when the banking system as a whole is known by the government to be in crisis, a soft bailout policy is preferable to a tough one because the cost of not sufficiently liquidating the loans of defaulting borrowers is greater than the cost of excessive recapitalization which deflects managerial incentives into overstating the needs of more solvent banks' (p. 201).

This conclusion would please the Japanese monetary authorities who seem to be considering taking 'soft' policies. The recapitalization that took place at the end of March 1998 did not ask executives to resign. More than 1 trillion yen was injected into 21 banks (18 large banks and 3 regionals). The banks had to submit 'restructuring plans', but they did not include any executives taking responsibility or accepting a bonus cut and reduced pay.

Theoretical results may be questioned in the light of the Japanese situation. The danger of this soft approach is not emphasized enough. The danger of hiding bad assets is not unique to the hard approach but can occur in the soft approach as well. In the soft approach the merit of honest disclosure may be greater than its cost for a bank, but the reverse may hold for bank managers. Benefits for bank managers, that is, hefty bonuses and severance pay, may still be affected even in the soft approach. The complete immunity of the bank executives may obviously cause moral hazard. Hence, even the soft approach may fail to induce full disclosure. The history of Japanese banking in the 1990s demonstrates this point.

The key assumption of Aghion's point (Aghion *et al.* 1998) is that the supervisory authority cannot know the exact situation of bad debts which bankers know. If the information is shared, then the result is obviously different. The policy implication is that it is important for the supervisory authority to strengthen the due diligence process.

The fourth section describes Japan's performance. For both the pre-crisis (1991–4) and the crisis (1994–) periods, policy developments are described. This section needs to be developed more carefully. For example, the Deposit Insurance Corporation (DIC) has gone through several institutional changes before arriving at its current status. Initially it was assumed that an institution would be allowed to fail and be liquidated. This left the DIC to play a role only as a 'paymaster' who dispersed the deposits to depositors as long as each payout did not exceed 10 million yen. Next, the DIC was reformed, which allowed it to give a payout equivalent to that of a white knight institution. Then, after the crisis deepened, the maximum payout equivalent was removed. Each change was in the right direction, but maybe a bit too late. These changes should be described carefully.

The description of the RCB and the Bridge Bank proposal should be strengthened to avoid any possible misunderstanding. The proposed bridge bank in Japan may be different from the US model in its legal power and its trigger.

The penultimate section is an assessment. Professor Corbett concludes that: (a) according to the theory presented, the Japanese policy of *ex ante* tough but *ex post* soft does not seem desirable; (b) managing assets of a failed bank is an unproven strategy; (c) depositors are fully protected, but the DIC has not been given full power to act; (d) with respect to recapitalization, 'Japanese policy seemed to have moved initially in precisely the wrong direction' (p. 212) because it was done across the board; (e) the best policy would 'be either to transfer debt along with a tough policy by the bad-debt bank on debt workouts, or self-reliance combined with an *ex ante* soft policy on bank closures which make recapitalizations conditional on observed workout performance by banks' (p. 212).

These conclusions are basically reasonable and agree with my assessment. The situation is still changing with each day at the time of writing this, and we can only hope for the best.

REFERENCES

Aghion, P., P. Bolton and S. Fries (1998), 'Optimal design of bank bailouts: the case of transition economics' EBRD Working Paper 32, London: EBRD.

Corbett, J. (1999), 'Japan's banking crisis in international perspective', in M. Aoki and G. Saxonhouse (eds), *Festschrift for Hugh Patrick*, London: Oxford University Press.

Dziobek, C. and C. Pazarasioglu (1997), 'Lessons and elements of best practice', in W. Alexander, J.M. Davis, L. Edrill and C-J. Lindgren (eds), *Systemic Bank Restructuring and Macroeconomic Policy*, Washington, DC: International Monetary Fund, 75–143.

Lindgren, C-J., G. Garcia and Matthew I. Saal (1996), *Bank Soundness and Macroeconomic Policy*, Washington, DC: International Monetary Fund.

Index